W9-COY-648

The Third World:
Premises of U.S. Policy

9 8 0 3

THE THIRD WORLD:

PREMISES OF U.S. POLICY

W. Scott Thompson, *Editor*
Dennis Austin
Peter T. Bauer
Max Beloff
Richard E. Bissell
Daniel J. Elazar
S. E. Finer
Allan E. Goodman
Nathaniel H. Leff
Seymour Martin Lipset
Edward N. Luttwak
Daniel Pipes
Wilson E. Schmidt
Anthony Smith
Basil S. Yamey

Institute for Contemporary Studies
San Francisco, California

Copyright © 1978 by the Institute for Contemporary Studies

Printed in the United States of America. All rights reserved. No part of this book may be used or reproduced in any manner without written permission except in the case of brief quotations embodied in critical articles and reviews.

Copies of this book may be purchased from the Institute for $5.95. All inquiries, book orders, and catalog requests should be addressed to the Institute for Contemporary Studies, Suite 811, 260 California Street, San Francisco, California 94111—(415) 398–3010.

Library of Congress Catalog Number 78–67593
ISBN 0–917616–30–8

CONTENTS

v

III

International Affairs

IV

The Economic Problem

V

Conclusion

CONTRIBUTORS

DENNIS AUSTIN
Professor of Government, University of Manchester

PETER T. BAUER
Professor of Economics, University of London

MAX BELOFF
Principal, University College at Buckingham

RICHARD E. BISSELL
Managing Editor, ORBIS

DANIEL J. ELAZAR
Director, Center for the Study of Federalism, Temple University

S. E. FINER
*Gladstone Professor of Government and Public Administration,
Oxford University*

ALLAN E. GOODMAN
*Adjunct Professor of Diplomacy,
Georgetown University*

NATHANIEL H. LEFF
*Professor of Business Economics and International Business,
Columbia University*

SEYMOUR MARTIN LIPSET
*Senior Fellow, Hoover Institution, Professor of Political Science
and Sociology, Stanford University*

EDWARD N. LUTTWAK
*Senior Fellow, Center for Strategic and International Studies,
Research Professor, Georgetown University*

DANIEL PIPES
*William Rainey Harper Teaching Fellow, College of
the University of Chicago*

WILSON E. SCHMIDT
*Professor of Economics, Virginia Polytechnic Institute
and State University*

ANTHONY SMITH
Associate Professor of Political Science, Tufts University

W. SCOTT THOMPSON
*Associate Professor of International Politics, Fletcher School of
Law and Diplomacy*

BASIL S. YAMEY
Professor of Economics, University of London

PREFACE

Demands for a New International Economic Order, echoed in their essentials by the U.S. Ambassador to the United Nations, have raised the Third World as a center of political and moral controversy. On the one hand, important elements in the American foreign policy establishment argue that the essential North-South problem involves the West's responsibility for Third World poverty and a complementary responsibility to solve that poverty by massive wealth transfers. Politically, these elements argue that the Third World has no strategic importance in U.S. relations with the Soviet Union, and therefore that little importance should be attached to such recent events as Soviet and Cuban military adventures in Africa.

This "progressive" view of the Third World has come increasingly to dominate public discussions of the Third World, as well as discussions of the direction of U.S. policy in North-South relations. Because this growing dominance seemed to be retarding the possibility of a genuinely balanced public debate on Third World issues, the Institute asked W. Scott Thompson, of the Fletcher School of Law and Diplomacy, to assemble a group of scholars from the United States and Europe to examine these issues.

This is the Institute's second venture into international politics, following our general assessment of U.S. foreign and military policies in *Defending America: Toward a New Role in the Post-Détente World* (1977). What follows in this current book is a humane and realistic account of Third World problems, both internally and in the external relations in global politics of many individual countries.

> H. Monroe Browne
> President,
> Institute for Contemporary Studies

San Francisco, California
October 1978

THE THIRD WORLD

Afghanistan
Republic of Afghanistan
Algeria
Democratic and Popular
Republic of Algeria
Angola
People's Republic of Angola
Argentina
Argentine Republic

Bahamas
Commonwealth of the Bahamas
Bahrain
State of Bahrain
Bangladesh
People's Republic
of Bangladesh
Barbados
People's Republic
of Barbados
Benin
People's Republic of Benin
Bhutan
People's Republic of Bhutan
Bolivia
Republic of Bolivia
Botswana
Republic of Botswana
Brazil
Federative Republic of Brazil
Burma
Socialist Republic of the
Union of Burma
Burundi
Republic of Burundi

Cambodia
Democratic Kampuchea

Cameroon
United Republic of Cameroon
Cape Verde
Republic of Cape Verde
Central African Empire
Chad
Republic of Chad
Chile
Republic of Chile
Colombia
Republic of Colombia
Comoro Islands
Republic of the Comoros
Congo
People's Republic of the Congo
Costa Rica
Republic of Costa Rica
Cuba
Republic of Cuba

Dominican Republic

Ecuador
Republic of Ecuador
Egypt
Arab Republic of Egypt
El Salvador
Republic of El Salvador
Equatorial Guinea
Republic of Equatorial Guinea
Ethiopia

Fiji
Dominion of Fiji

Gabon
Gabonese Republic
Gambia
Republic of the Gambia

Ghana
  Republic of Ghana
Grenada
  State of Grenada
Guatemala
  Republic of Guatemala
Guinea
  Republic of Guinea
Guinea-Bissau
  Republic of Guinea-Bissau
Guyana
  Cooperative Republic of Guyana

Haiti
  Republic of Haiti
Honduras
  Republic of Honduras

India
  Republic of India
Indonesia
  Republic of Indonesia
Iran
  Imperial Government of Iran
Iraq
  Republic of Iraq
Ivory Coast
  Republic of Ivory Coast

Jamaica
Jordan
  Hashemite Kingdom of Jordan

Kenya
  Republic of Kenya
Kuwait
  State of Kuwait

Laos
  *Lao People's
  Democratic Republic*
Lebanon
  Republic of Lebanon
Lesotho
  Kingdom of Lesotho
Liberia
  Republic of Liberia
Libya
  *People's Socialist
  Libyan Arab Republic*

Madagascar
  *Democratic Republic
  of Madagascar*
Malawi
  Republic of Malawi
Malaysia
Maldives
  Republic of Maldives
Mali
  Republic of Mali
Mauritania
  *Islamic Republic
  of Mauritania*
Mauritius
Mexico
  United Mexican States
Mongolia
  Mongolian People's Republic
Morocco
  Kingdom of Morocco
Mozambique
  *People's Republic
  of Mozambique*

Nepal
  Kingdom of Nepal
Nicaragua
  Republic of Nicaragua
Niger
  Republic of Niger
Nigeria
  Federal Republic of Nigeria

Oman
  Sultanate of Oman

Pakistan
  Islamic Republic of Pakistan
Panama
  Republic of Panama
Papua New Guinea
Paraguay
  Republic of Paraguay
Peru
  Republic of Peru
Philippines
  Republic of the Philippines

Qatar
  State of Qatar

Rhodesia
Ruanda
  Republic of Ruanda

Samoa
São Tomé and Prïncipe
  Democratic Republic of
  São Tomé and Prïncipe
Saudi Arabia
  Kingdom of Saudi Arabia
Senegal
  Republic of Senegal
Seychelles
Sierra Leone
  Republic of Sierra Leone
Singapore
  Republic of Singapore
Somalia
  Somali Democratic Republic
Sri Lanka
  Republic of Sri Lanka
Sudan
  Democratic Republic of
  the Sudan
Surinam
Swaziland
  Kingdom of Swaziland
Syria
  Syrian Arab Republic

Tanzania
  United Republic of Tanzania

Thailand
  Kingdom of Thailand
Togo
  Republic of Togo
Trinidad and Tobago
Tunisia
  Republic of Tunisia

Uganda
  Republic of Uganda
United Arab Emirates
Upper Volta
  Republic of Upper Volta
Uruguay
  Oriental Republic of Uruguay

Venezuela
  Republic of Venezuela
Vietnam
  Socialist Republic of Vietnam

Western Sahara

Yemen
  People's Democratic Republic
  of Yemen
Yemen
  Yemen Arab Republic

Zaïre
  Republic of Zaïre
Zambia
  Republic of Zambia

Countries which have social and economic characteristics in common with the Third World but, because of political affiliations or regimes, are not associated with Third World organizations:

China
  People's Republic of China
Cyprus
  Republic of Cyprus
Israel
  State of Israel
Kazakhstan
Kirghizia
Korea
  Democratic People's Republic
  of Korea
Romania
  Socialist Republic of Romania

South Africa
  Republic of South Africa
South West Africa*
  Namibia
Tadzhikistan
Turkmenistan
Uzbekistan
Yugoslavia
  Socialist Federal Republic
  of Yugoslavia

*Due to become independent late in 1978.

I

Introduction

1

W. SCOTT THOMPSON

The Need to Take Stock

The Western attitude toward the Third World in the 1970s. Currents of thought regarding regional development. Multinational corporate investment. Nonalignment and communist intervention. Political insecurity and alignment with the left. Nationalization. The need for intellectual curiosity.

The Third World, something of an over-the-counter stock in America during the 1960s, has clearly made the big board. It might even be said to have attained the status of a glamour issue by the late 1970s as new American leaders came to power, competing among themselves to shift their departments' traditional concerns more to those of the peoples and states of Africa or Asia.

3

There *is* something romantic and fascinating about regions and peoples who have been catapulted into modernity. Small wonder, then, that the Third World elicited an extraordinary percentage of new social science talent in the past two decades, propelling many students into the front ranks of scholarly fashion. In addition, many of those who came to make United States policy spent their formative years as Peace Corps volunteers, or as protestors against a war being fought in the Third World.

What is the result of this heavy psychological involvement of American scholars and administrators in the Third World? Our contributors do not speak with one voice, but there may well be a consensus among them that the romance of these once-exotic places attaches too firmly to the analysis of the Third World, particularly as regards American policy interests.

Although, in its official rhetoric, the Third World speaks of itself as an undifferentiated mass, these leaderships realize that their interests differ from region to region, indeed, from state to state; that "the peoples of the world" or the "downtrodden masses" cannot, in fact, speak with one voice, a point argued cogently by Dennis Austin. We would probably all prefer not to use the term "Third World" at all, had it not come to be so convenient, current, and generally accepted. For its use, to an extent, has the effect of a self-fulfilling prophecy, endowing those most radical leaders with a sense of mission, in reference to a disparate 114 states from Afghanistan to Zaïre.

The problem is that there are three quite distinct currents of thought and action with respect to the Third World, both therein and in the United States. One is a realistic current, of a sort endorsed by the contributors to this volume, by increasing numbers of Third World elites, by important segments of official America, and by increasing numbers of academics. The second current starts with idealism, of a kind enunciated both by Third World leaders at the United Nations and by American political leaders recently, but ends with illusions

Soviet allies for bestowing stability on conflict-torn African states. Thus, just when, for separate reasons, American bureaucrats and scholars were beginning to wake up to the problems of unreasonable and unrealistic Third World demands, and just when numerous Third World leaders were pressing Washington to deal with the Soviet-Cuban threat, the *political* leadership began acting on antithetical assumptions, vitiating in large measure the learning experience occurring elsewhere. Alas, the political naïveté—of which Professor Beloff writes so eloquently—was welcomed in Moscow where, though it was considered suspect, it was of great use in the media.

The point here is not to list the achievements of the Soviet Union since it began to project its power throughout the Third World, nor to criticize a particular American administration. It is, rather, to demonstrate the indissoluble connection, at every level of analysis, between the "North-South" and "East-West" axes. Fashionable analysis in the United States has had it for several years now that the two were separate, and that American policy would be successful inasmuch as it kept the two disaggregated. But it is in the Third World that the Soviets have achieved their most spectacular gains, and it also is there—as the most casual or the most rigorous examination of their own analyses, as published in *Pravda* and other journals, would show—that they expect to make significant gains against the West. It is under the shadow of the massive buildup of Soviet power throughout the world that Third World leaders have felt increasingly free to nationalize Western corporate interests. And the most critical Soviet moves have occurred at the mouth and heart of Western supply lines of critical minerals and oil, on which Western industry depends for survival—as the Soviet press so frequently reminds its readers. The 3,600 percent increase in the flow of oil from the Persian Gulf to the West in ten years, around the Cape of Good Hope, explains much of Soviet political/military activity in the Horn and in Southern Africa in the late 1970s.

The combination of an enfeeblement of Western will at a time of Soviet growth in strength—at the strategic level, to one of superiority no later than the early 1980s (and, in my own view, in late 1977–1978)—appears to be sufficient to change the assumptions of how the world is organized: from one previously dominated by the West and its friends, to one in which Moscow is predominant, with the rules of the game shifting *pari passu.*

So it surely is time to take stock of our interests in the Third World, and of what would compose good policies in these parts of the world. This book is not so much a prescription for policy as such, as it is an attempt to examine some of the premises of policy, and to ask hard questions about the assumptions on which too many policies have been based. Our contributors no more represent a school of thought, as such, than a political persuasion—which is evident from the extraordinary diversity of their scholarly interests and their known political attitudes. Intellectual curiosity, of the kind we sought in planning this book, would not only be more honest. It turns out, as our contributors have found, that it would be in the interests of the West and of those diverse countries of Africa, Asia, Latin America, and the Middle East as well.

2

MAX BELOFF

The Third World and the Conflict of Ideologies

Past ideologies and their present application. Defining the Third World and its aspirations. Nonaligned countries. Ideologies as weapons. Use of Third World nations by the superpowers. U.S. misconception of Third World problems. Racial factors in economic and political advancement. Western guilt and emotional blackmail. USSR and the West—issues of strategy.

The "conflict of ideologies" is, of course, only a metaphor . Men or groups of men engage in conflict; ideologies being systems of ideas have no existence outside the minds of individuals. The role of ideologies may be to justify men engaging in conflicts over issues which they might otherwise seek to resolve by peaceful means, or to furnish them with a picture of the world within which their own struggles become more meaningful and hence more satisfying. The element of ideology in past conflicts will tend to loom larger in the minds of those actively engaged than for later historians. Crusaders may have believed that they were going off to rescue the Holy Places of their faith from the grasp of the infidel; later historians talk about land-hunger and Mediterranean trade. Philip II may have launched the Armada hoping to restore England to the Catholic Church; we look at the logistical problems of the Spanish empire.

From the outbreak of the French Revolution, the principal conflicts in the world have always had an ideological flavor, however important the material elements may appear; radical republicanism, socialism in its various guises, Marxist and other, fascism in a variety of forms, have inspired peoples, parties, and states to try to remould society in the light of their value systems; conservatives and liberals have tried to halt or reverse their advances.* Most important of all, nationalism has proved the most potent of ideologies, and the one most likely to prevail in an ideological conflict—if we may return to the metaphor.

When we apply these general lessons from the past to the Third World at the present time, we have to add some further considerations. In the first place, there is a problem of definition. The Third World can be regarded as simply a residue: what is left when one has subtracted from the world as a whole the industrialized West—mostly living under a system of capitalist or mixed economies—and the communist empires of Russia, China, and their satellites. But that residue contains countries of very different degrees of economic advancement and with a vast number of different types of social and governmental organization. One could, therefore, argue that the phrase "the Third World" itself is a kind of ab-

*I use "liberal" in the European sense as equally antithetical to the absolutism of the *Ancien régime* and to socialism. As used by Americans, it becomes hard to distinguish from (non-Marxist) socialism.

breviated ideology. Those who use it in the Third World do so to justify claims for assistance in moving towards a higher degree of economic organization and greater material wealth; those who use it in the West implicitly concede these claims.

It is also, of course, a fact of great importance that most Third World countries have populations which are wholly or mainly nonwhite. The notion of the Third World thus contains some distinctly racial overtones. One could almost say that there has grown up as a kind of counterideology to the nineteenth-century ideas of the superiority of the white "race"—which reached their culmination in the Nazi "Aryan myth—a black racism which sees the "emancipation" of colored peoples as the overriding issue of our times and which recognizes no limits of prudence or humanity in pursuit of this end.

How deep-rooted such an ideology can become is shown in another ideological key word, "nonaligned." Originally a nonaligned country was one whose government regarded the conflict between the Soviet Union and the West as none of its business and refused to take sides with either. In that sense, it was merely a slightly different version of classical "neutrality," as exemplified by Switzerland. But in actual practice, the nonaligned have become a group of countries who, while not forming part of either the Western Alliance or the Soviet bloc, are nevertheless very close to the Soviet position in most of the issues that arise—particularly issues in or relating to the Third World; the "nonaligned" in relation to the Israeli-Arab conflict, for instance, are clearly nonaligned *against* Israel. Indeed, a Soviet bloc country like Rumania takes (no doubt, for good reasons of its own) a much more neutral stand than such "nonaligned" countries as Yugoslavia or India. Again, there is the fact that Cuba, which is even more dependent on and more subservient to the Soviet Union than some of the East European satellites is admitted to the ranks of the "nonaligned."

All this would point to some confusion, a confusion which is shared by some Western statesmen and diplomats, particularly, perhaps, in the United States. The reasons for this confusion demand some further probing. It is clear, to begin with, that the major ideologies are themselves products of the conditions and mental attitudes of the advanced world. They have been imported into the Third World, which has not so far developed bodies of ideas complex and all-embracing enough to be dignified by the title of ideology. The Third World itself has produced no fully developed ideologies, though Gandhi's peculiar blend of nationalism and "nonviolence" and rejection of the machine age came near to being one. Nor, on the whole, have any but the more sophisticated Third World countries—which means mainly those with a long history of European contacts—been able fully to absorb the complex doctrines of the major Western ideologies.

What one gets in the Third World in place of ideology are a number of words and phrases believed to be progressive in character—words like "socialism," "democracy," "equality," "nondiscrimination," "peace-loving"—which are then combined in various ways to give an impression that the ruling party or government has its heart in the right place. The result is to create a confused syncretism which can be no guide to practice, since it is based upon no analysis of either the material conditions or the mental attitudes of the peoples concerned. Words like "socialism," that have, whether one likes what they stand for or not, perfectly concrete and definable meanings, become transmogrified when one finds talk of "African socialism," which is no more meaningful than, say, "African mathematics."

In seeking for appropriate words in which to clothe their political aspirations, it is understandable that many Third World leaders should have found the concepts of Soviet communism easier to manipulate than the more subtle demands of Western ideologies such as liberalism. What Soviet communism appears to offer is a ready-made excuse for failing to produce the economic goods that independence has been supposed to guarantee—the failure can be put down to the survival of capitalism or to "neocolonial" exploitation.

The idea of the "class struggle" is helpful when it comes to finding a good reason for the "liquidation" of traditional authorities, of the educated classes, or of any other obstacle to those who wield power in the name of the "people." The horrors of Cambodia since liberation, the only slightly less horrific aspects of what has been going on in Uganda and Ethiopia, are testimony to the ample power of verbiage to cover up massacre.

It is not only against their own peoples that the present-day tyrants wield their ideological as well as their more lethal weapons; they also use them as a method of disarming the international community and preventing any reaction on its part—lest the governments which do react are assailed as reactionary and racist, not merely by the other communist or nonaligned governments, but even by elements among their own peoples whose minds are equally unready to unravel the deceptions and conclusions of the Third World ideologies.

Indeed, one could almost go so far as to say that the ideological aspects of the conflicts in the Third World are relevant not to the Third World countries themselves, but to the governments and peoples of the superpowers and their allies and satellites.

The Soviet Union can justify its military assistance and its armed intervention by proxy in the name of "anticolonialism" and respect for the rights of nationalities (not respected at home). Because the nation-state and its boundaries are, in much of the Third World, relatively recent and artificial, the Soviet Union can select the doctrines it applies according to the particular situation with which it is dealing. It can support the Somalis, whose national identity is not coterminous with the frontiers created by Ethiopian or European conquests. (From 1935 until after the fall of Mussolini's empire, the Ogaden was administered with Somaliland.) It can then change sides, and deny the Somalis as well as the Eritreans self-determination in order to tighten its grip upon the communist inheritors of the Ethiopian empire. Western and Central Africa—notably Zaïre—present similar possibilities in areas where there are important material resources which could be denied to the West with important consequences for the world balance of industrial and military power. Even in Southeast Asia, where the indigenous nationalisms are more deep-rooted and based upon more advanced and complex civilizations, both the Soviet Union and the People's Republic of China have been able to manipulate ideological appeals in competition with each other and to the general detriment of the West.

The rulers of the Soviet Union—speculation about China in this respect may be unwise—are, of course, ultimately inspired by an ideological commitment, but they have avoided allowing their activities in the Third World to be robbed of flexibility by considerations of ideological purity. Khrushchev may have gone further in the direction of accepting ideological idiosyncracies than his successors, but the point remains valid. Since the Soviet rulers preserve at home a highly structured bureaucratic regime, frozen almost into immobility, and since they can prevent their foreign instruments from being exposed to Soviet realities or the Soviet people from being enlightened as to the cost of overseas expansion, they are in a strong position to cultivate the advantages that the conflict of ideologies confers upon them. These advantages lie not in the Third World itself, but in the confused consciences of the West.

In Western Europe, inhibitions on acting to protect the West's own interests in the Third World, and to protect its peoples from both Soviet exploitation and the frightfulness that accompanies the imposition of communist rule, are encouraged by political parties actively sympathetic to the Soviet cause and by other circles which respond readily and uncritically to fashionable talk of "neocolonialism." On the other hand, West Europeans are still too close to the past, and have too many real contacts with their former imperial possessions, to accept totally without question some of the claims put forward for the Third World, its regimes, and its political movements.

The real victim has been the United States where, until quite recently, much of the Third World—particularly Africa—has been seen without the benefit of first-hand experience or understanding, and interpreted in the light of slogans that derive from external ideologies. It is not simply a question, as in Europe, of the follies of the Left. In America, both Left and Right, in their different ways, have subscribed to the same cardinal illusion—that the imperial or colonial period was a negative factor in the development of Third World countries, and that, freed from their imperial masters, Third World peoples would do as well as did George Washington and his contemporaries when they attained political independence.

The ideological curtain prevented Americans from seeing how ill equipped most of the newly independent nations were to prove themselves to be in managing their own economic inheritance, and in protecting themselves against externally aided communist subversion. Least of all could they perform these functions through American-style democratic institutions, or the fashionable "mixed" economies of the post-Keynesian world. Their need was not for American democracy, which their social arrangements and traditions made impossible—the earlier experience of Latin America is very cogent in this respect—but for American-style capitalism. In countries facing a population explosion, increased production and increased trade were what mattered most. The successes in the Third World—Singapore, South Korea, Taiwan—did not conduct their affairs with Jeffersonian rectitude, nor would they have been as successful if they had.

It might have been hoped that the Vietnam misadventure would have produced a greater sense of realism—that Americans would have come to realize that the objective of stemming the communist advance was not an ignoble one; that even the much derided "domino" theory was not in itself absurd. They might even take comfort from the fact that, after some false starts, they did learn to cope with the internal war of subversion, guerrilla activity, and terrorism. What vitiated their intervention in the end was that the communists had no intention of treating the frontier between the two Vietnams seriously, and were prepared to invade South Vietnam across it with the full panoply of conventional forces at a time when the domestic circumstances in the United States made any military response impossible. The fact that the United States had entered the war in a fog of intellectual confusion proved irremediable. Having lost their nerve and their national unity, they accepted withdrawal as a prelude to the defeat of their ally, with catastrophic consequences for the people of all Indochina, and perhaps for all Southeast Asia.

History suggests that nations often learn from their defeats. What is important is that the lessons should be the correct ones. It is not clear that the United States has fully assessed the political as distinct from the military lessons of Vietnam. It seems too readily taken for granted that because "intervention" failed, "nonintervention" will succeed; that "progressive" forces (as defined in Soviet-inspired ideologies) will always come out on top and must, therefore, be accepted or even supported unless very cogent material reasons suggest the contrary (as in the Middle East). It has also been assumed that the Soviet Union, which, after all, won the war in Vietnam through its own style of intervention, would accept a self-denying ordinance. Again, it was assumed that "race" would invariably be a more decisive factor in the choice of sides in a postcolonial situation than any other, and that the Russians would therefore be subject to the same suspicions as the West if their intervention was too visible.

There is, of course, something in this argument; "race" and "color" are powerful factors, and can themselves give rise to ideologies or to partial ones. But it is possible to press the argument too far. It was pressed too far when President Carter chose as his ambassador to the United Nations—and therefore a key figure in articulating the ideas governing American policy in the Third World—a man like Andrew Young, whose own strong racialism was not offset by any understanding of the political realities of the Third World or of the nature and purposes of Soviet communism. What is missing from the approach to Africa's problems, as defined by Mr. Young and as exemplified in his handling of the Rhodesian question, is an ability to get behind the ideological curtain and to perceive the material elements in the situation both of Rhodesia and of its neighbors. No country can do well by its own people—of whatever race—nor by its neighbors, if its own productive forces decline. In Africa, a low level of subsistence farming will not be enough to prevent deficiencies if countries like Rhodesia, that can produce a surplus through more advanced agricultural methods, are prevented from doing so. While some Third World countries—in addition to those mentioned and some oil-rich states, there are Malaysia, Kenya, the Ivory Coast, Tunisia—have done well since they attained independence, others, through inefficiency, or corruption, or the imposition of unreal socialist guidelines, have been unable to maintain their economic inheritance, let alone improve it. Where this means that their primary products, particularly foodstuffs, no longer figure in the channels of world trade, the loss is important. Some onetime food exporters like Nigeria have come to rely on external sources.

It is natural that the ideologies with most appeal are those that allow failures to be blamed on external factors, and that suggest it is possible (provided the right formula is adopted) to reach the levels of consumption of the advanced countries without undergoing the long and painful travail—not merely of the industrial revolution, but of the long centuries of state- and nation-building—that preceded it in Europe. It may be said that much Western investment before and since independence was based upon the needs of the capital-supplying country rather than those of the country in which the investment was made, and that its contribution to general growth was, therefore, limited. But the same is even more true of government-to-government ''aid.'' If a country has not developed its nationhood to the extent that it can rely on its rulers—whether civil or military—to regard the country's betterment rather than their own, their family's, or their tribe's, neither trade nor aid will benefit the majority. Moreover, the degree of political instability caused by the frustration of the revolution of rising expectations will imperil even the bare hope of national survival.

It is not a question of the degree of civilization attained by a people, or the length of its recorded history—the record in South and Southeast Asia is sufficient testimony to that. Nor is it a matter of "race." On the contrary, the poor performance of even the most promising African countries, Ghana or Nigeria, and their inability to produce elites able to cope with the demands of a modern economy, is highlighted by the successes as individuals in the New World of men of African descent. What African countries need is an infusion of Western and of Asian skills; they should be, in their own interest, hospitable to the skilled immigrant, as were European cities and states to their advantage in the Middle Ages and later. Instead, under the impulse of ideology, the Asians have been forced out of East Africa and Zambia; and recrudescent terrorism makes a similar fate likely for Europeans in Zaïre, Zambia, and—if the "patriotic front" and Mr. Andrew Young get their way—in Zimbabwe as well. As violence and corruption spread, so the economic prospects dim.

These are harsh words, and words rarely spoken in academe or in the political arena. For this there are obvious reasons. In the first place, the guilt complex that Europeans entertain over "colonialism"—and Americans since Vietnam—combine to make it conventional not to criticize the rulers of Third World countries, and to refrain, above all, from disputing with them over matters that could be classed as "ideological." Indeed, in a rather patronizing way, it is thought proper to flatter them and to extol their enlightenment unless, like Idi Amin, they pass the bounds of the decent— and even then it was left to the Israelis to show him up for the bully and braggart that he is. In the second place, there is the fear that any criticism will tend to shift such rulers and their countries into the Soviet camp. And this fear that the Russians will profit by any strains between Western countries and Third World governments is used by the latter for material as well as emotional blackmail.

Fears of this kind have little foundation in reality, since they rest upon a misconception of the nature of the Soviet appeal and of the sources of Soviet strength. The Russians are quite capable of making the necessary distinction between their long-run aim of extending the area of Soviet control—which is the way they interpret world revolution—and the more immediate objective of strengthening their own state and their own economy. Because of the nature of their economy and the resources available to them in the Soviet Union itself or in Eastern Europe, they do not need many commodities from Third World countries. In that sense, when they say they are disinterested in Africa, for instance, they are speaking the truth. What they can benefit from militarily, and because of its economic consequences in the West and elsewhere, is a denial of such resources to the West. They have little, if anything, to lose from upheavals and anarchy, provided they can secure for themselves or deny to others important staging points in the world's sea and air routes. Their thinking is strategic, not economic. This fact explains the relatively small part that "aid," in the Western sense, plays in the Soviet handling of Third World issues. It is reckoned that the Soviet and East European contribution (if the military aspect is excluded) comes to about 4 percent of that of the OECD countries. The Russians have realized that Third World regimes want to know, not who is going to be nicer to them, but who is going to come out on top. The clumsiness of Soviet diplomacy at a personal level is counterbalanced by the growing conviction that the West can be trusted not to resist Soviet advances, and that the path to safety lies in maintaining or extending links with Moscow.

The question of racial feelings hardly comes into it. By definition, Marxism is an international doctrine that should apply equally to all men. But, like its founders, its modern adherents remain wedded to their prejudices. Accusations of "racism" are something with which to tax the West; they have no bearing on the Russians' own conduct. As a people, they seem to be less affected by prejudice than are other peoples, and their own commitment to the values of a materialist culture makes them less rather than more ready to make allowances for other cultures. In the Third World countries in which they maintain a presence, it is through groups deliberately and effectively insulated from the local population, just as those who are brought to Russia for education or training are kept separate from the indigenous student body. To get the point, one has only to try to imagine a Russian "Peace Corps." But although this form of *apartheid* may be an irritant, it will not affect interstate relations so long as the Third World countries concerned are getting what they want—which may be arms simply for their local battles, not for the pursuit of ideological aims.

When ideology is involved in overthrowing existing foreign or traditional rulers, and where "liberation" or revolutionary movements have been powerfully assisted by Leninist ideas of party structure and Maoist ideas of guerrilla warfare, its role should be distinguished from that involved in the actual construction of new states. For these purposes, the communist ideology is as irrelevant as is Western democracy. Both presuppose a high degree of authority on the part of the state, and a governmental machine that has a conception of common goals and is not simply a means for personal enrichment or social promotion; they also presuppose already existing cadres of skilled workers and professional people. Over a large part of the Third World these preconditions are not met. Where they exist at all, they result from the legacy of the imperial or colonial period in both the civil and the military fields. Unless the imperial power failed to train the local population in technical and administrative skills and relied too entirely upon expatriates, it would seem to follow that the longer a country was under European rule or influence, the better its chances of making a success of independence.

For these reasons, neither of the great world ideologies of today, liberal-democratic and communist, fit easily into the outlook of most Third World countries. They are more likely to regard them as the way in which the superpowers dress up their own rivalries. Their choice between them will depend, as has been said, upon which side offers the most in their own terms, and, above all, on which side they think is going to win.

It took a thousand years for an embryonic European civilization to emerge out of the ruins of the Roman Empire in the West. A thousand years is not very long in an historian's perspective, but for those living through Dark Ages and Times of Troubles, that is no consolation. We can certainly see the possibility of a long period of violent anarchy descending on parts of the Third World. How long will it take for Uganda to recover from Amin? Who will be left to be instruments of the recovery? In Ethiopia and Cambodia we have seen the same use of massacre as an instrument of policy, in the former case putting an end to hopes once entertained that it might peacefully transcend some of the handicaps of its inheritance.

It would not be surprising if peoples so afflicted were to accept indirect rule by instruments of Soviet power as preferable to total uncertainty. Each successive step towards establishing Soviet power will make the subsequent ones easier. From Afghanistan to Angola, the omens are, therefore, bleak. Unless the Western world can recover confidence in its own ideas, and cease to rely on some imaginary innate resistance to Soviet power in the Third World, the so-called conflict of ideologies may yet contribute to its own isolation and eventual ruin.

3

ALLAN E. GOODMAN*

Myth versus Reality in North-South Relations

The Arab oil embargo as an example to less-developed countries. The Third World as a bloc. International conferences on economic cooperation, trade, and development. GNP expansion in the developing countries—internal resources and policies. The NIEO Action Program and its lack of support. Bilateral and international relations. Differences in approach by industrialized nations.

*This paper has been reviewed for possible disclosure of classified information, sources, or methods, and has been approved for publication by CIA's Publication Review Board. This review does not imply U.S. government endorsement of the contents of the paper. All ideas and opinions expressed are the author's own.

Ever since the 1973 Arab oil embargo, three myths have
dominated multilateral negotiations between the industrialized
and the developing countries of the so-called "Third World."
They are:

1. LDC (less developed country) development prospects
have been seriously hurt by the global economic disorders
since 1973.

2. The LDCs have a clear view of the relief they want: a
"new international economic order" (NIEO).

3. The LDCs, acting through their negotiating bloc—the
Group of 77 (G-77)—constitute a cohesive force that makes
them influential in international affairs.

These myths have had enormous significance for multilateral diplomacy. In brief, they have encouraged LDCs to demand radical and often poorly thought-out changes in the international economic system, and they have encouraged responses from industrialized countries in which concern for
political appearances has outweighed a concern for bringing
the LDCs down to earth. The result has been nearly five years
of desultory "North-South dialogue," which has brought the
LDCs little in the way of concrete results, and has complicated relations between industrial and developing countries
on important international and bilateral issues.

How did these myths arise? What accounts for their currency today? What is the reality? These are the central questions to be explored in this chapter. They are designed to set
in context some of the key issues—and their implications—
with which this book is concerned.

ORIGINS AND POLITICAL/DIPLOMATIC SIGNIFICANCE

Before these myths can be exposed, it is essential to understand the political events which gave rise to them and which

led policymakers in industrialized countries to take them seriously.

In October 1973, a few developing countries did with one bold stroke what many had sought for years. The Arab oil embargo ''proved'' to LDCs that their joint actions could influence, if not determine, the course of international events. It was a powerful tonic, and led to a sharp rise in LDC militancy and assertiveness, especially in UN politics.

The chief result of these tendencies was the injection into the UN's work on economic development of a political attitude which stressed, not the positive contribution that the international economic system had made and could make to the developing countries, but its inequities. The demand for an NIEO amounted, in effect, to a call for ''reparations'' for the alleged exploitation (primarily in the area of raw materials) of LDCs by industrial countries and multinational corporations.

What some LDC leaders had in mind was the spectre ''one, two, . . . many OPECs''—a slogan frequently heard in UN corridors at the time—and the effect it could have on the attention paid to LDC demands for changes in the international economic order. With the example of OPEC (Organization of Petroleum Exporting Countries) still fresh in mind, the LDCs called *en bloc* for a special session of the UN devoted to the problems of development. When the session was held in April 1974, LDC militancy had been transformed into an unprecedented degree of bloc cohesion. This, in turn, facilitated the adoption by the UN General Assembly of a statement of the LDCs' most radical demands, those embodied in the NIEO ''action programme.''

Little is substantively new about these demands; in fact, many date from the founding of the UN Conference on Trade and Development (UNCTAD) in 1964, and had been pushed (with modest success in such areas as trade preferences, compensatory financing, and new SDR [special drawing rights] allocations) throughout the 1960s in UN circles. What gave NIEO such prominence was its political impact on multilateral diplomacy. Of greatest significance has been the tendency of some key leaders of the G-77 (especially Venezuela, Nigeria, Algeria, Mexico, Indonesia, Iran, and Argentina) to link their cooperation in negotiations—over law of the seas, energy prices and supply, the quality of the environment, the regulation of the export of nuclear technology, and international measures to combat terrorism—to progress toward an NIEO (Gosovic and Ruggie 1976:309–45). Consequently, it was widely believed in Western government circles that progress on the key global issues mentioned above would not be possible without the support and active cooperation of the G-77.

In addition, it was also widely believed that engaging the LDCs in a North-South dialogue could serve as a means of "bringing the LDCs into our system." The hope was (and still is) that involving LDCs in discussions of complex trade and development problems would dissuade many from insistence on the NIEO.

This dialogue has taken place in two main arenas. Of primary importance in 1975–1976 was the twenty-seven–nation Conference on International Economic Cooperation (CIEC), which dealt with energy, development, trade (especially LDC commodity exports), and finance. CIEC was plagued from the outset by the inability of the nineteen participating LDCs to act as representatives of—or actually bargain over—the G-77's bloc demands. When CIEC formally ended in June 1977, the communiqué listed some twenty areas where agreement had been reached, and twenty-one on which it had proved impossible. Most LDCs have branded CIEC a failure, on balance, and there is little prospect that it will be revived. Currently, the bulk of the North-South dialogue is conducted in the Geneva-based UN Conference on Trade and Development. While in UNCTAD all LDCs are represented, they have proved no more able to reach an accommodation with the industrial countries over the NIEO than they did in the CIEC.

Who or what is to blame for the lack of progress in the North-South dialogue? This is a question frequently heard at

UN conferences, and one which especially preoccupies LDC-oriented interest groups in the industrial countries. Certainly the intransigence of both groups of countries has done little to enhance prospects for reaching "global bargains" on the issues involved. But I think that the root cause of the problems experienced to date lies in the fact that the premises on which the North-South dialogue is based are more myth than reality.

Myth No. 1: LDC development prospects have been seriously hurt by the global economic disorders since 1973.

The quadrupling of oil prices and the recession of 1974–1975 have been singled out by the LDCs as having dealt a major blow to development prospects. Particularly hard hit, it is claimed, were the poorest LDCs and those which depended on earnings from exports of raw materials, the prices of which plummeted because of the global recession. The longer-term consequence of these events, UN-sponsored studies now suggest, is that without major resource transfers and fundamental changes in the international economic system, most LDCs will not achieve even the relatively low target of $500 gross national product (GNP) per capita (set by the UN General Assembly in its International Development Strategy) by the end of the century.

What is reality?

The answer to this question depends on what you hold responsible for LDC development problems today. The global economic disorders of the 1970s have unquestionably had a profound effect on LDCs, adding billions to the costs of their imports of oil and manufactured goods. But are these added burdens really the source of development problems, especially that of widespread poverty, and do they represent permanent impediments to LDC economic growth?

In the rhetoric of the North-South dialogue, one theme frequently neglected is that LDC development problems today are the result more of government policies and performance than of the operation of the international economic system per se. Since the 1950s, LDCs have been important beneficiaries of freer international trade and capital movements. The steady, vigorous expansion of the economies of the industrialized countries has permitted LDCs to make impressive economic progress. For example, their real GNP growth— 5.5 percent per year between 1960 and 1973—represents a sustained expansion that surpassed that of any other region or country during any previous period.

There have, of course, been considerable differences in performance among the LDCs. Countries like Korea, Taiwan, Brazil, and the Ivory Coast have sustained a growth of between 7 and 10 percent annually, while for many African and Southern Asian countries economic growth rates have scarcely stayed ahead of population growth. Despite differences in size and natural resource endowments, those countries doing well clearly have several important common characteristics: a skilled and literate populace, political stability, and export-oriented development strategies. The important point to note here is that these characteristics depend on what a government does for its people, not on the magnitude of resource transfers from rich countries. For, as World Bank President Robert McNamara observed in his 1977 address to the Board of Governors, "what is required [for development] . . . is that developing country governments adopt policies that will assist the poor to enhance their own productivity, and that will assure them more equitable access to essential public services."

When viewed in this context, it is also important to note that the international economy has generally helped— particularly in times of crisis—those LDCs whose governments have set policies to take advantage of it. Without serious tampering, for example, the present system brought many LDCs through the oil crisis and the recession. Of greatest significance has been the development of new oil resources, and the expansion of LDC access to capital markets. These include enlarged facilities at the International Monetary Fund (IMF) for compensating exporters of primary products in bad years, and greater access to private lenders. Today, in fact, foreign private sources meet over half of the Third World's financial needs. This development has meant a greater role for foreign bankers in establishing standards of economic performance and shaping stabilization policies in the LDCs. The resulting interaction has promoted greater understanding on both sides of LDC development problems.

These important facts are all but forgotten in the rhetoric of the Group of 77's various declarations and statements of demands at international negotiating sessions. There are two reasons for this. The first is the quiescence at such negotiations of the LDCs who have benefited most from the present international economic system. While these LDCs are ambivalent about many of the G-77 demands, they are also unwilling to be perceived as a source of division within the LDC bloc. The explanation for this behavior will be discussed below. The second reason for the tendency to downplay the positive contribution that the present economic system has made to development is the attractiveness of NIEO itself. As a political manifesto, it appeals to deeply held, anticolonial, antiimperial emotions of LDC leaders. If enacted, the NIEO proposals would eliminate any tinge of dependency or inferiority in LDC dealings in the international economic system (e.g., aid would no longer be dependent on political or economic performance), and LDCs' status in—and authority over—international institutions (especially financial ones) would be substantially enhanced. Fortunately for me, the case of dependency theory and its appeal among LDC leaders is well covered by Anthony Smith in Chapter 11. The important point to keep in mind here is that NIEO is as much about politics and political power and status in international affairs as it is about economics.

This brings us to the issue of the ever-widening (or nevernarrowing) income gap between developing and developed countries. Despite the pace of LDC economic growth over the past two decades, it seems to all LDC leaders that the rich are simply getting richer. And, if the calculations of Dr. David Morawetz of the World Bank are correct, it would take most LDCs, growing at twice their present rates, more than a century to close the income gap. By the end of this century, many LDCs may not even achieve a level of growth that would permit them to match the minimum per capita income target set by the UN General Assembly.

There is now considerable debate—even among LDC economists—about the appropriateness of such targets, and the use of the gap as a rationale for LDC demands on the international economy. As one LDC spokesman has argued, "the concept of catching up must be rejected. Catching up with what? Surely the Third World does not wish to imitate the life styles of the rich nations? It must meet its own basic human needs within the framework of its own cultural values" (Ul Haq 1976:2).

As I have attempted to indicate, moreover, the present international economic system appears on balance to have contributed more to development than is commonly assumed. It will continue to do so. What has made the most critical difference between governments which have succeeded in meeting their development objectives and those which have not has been government policy. Governments which put development first, and which take advantage of the international economics system, will continue to achieve the growth they desire. Standards of living will rise. Governments which are unable to do this will not be able to deliver on their development promises, just as they have not been able to do so in the past, despite the help of massive resource transfers. Even if NIEO became a reality tomorrow, the development of those countries which have been most vociferous in the North-South dialogue would still depend primarily on the effectiveness of their governments and not on the generosity of the new economic system.

Myth No. 2: The LDCs have a clear view of the relief they want: a "new international economic order."

LDC spokesmen have supported the NIEO Action Program with unexpected tenacity through more than a dozen international conferences and negotiations. Despite diversity in outlook, economic philosophy, and political objectives among the LDCs, numerous studies, working groups, and intrabloc ministerial conferences have consistently supported the basic resource transfer schemes and proposals contained in the NIEO Action Program. This process has transformed many elements of the "action program" into powerful political symbols. But such symbolism has had relatively little effect on the economic policy of most LDCs, or on their trade and aid relations with individual industrialized countries.

One and three-quarter billion people live in the 114 LDCs (the 115th member of the G-77 is the Palestine Liberation Organization [PLO]). Of this number, roughly a third (620 million) live in some twenty-four countries that are either resource-rich (e.g., the OPEC states, Zaïre, Zambia, Jamaica, Morocco, Malaysia), or have reached a level of development and possess the human resources essential to attracting foreign investment (e.g., Taiwan, Singapore, South Korea, Mexico, Brazil). The basic objective of these states is to maximize revenue from the sale of their resources and manufactures, and to secure access to stable sources of commercial capital and technology in the industrial world.

Roughly one-half (930 million) of the inhabitants of the developing world live in some seventy-two countries that have only some of the ingredients necessary for economic growth and development. These countries (e.g., India, Peru, Jordan, Liberia, Thailand) seek trading preferences, technical assistance, and government-sponsored "soft" development loans from the industrial world. Finally, nearly 200 million people live in extremely poor countries that basically lack sufficient resources to sustain economic growth. These countries (e.g., Bangladesh, Ethiopia, Laos) are wholly dependent on external assistance to survive, as constituted at present.

Given such profound differences in objectives and capabilities, LDC support for the NIEO Action Program has been only skin deep, and probably reached its high point in 1976 when the G-77 agreed on the Manila Declaration in preparation for the fourth ministerial meeting of UNCTAD. The next such meeting will be held in May 1979 in Manila, and it is highly unlikely that the basic outline of the Manila Declaration will change. This manifesto contains the most extreme formulation of the LDCs' demands, and was adopted to paper over substantial differences between the Asian, Latin, and African regional groups that plagued G-77 strategy and tactics throughout 1975. Since its adoption, the bloc leadership has not deviated from it for fear of fracturing unity, despite substantial differences among the LDCs over the desirability of many key elements of the NIEO program, especially in the areas of commodity trade and debt relief.

The dynamics of the dialogue have also facilitated the maintenance of the NIEO in the light of Manila, because the industrial countries have made no "take it or leave it" offers or enforced other penalties for LDC intransigence. The industrialized country responses to LDC demands, in fact, have virtually eliminated any need to consider critically the practicability of some of the key elements of the NIEO. For most LDCs, moreover, the NIEO program still requires no choices about which of its provisions should have priority.

Myth No. 3: The LDCs, acting through their negotiating bloc (the G-77), constitute a cohesive force that makes them influential in international affairs.

Thus far, the leadership of the G-77 has been remarkably successful in subordinating the differences among the LDCs—over both the appropriate tactics to use in the North-South dialogue and the desirability of particular demands—for the sake of confronting the industrialized countries with a unified bloc. Created at the first ministerial meeting of UNCTAD (Geneva 1964), the G-77 has served as the LDCs' UN caucusing group in New York, Geneva, Rome, and Paris, and has surpassed in influence any other LDC bloc.

But it is essential to view the relative influence of the G-77 from the perspective of its components. Of central importance is the fact that only a handful of LDCs can actually influence international affairs. The major actors are those LDCs whose actions directly affect world trade and financial flows. Aside from the oil-rich members of OPEC who possess substantial financial reserves (Saudi Arabia, Kuwait, the United Arab Emirates, Iran), the ranks of the group of export-oriented countries, sometimes referred to as "upper-tier" LDCs, are small (Mexico, Brazil, South Korea, Singapore, and Taiwan), likely to remain so, and far from monolithic or unified in outlook on international affairs.

The fact that such countries are not viewed as "LDCs" by many members of the G-77 complicates their relations with the Third World. Especially in the context of international economic negotiations and UN multilateral diplomacy, upper-tier countries are clearly ambivalent about identifying with the New International Economic Order, particularly when it would adversely affect investor confidence or threaten to disturb already satisfactory trading relationships. Nevertheless, each has been able to move with ease in multilateral diplomacy by rhetorically siding with the G-77, and by privately assuring industrial countries and multinational corporations that their respective interests are hardly threatened by the inchoate resolutions and actions likely to result from such bloc politicking.

The momentum behind the North-South dialogue, moreover, is largely due to the efforts of a small, fluid group of *activist* countries. They derive their influence primarily from their ability to control institutions of multilateral diplomacy (e.g., the UN General Assembly, UNCTAD, the G-77), rather than their economic importance.

The activists (e.g., the Philippines, Indonesia, India, Algeria, Venezuela, Nigeria) argue that there should be a redistribution of both wealth and political power in international affairs. To that end, they contribute resources in perpetually short supply in international organizations—i.e., capable diplomats and technicians who can devote their full time and energies to running caucus meetings, staffing ad hoc drafting groups, and lobbying. Their influence is enhanced, consequently, not only because they provide what many Geneva- and New York–based Third World diplomats lack (expertise, staffing assistance, social occasions, and the prestige of occasional chief-of-state endorsements), but also because the latter often operate in the absence of any firm instructions—other than to avoid jeopardizing LDC bloc unity—from their national capitals.

Because they are explicitly concerned about power relations, and especially about increasing their authority in regional and international affairs, the activists tend to evaluate the policies and preferences of industrialized countries in terms of their impact on national prestige. What matters to the activists seems to be the degree to which the initiatives and preferences of the United States and other industrial countries reinforce or detract from such immediate objectives as the consolidation of regional status and influence and the expansion of authority over international institutions and affairs.

Most activists are more realistic in private about prospects for changes in international affairs than they are in G-77 and UN arenas, and they are increasingly pragmatic about the progress that can be made. However, events to date—especially the unity of the G-77 and the continued (albeit grudging) attention the industrialized countries have paid to bloc demands—have only caused the activists to scale down their short-term expectations, rather than to revise fundamentally their basic demands for systemic change.

The continued North-South polarization of international economic and political issues will thus complicate the conduct of multilateral diplomacy, and could generate strains in U.S. relations with some of the LDCs who are among the most influential in UN politics. Aside from the Arab oil-producing states, however, the nonindustrial states do not have the leverage to extract any of their basic demands against the will of the major industrialized countries. And they clearly wish to avoid any net loss of support for their modernization efforts.

Nevertheless, the need to manage the problems of scarce resources will require the active cooperation and support of key LDCs. Some will continue to see the arenas in which solutions to their problems are discussed in North-South terms, evaluating U.S. diplomatic initiatives in terms of political power balances in international organizations. Others, while they may be realistic about the utility of dealing with such problems on a global basis, will continue to find rhetorical support of LDC bloc approaches useful for enhancing their status within the context of regional rivalries and ambitions. And still other LDCs will contiue to insist that the problems mentioned above can only be handled on a case-by-case basis, and in the context of specific bilateral relationships. Sensitivity to these differences in outlook among the LDCs, and to their preferences for dealing with what are nominally called ''North-South'' issues, will thus remain a central challenge to U.S. diplomacy for the foreseeable future.

IMPLICATIONS

It would be erroneous to conclude from the foregoing discussion that to do nothing about the demands of the developing countries for an NIEO is the wisest course. The issues of aid and trade policies toward the LDCs, as well as their role and authority in international institutions, show no signs of disappearing from the international scene. The LDCs, singly and *en bloc,* are likely to continue to be assertive—and to speak with increasing confidence—when their interests are at stake.

In addition, the North-South dialogue has uncovered differences in approach and outlook among the industrialized countries that have complicated and burdened the agenda of OECD (Organization for Economic Cooperation and Development) relations. France, Italy, and the Scandinavian countries, for example, support the LDCs' overall program to protect purchasing power in the international commodity trade; the U.S., Germany, and Japan do not. Differences also exist over the appropriateness of specific negotiating arenas, the institutions and mechanisms through which resources should be transferred from North to South, and responsiveness to LDC pressures for increased power and authority in international organizations generally. The coordination of OECD policies on North-South issues will, therefore, be a continuing problem. In any case, the foregoing would suggest that the possible tactical value of inaction—a course favored by those seeking to "break the bloc"—should be weighed against the longer-run costs to relations among the OECD countries, and international relations generally, of the tensions that could be generated by the continued polarization of important international issues along North-South lines.

At the same time, it would also be erroneous to conclude that the initiative for accommodation and concession to LDC demands rests solely with the industrialized countries. Indeed, the foregoing would suggest that *demonstrating no willingness to go beyond current offers in the framework of the North-South dialogue is essential* to reinforcing tendencies toward realism and pragmatism on the part of key LDCs.

Thus far, the industrialized countries' policy has been to avoid confrontations with the LDCs, and to promote a spirit of accommodation that would carry over from *venue* to *venue.* The trade-off for maintenance of this atmosphere has been freedom of action; that is, in many cases the industrialized countries have had to accept LDC conceptions of key issues, and to commit themselves to a schedule and negotiating agenda over which their influence has been minimal. The significance of this trade-off is that if, as is currently believed, most industrialized countries have reached the maximum extent of flexibility on NIEO issues, there may be little that can now unilaterally be done to promote a tension-free atmosphere in multilateral diplomacy.

At the same time however, intransigence—originally used by G-77 leaders to accommodate the Africans and radicals—has produced little in the way of results from the LDCs' viewpoint. Some G-77 leaders, in fact, argue that progess in the North-South dialogue is now dependent on *LDC initiatives* to reach an accommodation with the industrialized countries. This changing outlook—combined with the concern of many in the G-77 that a return to confrontation would be counterproductive—is thus likely to serve as a check on those who favor confrontational tactics.

If the stage were thus set for more down-to-earth discussions with the LDCs, where should such bargaining take place? The chief implications of this analysis are that efforts to achieve greater industrialized country control over the present mechanisms of the North-South dialogue (e.g., UNCTAD, the UN "overview mechanism," and the General Assembly itself) will only further enshrine the myths described above. This would, in turn, virtually assure the tendency on the part of most LDCs to continue to support a bloc politics approach, and protract the search for less-politicized ways to negotiate with the industrialized countries. Hence, what is most needed now in North-South relations are initiatives, by industrialized and developing countries alike, to change the *venues* in which LDC demands are surfaced and negotiated.

Promising starts have already been made toward transforming the North-South dialogue from a confrontation into a meaningful discussion of complex economic and political issues. Among these, the following stand out in terms of the pragmatic directions taken: the creation of the International Fund for Agricultural Development, Association for Southeast Asian Nations (ASEAN), consultations with the United

States, Japan, and the European Economic Community, the
expansion of the soft loan windows of the regional development banks, and the individual commodity negotiations taking place at Geneva. But these efforts are hampered, in part,
by the currency given to the myths described in this chapter,
and by the tendency among some LDCs to equate compromise and accommodation with industrialized countries at
this level with selling out G-77 interests as a whole. Tacti-
cally, the industrialized countries can divest these myths and
presumptions of their self-fulfilling character. However, the
future of the North-South dialogue now appears to depend as
much on what the LDCs do to establish their own priorities as
on the willingness of the industrialized countries to participate in the creation of a new international economic order.

II

*Social and
Economic Realities*

4

DENNIS AUSTIN

Prospero's Island

The worlds of the haves and the have-nots. The projected fears at the end of colonialism. Tyranny as a product of national self-assertion. Postcolonial differences among formerly dependent nations. The economic range between poverty and wealth among nonindustrial states. Managed economies and private enterprise. Political stability independent of national prosperity. Amnesty International.

Belief in the existence of a "Third World" is now almost an article of faith. Like most beliefs, it is held doctrinally under one form, but under quite another in practice. There are not three worlds but two, a developed world and an underdeveloped world—a world of those who have and those who have not. The haves not only possess more goods; they have a richer life, enjoying political stability, old age, full stomachs, freedom from anarchy, warm houses in winter, cool homes in summer, the advantage of travel, and the marvels of technology. Such are the attributes of the developed world, whether under capitalist or communist rule, whereas those who are categorized as "Third World countries" suffer fearfully by comparison. As with most faiths, there have been definitional amendments. There are now a number of subdivisions within the circle of description of the first United Nations Conference on Trade and Development (UNCTAD).[1] Yet despite the qualifications, the dogma persists that a sharp line divides the powerful and dependent, rich and poor, bad and good. What began as economics has widened into political economy, politics and morality, but still the shadow line between the developed and underdeveloped worlds is maintained in conference declarations and popular reference.

So widespread a conviction must reflect more than the obvious difference between, say, California and Papua New Guinea. It seeks to divide the world between light and dark, and any myth of that nature has great power, although (like all myths) it has grown and changed in the making. More than twenty years ago, the French scholar Manoni (1956) noted that within the managed world of the European empires there was always a Caliban-Ariel division between the bad (recalcitrant) native and the good (obedient). It had been marvelously represented, he observed, in *The Tempest*. The loyalty of the obedient Ariel was retained by promises underpinned by threats; Caliban was held in check through fear of reprisals. The problem is solved eventually, at least in Shakespeare's drama, by separation. Prospero returns to Milan, Ariel goes free, and Caliban rules his island; he is again all the subjects that he has, and is once more his own king.

But within the tormented pattern of relationships among twentieth-century governments there is no such easy end to the problem of dependency between the rich and the poor, and the powerful and the vulnerable. Prospero's island has become the world. And the myths, too, have been enlarged. As the colonial world dissolved in the 1950s, a dualistic view of the new international order reappeared in the United States and the Soviet Union. It was as if the old Ariel-Caliban division within the colonial territories had been internationalized and, indeed, made worse by there being, so to speak, rival Prosperos trying to weave their spells from Washington and Moscow. There was the same neurotic projection onto the weak of the fears and dreams of the powerful.

By the 1960s, however, the doctrine had put out new forms. The configuration of good and bad had changed again. Caliban and Ariel (however defined) had begun to join forces. Or so, at least, it was assumed. And it is true that a number of Asian, African, Caribbean, and Latin American governments, dispirited by lack of success in controlling their own societies, moved bad-temperedly towards the assertion that the rich and powerful were all culpable. Their continued dependence on the money and markets of the wealthy, as of the rich on the resources of the poor, added to that exasperation, and the effect is now plain to see. We are regularly presented internationally with what is loosely described as a North/South, or non–Third World/Third World, or a haves/ have-nots division.

The distinction is confirmed among the generous-hearted young by a kind of paper radicalism which, crudely expressed, often takes the form: the Third World is poor because it is dependent, helpless because it is poor, and blameless because it cannot help itself. The belief rests comfortably on a number of related dogma; for example, that although African and Asian governments buy arms to fight local wars and to maintain internal control, they are enticed to purchase them by the governments of the industrial nations, among whom the dynamics of growth and its surplus wealth are predicated on the dependence of others. It is also recognized that Third World societies are often governed corruptly; but that, too (it is said), comes from the dislocation inflicted by colonial rule or from the intrusion of foreign capital. Even the bloody tyrants among the new leaders—Amin, Bokassa, the archetypal Papa Doc, or the more brutal of the Latin American dictators—can be explained away as atavistic reactions to the need for a national self-assertion against the past, quite apart from the fact that many of them are propped up from outside: Pinochet by the United States, Mengistu by the Soviet Union, Bokassa by the French, Mobuto by the International Monetary Fund (IMF).

It is easy to understand why such a dualism is endorsed. It projects a simple picture of the whole globe, including the moral helplessness of the poor—an easier view than that of a changing, multiple, uncertain world of the quite good and the not very bad, or the more or less wealthy and the more or less poor. Moreover, dependency is not only exculpatory. It *transfers* the blame, and it ties in neatly with the allied belief that all would be well if only this or that particular obstacle, beyond one's immediate grasp, were to be removed. Those who lack power can actually take comfort, therefore, from their impotence. Since it is beyond their capacity to change the world, they need only demand action by others. At their most romantic, such arguments reflect a deep sentiment of longing, a longing for Prospero's island without Prospero and the computations of wealth and power. The world, it is said, must be remade until a new international order emerges, transformed by a radical restructuring of its society and economy, within which there will be neither wealth nor poverty, nor power and dependence. Then, and only then, will Prospero and Caliban, and even Ariel, be changed into self-reliant creatures, and man will cease to be a capitalist wolf to his fellow men.

So runs the creed. And even the industrial rich have been half-persuaded in public declarations, if not of their guilt, at least of their need to respond to such assertions—in marked contrast, one might note, from earlier, more robust beliefs. It is not very long since it was argued that the world could be put right politically—and enabled to grow economically— not by expiation, but by imitation. The formulae varied, but the confidence was there. Newly independent countries had only to adopt the Westminster Constitution, or accept *La Ré-*

publique Française, or turn communist, or listen to Washington or the IMF, in order to follow in the wake of the successful. That kind of optimism is almost gone, although it may perhaps linger among the party faithful in Moscow or the more devout of Carter's followers. To each, then, today, his own political culture. But it is still possible, it seems, to believe that all the poor are one poor, and all the rich are culpable.

The actual effect of such beliefs has been very bad. It has produced a crude, distorted picture of the world of sovereign governments. It ignores the diversity of states even within those that pass for the founding members of the Third World. Its rigid fixity of belief also leaves out the politics, not of dependency but of morality, avoiding the awkward fact that the desperately poor and extravagantly rich are as likely to be found within a single state as in the division between states, and that the cruel and the tolerant are at opposite ends of a broad spectrum of new and old states alike. It also posits a loose kind of international morality which a number of uneasily based governments have used as cover for their own deficiencies at home. Underlying the distortion, there is a disregard of the capacity for ameliorative change among non-European societies—perhaps a residual belief still in Prospero's magic? In short, there has been an old-fashioned and an ill-fashioned look to such arguments.

They also lack substance. Even without such subcategories as the oil-rich and oil-poor countries, there was always something very odd about a dualism which omitted the huge fact of China—powerful, poor, nondependent, and immensely distinct by its long history and self-contained culture, yet no longer able to be left out of any full view of an international order. Nor have the imprecise boundaries of a Third World, however modified, been able to take proper account, in or out, of a number of intermediate countries such as Turkey or Israel or South Korea or Iran and the poorer communist states. (By 1977 Cuba, for example, was numbered among the members of a New Economic Order, Albania was not.) *Excepciones probant regulas*? Perhaps. Yet even among the former colonies, most of which have been independent only since World War II (though Latin America is a huge exception to *that*), even there, among the states which are commonly said to comprise the central core of the Third World, the range of political experience and economic attainment has been very wide. The difficulty of attaching a single label to whatever is meant by such a category can be seen by examining the indices generally adopted.

COLONIAL RULE?

It is only a generation or so ago that colonial governments were internationally recognized and legally administered; but as they surrendered control in the 1950s and 1960s, the post-colonial differences became very marked. It was hardly surprising. Colonialism had been diverse, different in its British and French, or Belgian, Dutch, and Portuguese settings; distinct also from one part of the globe to another, even within the same empire. It was molded to—and by—the pattern of local culture. French rule in Algeria was not only unlike that of Belgium in the Congo, but unlike French control of Indochina; British rule in Barbados was different from its administration of Kenya or Sri Lanka or Cyprus. Only from the commanding heights of Marxist theory, or a simple American morality, could colonialism be seen as an undifferentiated phenomenon. The distinctions have widened into sharp contrasts now that European empires (and the shorter-lived Japanese and American possessions) have come to an end, and a good deal has happened since independence to accentuate the difference, including civil wars, *coups d'état,* the rise and fall of particular leaders, changes in commodity prices, and the change of patrons from old to new masters.

The mistake in referring back what *is* to what *was* comes from too close a stress on continuity in history. Politically, before-independence was unlike after-independence in one critical aspect, namely, that rule by foreigners is always different from government from within one's own society. Form, too, is different from content. Whatever the similarities, there has frequently been a sharp political contrast between a colonial administration and its nationalist successors. The former was an intrusion, however locally devoted its officers might be to those over whom they ruled. They were always a foreign elite, banded together under the governor as much by a code of colonial behavior as by instructions, and although there might be some backsliding— "going native"—they were, as Kipling portrayed them in India, always a disciplined hierarchy. It was not the lawlessness but the law of the jungle which ruled their conduct as a set of guardians whose strength lay in the pack.

> Now these are the Laws of the Jungle, and many and
>   mighty are they;
> But the head and the hoof of the Law and the haunch
>   and the hump is—Obey.

Their nationalist successors have no such code of ethics or surety of racial solidarity. They are party or military leaders who retain control by exercising power over their own kind. The difference can be sharply expressed at its extreme by noting that no governor ever hanged one of his colonial officers, whereas Nkrumah in Ghana imprisoned his own party colleagues, and Idi Amin in Uganda beats to death civil servants, judges, university teachers, and his fellow army officers, alike. One needs to be careful when looking at the persistence of colonial characteristics to note also the interruption of the legacy or, more truly, the new departures as well as the old continuities.

Colonial rule, therefore, is a "variable" in the experience of many new states. On the one hand, the effect is now a diminishing force. On the other, it has bequeathed different legacies. For there must be some carry-over from the past, however attenuated. The long history of British rule in Barbados has preserved an unbroken structure of parliamentary government since 1626. The gruesome quality of Leopold's misrule in the Congo, though redeemed by government from Brussels, pointed the way forward to Mobutu's Zaïre, where it frequently seems as if time has not simply stopped but turned back, its local forces in rebellion, and large tracts of the eastern and southern provinces

> . . . a darkling plain
> Swept with confused alarms of struggle and fight
> Where ignorant armies clash by night.

ARTIFICIALITY?

At a more abstract level of expression, it is sometimes argued that an overriding characteristic of Third World states is that they are flawed by communal division, a point Seymour Martin Lipset makes below in a different context. They bear the stamp of artificiality. They lack, it is said, identity, with the result that national loyalties are weak and without any strong center of allegiance. They may include old societies, but for the most part they are new states. No wonder, therefore, that the location of political authority is uncertain and that, in consequence, institutions and procedures fail to command respect.

There is a good deal of truth in such descriptions. Yet even among countries generally singled out as "Third World," variations in the degree of heterogeneity, whether of an ethnic, religious, racial, or linguistic nature, and in the relative strength of national loyalties, are also notable. Nor can it easily be said that diversity breeds instability and/or political coercion. If that were so, Sri Lanka would be less liberal and less steady than, say, Turkey or Libya. And that is certainly not the case. Malaysia, too, is plural and relatively noncoercive; Uganda is plural and murderous. Of course, at the extremes, as in the Lebanon or Cyprus, where local conflicts are reinforced from outside, communal division and political collapse are clearly linked.

But the growing literature on pluralism does not point easily in any direction, nor can it isolate a category of states even nominally "Third World" in character. For example, despite what might be thought an excessive pluralism, India, one might argue, has a sufficient historical identity, both colonially rooted and precolonially derived, and is sufficiently self-aware as a political community, to maintain free institutions; at least, it has kept the military at bay and has changed its politics without massive violence. Yet Egypt—a very ancient state—is constantly and precariously poised between order and breakdown. Nor is there any clear demarcation between industrial and nonindustrial states in this respect. The politics of ethnicity have plagued states which might be thought to have the resources to cope with the problem: Belgium, Canada, the United Kingdom (of which Ulster is still a part), France, and substantial urban areas of the United States. Moreover, if it is Canada today, who can swear that the USSR will not be broken by communal violence— whether regional or national—tomorrow, once the steel hoop of its party apparatus is weakened, a question not unrelated to that discussed in Daniel Pipes's article (Chapter 10).

RESOURCES?

Between Prospero and Caliban-plus-Ariel, it is assumed, there lies not only power, but the wealth on which power is based and from which the comfortable life of the industrialized nations is derived. It is certainly true that many Asian and African states are poor, particularly those affected by drought and famine. But the economic range between extreme poverty and quite substantial wealth among nonindustrial states is very striking, Gabon is oil-rich beyond the dreams of Lesotho; Jamaica and Kenya are far wealthier than Rwanda and Upper Volta. Even within the literature of dependence, there are MDCs and LDCs—greater and less de-

veloped countries—and the "most seriously affected." Even
the dependent poor have weaker and poorer states dependent on
them, just as the rich have the not-so-rich dependent on *them*.
The bland assertion that there is a Third World unable to break
the bonds of a world economy which holds it in thrall—in the
grip of growth without development, or within an enclave
economy of benefit only to a parasitical state bourgeoisie—
makes little allowance for the relatively well off (Venezuela,
the Ivory Coast, Mexico, Brazil, Malaysia), and no allowance
at all for the very successful (Singapore, South Korea, Hong
Kong, the ex-colonies of New Zealand and Australia, or the
once politically stunted and feudal Japan).

The Japanese are, indeed, a remarkable example of those
who convert feudal rags into industrial riches. In 1847 an
official of the emperor informed a persistent Dutch envoy that
"His Majesty charges us to inform you that it is of but slight
importance to the Empire of Japan whether foreigners come
or do not come to trade." By 1853 Commodore Perry had
forced upon a reluctant Shogunate the market economy of the
West. But still the British shook their heads in sorrow, because "for nearly two centuries and a half Japan had been cut
off from the atmosphere of competition, and had never had
the opportunity of warming her intelligence at the fire of international rivalry." Who is getting scorched today? By the
1970s British ministers were flying to Tokyo to ask for a
curtailment of exports into Western Europe. A reversal of
dependencies?

I have heard it argued that it was easier in the nineteenth
century for the non-Western world to catch up and overtake.
But there are late twentieth-century states which are both dependent and becoming dominant. They, too, are busily "in-
digenizing," in the sense of bringing into one national
economy the duality of domestic and foreign sectors. Japan is
ceasing to be singular. Other Asian countries, notably South
Korea, Singapore, Taiwan, Hong Kong, and some Latin
American states, particularly Brazil and Venezuela, have
begun to frighten the life out of older industrial nations.

South Korea has even managed to alarm the Japanese by its combination of low wage costs and modern technology in textiles, shipbuilding, electronics, steel, and petrochemicals.[2] It is hardly a question of Caliban and Ariel distancing themselves from Prospero, but of their capturing and using his skills against him.

There is, to be sure, a distinction between totally managed economies and those in which private wealth is allowed to have its say. When the state is all-powerful, one may fear that the cruel and strong will seek not wealth but power; where mixed economies sustain the state, it may be, as Keynes (1961:374) observed, that "dangerous human proclivities can be canalised into comparatively harmless channels by the existence of opportunities for money-making and private wealth. . . . It is better that a man should tyrannise over his bank balance than over his fellow citizens." But that has nothing to do with contrasts between Third World and industrial countries. Between the worship of power, leading to tyranny, and the worship of riches within a privileged elite, lies the entire spectrum of states which comprise the present international system—not a dualistic world of those with, and those without, resources.

What should be done, then, about the many desperately poor who lack resources, power, and skills? No one seems to know. El Salvador or Tanzania is unlikely to reach the level of the Ivory Coast or Kenya, neither of which can as yet hope to rival Trinidad, nor can Trinidad equal Singapore and Taiwan. But what can be done about the truly destitute? Within the present century, it is inconceivable that the huge disparities between the poorest of the poor and the very prosperous can be more than diminished a little by an intelligent and generous use of the power of the latter. Whether that is best done by market access, or un-tied aid, or commodity agreements, or a different pricing mechanism in petroleum products, is a matter for argument in each instance. But simply to divide the world between a notional Third World and non–Third World is no help at all. It is likely to conceal the

plight of the worst. Hence, the subdivision into the "less developed," although even that is a crude categorization, since
the very poor are often more dependent on the poor than on
the rich.[3]

POLITICAL ORDER?

It is easy enough to conjure up a Third World of tormented
states and an industrial world of steady societies under firm
political control, although such an image ignores a whole
area of recent argument concerning the ungovernability of industrial and postindustrial states, and there must be few who
see Italy in the 1970s as under firm control. Still, it is true
enough that many of the recently independent states and most
Latin American societies are badly governed. It is certainly a
singular fact that no independent government, in all the fifty
or more states of the African continent, has been removed
from office by an election alone: only by the army or an as-
sassin.

Yet the picture is not quite so unrelieved. Such general
phrases as "the instability of the Third World" may give too
permanent a title to what may be a passing phenomenon. If a
single explanation of the present unsettled pattern of military
coups and unsuccessful governments were needed, I would
not emphasize the paucity of resources, or the effect of dependency by multinational companies and distant agencies of
control. After all, a society or state may be held in a steady
subservience, as one might say of Liberia under the former
president, Tubman. Poverty, too, may immobilize a society
and confirm one or other sections of its rulers in power by
passivity, as might be said of Upper Volta.

No, I would argue that the breakdown of authority in many
new states, and its broken-backed misrule, are due primarily
to novelty—the novelty of elites and their nervous incapacity
in office.

In the broadest sense possible, the effect of the dissolution of a major empire is invariably calamitous. It leaves behind an uncertainty about successors and the institutions they inherit. The "proof," so to speak, may be seen by the avoidance of breakdown when the last-hour efforts of the imperial power have been more successful than elsewhere, as in the Ivory Coast under French rule, or in Ceylon under the British. But time may repair the omission even among the most unsuccessful, as leaders become established as ruling elites or even as classes, some tolerant, some brutal. To put the matter crudely: if Africa and Asia cannot settle down to their inheritance of colonial procedures and institutions, they may yet settle down to tyranny. Stability is an ambiguous virtue. The regime of Papa Doc at one extreme, and that of Stalin at another, were both, in a sense, "stable." But that, too, is over-simple. The variety of political experience is bound to be as complicated politically throughout the former colonial states as it is likely to be in relation to economic performance. Already, a number of such governments, including those commonly seen as controlling Third World countries, have preserved a relatively peaceful continuity under changes of regime: India, Malaysia, Jamaica, Costa Rica, Colombia, Fiji, Sri Lanka.

Nor is it at all certain that the world of industrialized states will remain politically steady. They may take any loss of wealth more hardly than others. He that is down need fear no fall. It is perhaps the rich, not the poor, who are at risk. The little state of the Gambia is dependent, without resources, ex-colonial, ethnically divided, and overshadowed by its neighbors; yet its half-million citizens have a freedom of political expression, a steady government, and civil liberties very different from the history of many richer, more tormented states. Naturally, it would be helpful if across the world—Third, Fourth, First, and Second alike—there were ancient traditions harmoniously related to the present, a benign period of political history, adequate resources (assuming there are such assets), a clear location of power, skillful leaders of clear moral perception, and a close identity between citizens and state. The world unfortunately is not like that at all, and, even if it were, the sinfulness of civic man might still corrupt it. The future is much more likely to reflect the past—an unsure pattern of confident as well as sickly governments, strong as well as feeble regimes. All history in this sense is the history of uncertainty.

It is in respect of morality—political morality—that one can actually bring back a division of the good and the bad, not in relation to dependency and power, or wealth and poverty, or old and new states, but between liberty and oppression. If a dualistic picture of the world were needed, I would take what might be called "the view from Amnesty," and the sight of that political landscape would soon put "paid" to assertions that the wealthy are democratic because they are rich, or that the dependent are brutal because they are poor, as if political freedom was a commodity which went only to the highest bidder.

THE VIEW FROM AMNESTY?

One does not have to be so simple as to believe in the totality of darkness on one side and the purity of light on the other. There are no unreservedly good governments, though there may be unredeemably bad ones. The moral yardstick that can be used is plain enough. First, the number of political prisoners and the use of torture; second, freedom from imprisonment without trial (of rich and poor, political and nonpolitical alike), and the right to own and freely use a passport.

Very few states, indeed, grant such rights today. How many are being tortured—now, in 1978—in the prisons of the Soviet Union or Cambodia, South Africa, Uganda, South Yemen, Chile, Vietnam? It does not matter whether the gaoler and the prisoner, or the torturer and the tortured, are rich or poor, or white or black or piebald. The greatest evil of this century occurred in an industrial country of Western Europe, that same country from which the most passionate expression of freedom had been heard a century earlier. Was *Fidelio* written for a Germany controlled by Napoleon or a Europe tortured by Hitler? Nor would it be difficult to group together those states where there are no political prisoners, no dark cellars or closed rooms where men and women scream out in pain. A single postage stamp would bring a list of the not too bad and the atrocious from the headquarters of Amnesty International.

Its *Annual Reports* make grim reading. They tell of man's political cruelty, and no distinction is drawn between one part of the world and another. The picture is too bleak to be divided into north and south, or between ''the rich and the bad'' and ''the poor who can't help it.'' The introduction to the 1977 report states quite simply: ''As many as 117 countries are mentioned in this publication. In most of them serious violations of human rights have been reported. . . . Government-sanctioned torture is still practised in a horrifying number of states in spite of the newly adopted U.N. Declaration against all forms of torture.''

Torture is the vilest crime, under practices of medieval barbarity. But there are other cruelties, including the policy adopted by some Latin American governments of destroying all traces of their victims—''disappearance''; or long periods of solitary imprisonment without trial in a number of Asian countries; or the legal base of state victimization in the Soviet Union. As the report states: ''human rights are violated in a majority of countries all over the world. All major regions, all political or ideological blocs are involved—in spite of the Universal Declaration of Human Rights.'' Countries are described one by one, from which it appears that

the techniques of repression and the impact of these techniques vary. There are differences not only in number of victims, but also in methodology, objectives, duration and both short-term and long-term consequences. In some countries, regimes allow para-military groups to kidnap, torture and assassinate political activists; in others prisoners are kept in detention for years without trial. In some police stations torture is carried out with electric shocks; in others with psychological methods. In some prisons the inmates are refused all communication with their families; in others they are starved. There is absolutely no point in trying to judge which measures are categorically "better' or "worse" than others. Similarly it would be a misleading exercise to grade or rank regimes. In the end, what matters is the pain and suffering the individual endures in the police station or in the cell.

There is also no point in defining the worst, if only because the view from Amnesty is incomplete. Some countries are cleverer than others at concealing their crimes. "Amnesty International has carefully monitored all available information from North Korea and can only report that it contains no detailed evidence whatsoever regarding arrests, trials and imprisonment. . . . There appears to be a complete censorship of news relating to human rights."

The descriptions, country by country, are calm and precise, and—if it were not so grim a catalogue of horrors— almost schoolmasterly in tone, in the fashion of end-of-term reports. "Generally, Burundi appears to have settled down to a period of relative stability and reconciliation after the massacre and huge exodus of Hutu refugees during 1972." Tanzania, it is interesting to note, does not appear at all favorably. The level of coercion has risen, and there are "reports of torture still being carried out," in marked contrast with Kenya where, at the time of the 1977 report, the "total number of detainees is probably less than 10." Even so, there are much worse countries: Ethiopia, Cambodia, Guatemala, Chile, South Africa, and, in particular, Equatorial Guinea which, as the report notes, is said to be among "the most brutal and unpredictable in the world."[4]

Interestingly enough, such lists can be seen as constantly changing over time, although some countries remain steadily at the freer end of the scale, others no less steadily at the oppressive end. There is a broad middle band along which there is a good deal of movement, oppressive regimes becoming less oppressive—India, Greece, Venezuela, Sri Lanka; others moving up the scale of oppression—Sierra Leone, Tanzania, Burma, Bangladesh. Some of the worst governments, and the best, might be said to be on the left; others, on the right. Some have state-controlled economies; others, a mixed economy. But the bad and the not-so-bad are to be found in both camps. Size is not important; Nigeria is politically free to an extent unknown in South Africa or China. Barbados is a small free island a whole world apart from Haiti, or even Grenada.

Nor is wealth, or poverty of resources, a conclusive factor. That *is* a little surprising, perhaps, since a general belief in the freedom bestowed by wealth is commonly expressed. Get rid, it is often said, of unemployment, or ghetto housing, or famine, or disease, and you will enable not only citizens to trust their governments, but rulers to elicit support without coercion. In other words, if all the world were as rich as Scandinavia, humanity would be as free from torture and arbitrary rule as Sweden. Well, perhaps. Yet I would not swear to it. Over the past century, the industrial states have been murderously cruel to each other: war, gas chambers, and concentration camps have destroyed far more human beings than the feeble attempts of many non-Western, noncommunist states.

Nor does there seem to be any direct correspondence between wealth, on one side, and freedom from internal oppression, on the other. The Soviet Union is comparatively wealthy; India is relatively unoppressive, and the poverty of India did not prevent a move back in 1977 towards a less authoritarian regime. Of course, poverty itself is oppressive. But who is to say that political oppression is a counterweight to the burden of poverty? It is very often not a remedy for economic distress, but an added trial and, not infrequently, an additional source of economic misery.

It was neither poverty nor dependence, but inflation, which moved the politics of Latin America further towards dictatorship and toward the would-be populist dictators who raised the level of inflation. Nor, in this respect, have the Latin American countries moved in the same direction. Nicaragua and Costa Rica might be thought to be in much the same category of "Third World dependence"; yet the former is brutally governed, the latter is an open society free from prisoners and torture. From a lofty height of theory, the difference may not be very important. But it must matter a good deal to Costa Ricans and Nicaraguans.

There is, to be sure, an authoritarian argument, used by radical and conservative critics alike, which defends the need to place order above justice, based on the belief that disorder may be worse than injustice. Left-wing critics use the argument to "defend the revolution"; conservative writers uphold the belief in order to avoid anarchy. If states without justice are robbers, are not societies without obedience murderous? But there is an extremism about such aphorisms which is often the ground for more injustice, more enforced obedience, and more authority than are needed. *Sub specie aeternitatis,* as saints and poets have told us, good and evil may be the opposite sides of the same coin of a divine order imperfectly understood by men. Dante could place above the Gates of Hell the inscription:

> *Fecemi la divina Potestate*
> *La Somma Sapienza e il primo Amore.*

But, brought to earth, the divinity of love is all too quickly corrupted to a state religion of necessity, and a placing of party slogans above the labor correction camps. In this temporal world of political uncertainties on Prospero's island, we have to choose, and the "view from Amnesty" may help us to see a little more closely the not-so-good and the very bad.

Exactly why the view of the world should be as it is, frightening in one direction, often comforting in another, is a great puzzle. Why should Botswana be very poor and politically tolerant, the Soviet Union technically advanced and politically brutal? Why is Taiwan dependent and prosperous, Burma much poorer and less dependent? In many ways, such questions are so wide as to be meaningless. Even if one is talking only the economics of trade access and debt cancellations, the boundaries of the Third World are stretched beyond definition. When S. Rajaratnam, the Foreign Minister of Singapore, can speak of "We the poorer countries [must be] willing to practice the old-fashioned virtues of hard work, thrift and sacrifice" (quoted by Feulner [1976:12]), he is a long way from Niger or the Solomon Islands. There are many differences, too, to sustain the comparison.

But that is precisely the difficulty of talking loosely about the Third World or a New International Economic Order. Nor can it be sensible for the seventy-seven or ninety-nine or hundred-and-six countries to go on acting as if the world were dyadic or a triad. The effort to achieve a collective will defeats its purpose. Only when there are relatively clear common interests, as among the oil-producing states, is there likely to be the strength of joint action—and even they have had to struggle to preserve a common policy. The recent and abortive meeting of what were once said to be "nonaligned countries" is a good illustration of the worn-out inutility of beliefs that try to separate the world into divided camps. But it is primarily on grounds of misconception that it is surely time to discard outworn arguments about a Third World and its subdivisions, or a North-South division of the globe.

Prospero's island is now too crowded and too complicated to bring all its difficulties under a pseudo-doctrine of a belief which, since it no longer carries conviction, dangerously darkens counsel.

5

S. E. FINER

The Military and Politics in the Third World

Political origins of the Third World. The military, its motives, and its *coups*. Organization of the political public. Tribes, classes, and parties. Regimes and political systems—civilian and military. Military rule and the people it affects. Economics, modernization, and stability. Power and dependency. The need for political community and military neutrality.

The armed forces are the single most important political actor in the Third World. Nearly half its component countries are ruled by their nominees, and in at least half the remaining states, only the military stand between the regime and its downfall.

So much for today, but what of the future? Over the last twenty years, one military *coup* has followed another at the average rate of some eight per annum, and this rhythm, remarkably steady from year to year, shows no sign of slackening. Indeed, last year—1977—showed a total of no less than ten military *coups*.

Yet, on the other hand, when we look at certain individual countries we find that somewhere, after decades of military intervention, there has come a long period of calm. Mexico witnessed one thousand *pronunciamentos* in its first century, but experienced its last—and unsuccessful—uprising in 1938. Venezuela, which suffered fifty armed uprisings in the first century and a half of its history, has been a civilian state for the last twenty years, and even Syria, which experienced fourteen military *coups* between its independence in 1946 and 1970, has seen no more of them since.

May what has happened in some individual countries come to apply to all of them? Will the military return to the barracks, and if so, what kind of regimes will they bequeath? And, again, does it matter? Will it make a substantial difference to the material and moral circumstances of their peoples?

To explore these questions, we shall first lay out the bare facts. The second section will examine the claims made in favor of military regimes. Only then shall we be able to address ourselves to the questions stated above, and turn to the prospects for the future.

MILITARY INTERVENTION IN THE THIRD WORLD

Almost all the Third World states are ex-colonies of European powers. There are, indeed, a handful of very old states like Iran or Yemen which were never formally colonized by the Europeans, but which, in the age of imperialism, were either dominated or controlled by them. There are also the twenty Latin American republics which, although certainly ex-colonies of Spain or Portugal or France, became independent about a hundred and fifty years ago. They are "old" states by today's standards. The great majority of Third World states are, however, the fallout of the European empires after 1945.

If a first striking characteristic of the Third World is that it is overwhelmingly ex-colonial, and a second is that it is predominantly a post-1945 creation, the third is that, politically, most of its component states started their independent lives under some variant of the Western-style, party-competitive, representative government system. The exceptions are few and, paradoxically, lie at oposite ends of the scale—the revolutionary regimes (North Korea, North Vietnam, Guinea, Burma, Algeria, followed by Cuba [1959], and then, in the 1970s, Vietnam, Laos, Cambodia and Angola, São Tomé, Mozambique, and Guinea-Bissau), on the one hand; on the other, the traditional monarchies like Saudi Arabia. The remainder, some hundred states, started off with the Western constitutional and competitive party model; it includes Morocco, Jordan, and Iran, which are supposedly "constitutional" monarchies. The traditional monarchies and the revolutionary regimes are unashamedly authoritarian in theory and in practice. In contrast, the remainder began as democratic, representative, and constitutional. So we come to the fourth striking characteristic of the Third World: in more than three-quarters of its component states the liberal-democratic order has been swept away and, in one form or another, a tyranny has been installed in its stead.

This has come about by three main channels. In a few cases, the duly elected authorities have declared a state of emergency and, under cover of this, have suspended political activity and individual freedoms (India, Sri Lanka, and the Philippines).

More numerous, but still limited in number, are the states where the competition of parties has been suppressed in favor of a single official party, as in the Ivory Coast, Senegal, Zambia, Malawi, or Tanzania. The first characteristic of these regimes is that they are unquestionably civilian, but the second—the operative role of the single party—is much more problematical. In Tanzania, the party has a real rather than a token significance; in the Ivory Coast, it has long ossified, to become a more dues-collecting and legitimizing device for the president and his chosen advisers.

The principal way in which liberal democracy has been subverted in the Third World, however, is by military intervention.

Here we must beware. Military intervention in politics is not necessarily illegal or violent. Military intervention can and does take place at a number of levels. Even in the best-ordered civilian polities, the military will have a view to express, and they may move into the grey area.

Military *coups*, 1958–1978

I have selected the last twenty years as the time period for the analysis of military *coups* in the Third World, for it is from 1958 onwards that the spread of the *coups* becomes much more diversified beyond Latin America, as the number of independent states rose from ninety-five in 1958 to 157 at the end of 1977, almost all of them in Asia and Africa.

From a fill list of *coups*, we can derive these conclusions:
(a) The total number of *coups* amounted to 157—nearly eight *coups* per year. Of these, only six occurred in Europe, which is in itself a signal proof of the immensely greater vulnerability of the Third World as compared to European and European-type industrialized countries in North America and Australasia. Of the other 151 *coups*, ninety-seven were successful and fifty-four unsuccessful.

(b) Analyzed by region, there were six *coups* in Europe, fifty in Asia (including the Middle East), thirty-six in Central and South America, and sixty-five in Africa (including the North African states).

(c) However, although the number of *coups* has continued at a fairly even rate and shows no sign of abating, the number of countries affected by such *coups* is sharply lower, because some countries have suffered many more than one *coup* during this period. In all, sixteen states in Asia, twenty-seven in Africa, and thirteen in Central and South America have been affected.

(d) Further to this, two additional features are worth noting. First, the number of *coup*-struck states to reappear, as they suffer yet again at a later date, shows a continuous rise. Obviously, if the time period is set to begin at 1958, then all the states struck by *coups* in the 1958–1962 period will appear as "first-timers." However, the proportion of the "first-time" states to the total number of military *coups* launched during a given period has fallen as shown in Table 1. Table 2 shows that this trend is particularly striking over the last five years.

The second noteworthy feature is correlated to the former: it is that the distribution of *coups* to affected states is very disproportionate indeed. Some states have suffered very large numbers of *coups*, others have suffered one or two at most (see Table 3). Thus, twelve states account for seventy-nine of the *coups* or 52 percent of the entire total; and there are eight states which, between themselves, have accounted for fifty-one *coups*, one-third of the total. These extremely *coup*-prone states are Iraq and Syria (eight apiece), the Sudan (seven), Ecuador, Bolivia, and Benin (six apiece), Thailand and the Congo Republic (five apiece).

One final point is worth remarking. Whether one examines the earlier 1963–1967 period or the latest 1973–1978 period, approximately half the military *coups* were launched, not against a civilian regime, but against one that had already been taken over by the *military*. This is not surprising. Military *coups* tend, almost always, to generate military regimes; at the most conservative estimate, these constitute one in three of the Third World states at the moment of writing. Before turning to examine them, however, it is necessary to ask why the military intervene.

Table 1

Number of Third World States Struck by *Coups* for the First Time, as a Percentage of the Total Number of *Coups*, 1958–1978

Period	"First Time" States	Total *Coups*	Percentage of States to *Coups*
1958–1962	19	27	70
1963–1967	17	48	35
1968–1972	9	35	26
1973–1978	11	41	27
Totals	56	151	—

Table 2

Number of Third World States Struck by *Coups* for the First Time, Compared with the Total Number of *Coups*, 1973–1978

Year	Number of "First-Time" States	Number of *Coups*
1973	4	6
1974	1	7
1975	4	11
1976	0	7
1977	2	10

Table 3

Distribution of *Coups* per State, 1958–1978

Number of *Coups* Suffered	Number of States Affected	Total *Coups*
1	15	15
2	18	36
3	7	21
4	7	28
5	2	10
6	3	18
7	1	7
8	2	16
Totals	55	151

The Causes and Motivations of Military Intervention

A military *coup* is, obviously, an act of *will*. Soldiers must want to act thus. In principal, therefore, military *coups* ought to occur randomly throughout every type of state in the world. But as we have seen earlier, only four European states have been affected since 1958, compared with fifty-six Third World states. This suggests that the explanation of military intervention must be sought in the nature of a society, as well as in the outlook and organization of its armed forces. Briefly, the conditions of some societies are conducive to military intervention, while in others they offer impediments. In the latter, a rational soldiery will not lightly take the chance of intervening—at least, not intervening overtly by a military *coup*. Sometimes they are rash or misjudge the conditions, and in such cases we do indeed find *putsches* like the Kapp *Putsch* in Germany in 1920 or the Four Generals' Revolt in Algeria in 1961. On the whole, the conditions for successful takeover do not at present exist in the industrialized, well-organized, and civically conscious societies of Europe and North America/Australasia. Nor, in most cases, do the armed forces entertain a wish to do so. Over a long period, they have internalized the dogma of civilian supremacy, and experience shows that a society would have to undergo enormous social convulsions and polarization before this affected the military's view that politics was a thing to be left to the politicians.

In the first group of societies (those which possess features conducive to military intervention), the outcome depends on the motivation and mood of the armed forces. For it must not always be supposed that these are anxious to play an active political role. Many are those Third World countries where only the support of the military stands between regime and internal anarchy, but where, for all that, the military are politically disengaged from politics. Morocco, Iran, Jordan, Colombia provide examples. But these countries are always at risk. The Libyan *coup* of 1969 may serve as a paradigm. For decades the organized social base of the monarchy—the Senussi tribe, of which King Idris was the ancient and venerable head—had decayed, leaving no other solid basis of public support. Only the small army stood between the monarchy and its overthrow, and when it decided to act, as it did in 1969, it took over power at a stroke. It is, therefore, in those states where the societal conditions are conducive, and the military have motive and capacity to act, that the military *coups* occur. What we must ask now is, first, what comprise these "conducive" societal conditions, and then, what constitutes the military's motive and capability?

The societal factor.   Abstractly, what conduces to military intervention may be summed up as the "absence of organized and public opinion." Where "opinion" does not exist at all, or is confined to a tiny and unrepresentative minority, the military—with their enormous differential advantage over other bodies by virtue of their organization, hierarchy, discipline, intercommunication system, and corporate pride—will be able to impose their *fiat* without having to anticipate let or hindrance; whether they act or not will be at their own discretion. Countries in such a condition are Equatorial Guinea, Haiti, and the Central African Empire. The army will still be the most powerful coherent single force in society in more advanced political cultures where, although an "opinion" may be said to exist, it is unorganized or its organization is very fragile. This will be true even if such opinion as exists is highly public, i.e., very consensual. But it will be even more true where, on the contrary, this opinion is fragmented and—even worse—polarized. In these conditions, the lawlessness and disorder which ensue from its manifestations are apt to tax a civilian government and induce the military to take over in the name of "law and order."

A vast majority of Third World states are in this condition, but there are others which suffer from the opposite form of malady. These are countries where there is, indeed, an opinion, and this is well organized in political parties, trade unions, agrarian leagues, and the like, *but* is bitterly polarized into two uncompromisingly inimical factions. In such circumstances, no civilian government, irrespective of even the best civic tradition, could hope to survive since, if it supported one faction, it could do so only by drawing on itself the enmity of the other. The examples of Chile or, more latterly, Pakistan (1977) spring to mind. In these circumstances, the military may intervene to support the faction they favor over the other (Chile), or simply to try to guarantee public order (the original, and now abandoned, motive of General Zia's intervention in Pakistani politics).

In short, the higher the consensus in a society, and the stronger the width and the organization of this consensus, the less the likelihood that a rational military will contemplate intervention. To find out whether or to what degree the societal conditions conduce to intervention—or, if you will,

to what extent a state is at risk from its own armed forces—
we should need to pose two questions and find their answers:

(1) How far is there widespread public approbation of the
procedures for transferring power, with the corresponding belief that no exercise of power in breach of these procedures is
legitimate, and a similarly widespread public recognition of
who or what organ constitutes the sovereign authority, with
the corresponding belief that no other person or organ is a
legitimate one?

(2) How wide is the political public and how well organized
is it into communities, or into secondary associations like
trade unions, churches, corporations, and political parties?

Note that a positive answer to one question does not entail
a similarly positive answer to the other. In Chile (1973) or
Pakistan (1977), the political public was strongly organized,
but sharply polarized. This is equally true of Argentina and of
Turkey. These were countries where the political crisis was
overt. On the other hand, opinion may be consensual, but so
weakly organized that the military can move in without hindrance; and they will do so *a fortiori* if the opinion is not
merely weak but self-divided, since this not only creates the
political preconditions for the *coup* (that is to say, public disorders), but also promises some partisan support from
civilians—and this both helps legitimize the *coup* and affords
useful allies.

Most, though not all, of the Third World countries are
societies which generate precisely these conditions. On the
whole, then, such political opinion as exists is compartmen-
talized by the persistence of clan, by localism, by the hermet-
ic villages, by immemorial tradition, by the inadequacy of
postal, road, and rail communication, by feeble mass media.
Even where opinion does exist, it tends to be weakly organized. The secondary associations, whose integration with
the processes of government is an organic feature in the industrialized states of the First and the Second Worlds, are
fluid in the Third World, while it is the primary group like

family, clan, and region, religious or linguistic community, which is tough and durable. And these, unlike the secondary associations named above, are *divisive*. Even where opinion is, indeed, organized strongly, class, communalism, micronationalism, or all together, put it at bitter odds with itself. Furthermore, most of these states were for centuries ruled by traditional headmen, chiefs or sheikhs, and absolute monarchs, moving from the grass roots upwards; this rule then was either harnessed to or supplanted by the imperialist interlude of rule by an alien bureaucracy. The "Western" institutions with which the ex-metropolitan states endowed them were—except in interestingly rare cases like India's—utterly novel. Thus, in such countries, popular views about legitimacy—even supposing it is so sophisticated as to make such a distinction—are fragmented; even where they are not, the state is too weakly mobilized to support regime or government against an insurgent soldiery.

The military factor.　　*Size and firepower.* It is still customary for students of our problem to print tables of the size of the armed forces of the Third World countries. There is absolutely no reason for them to do so. Size bears no relationship whatsoever to the likelihood of a military *coup*—though the number of soldiers and, more important, of officers, may have a great deal to do with the style of government the military adopts if they have taken power. Less than 150 paratroopers subverted the government of Gabon in 1963; 600 troops out of a 10,000–strong army destroyed Nkrumah in 1966; the Northern Region of Nigeria, with some 30 million inhabitants, was subverted in January 1966 by a mere 500 men and thirty officers. The reason for this apparently paradoxical fact is really quite simple: it is that the very last thing on which intervention-minded officers wish to embark is protracted civil war, the more so if this is likely to force them to fire on brother soldiers. The interventionist officers are not interested in civil war, but in a *coup*—and a *coup* is to civil war what jujitsu or judo is to a prizefight.[1]

Unity. It has been shown in monograph after monograph that in the majority of Third World countries the social mobilization of the public is so poor that the military—with their five-fold advantage in organization, discipline, hierarchy, intracommunication, and corporate spirit, *plus* the fact that they are armed with heavy weapons—become overwhelmingly the most powerful organized corporation in society. However, this unity, discipline, etc., is consistent with considerable latent divisions inside the armed forces. Where these are large and modernized—as, for instance, in countries as dissimilar as Brazil and Argentina, on the one side, or Egypt and Syria, on the other—there are divisions which may be reflected in political differences between the three services. Next, the military may be divided into ethnic or regional components like the Nigerian army in 1966 or, to take a recent example, the Lebanese army in 1976, which simply disintegrated under the influence of the society's intercommunal vendettas. Similarly, the forces may be split by political allegiances; the highly politicized armies of Syria and Iraq offer striking examples of this. And it has been noticeable of late that the officer corps (which in almost every case is what we mean when we talk of the "military" in cases of military intervention) may be divided by rank/age strata. Sometimes generals lead the entire armed forces. In many cases, however, the *coups* are led by the younger members as much against these generals as against the regime.

It is an act of oversimplification to talk of *the* military, and it is very misleading for two most important reasons. The first is that it is infrequent that a military *coup* is staged by a consensus of the officer corps. On the contrary, most are staged by quite small groups of officers who have neutralized their expected rivals, and who acted without any complicity—or even knowledge—by the remainder. In short, the great majority of military *coups* are made by a *faction*; and this relies on surprise to capture the government, after which, it believes, the doubters—and even the outright opponents of the *coup* in the armed forces—will prudently decline to react against it. The second reason that the generalization is misleading is this: that the more self-divided the armed forces from which a successful *coup* has been launched, the greater the likelihood of successive counter-*coups*, and the feebler the military governments are likely to be.

Motivations. The military—or rather, in view of the caution expressed above, the military faction that intervenes, does so for any one or combination of five major motives. (It should be noted that this permits of no less than *thirty-two* different combinations of motives.) The first is the one that is always proclaimed by the *coup*-makers—namely, the national interest. Here, two points must be noted. First, the plea that a group of officials, constitutionally subject to the government of the day, has acted illegally and seized power by force or the threat of it because the national interest so demanded, is itself a remarkable phenomenon. It implies—and is meant to imply—that the armed forces have a special obligation to the nation, viewed as a continuing corporation in terms that Edmund Burke might have expressed,[2] and that this entails a special protective role which overrides constitutional obligations to obey the rulers of the day. This was not the viewpoint of the armies of the African states at the point of independence, but as they got rid of their European officers, they very rapidly adopted this standpoint.

The second point follows from this. Given such a perception of their role, it is unsurprising that "the defence of the nation" should always be the justification which the soldiers put forward for their intervention in politics. Most often it is a simple rationalization, a political formula, and it will not survive empirical investigation. But in certain cases the plea that the intervention was motivated by a concern for the nation is indeed a valid one. When the Ethiopian army intervened in 1974, it was on the valid ground that the imperial government had failed to tackle the terrible drought that had killed off tens of thousands of the population. When General Zia intervened in Pakistani politics in 1977, it was to stand between two armed civilian camps that threatened to plunge the country into civil war.

However, there are other motivations that can and do run concurrently with concern for the national interest, and which stand as sufficient motives for intervention independently of that claim—and, arguably, often in direct opposition to such a concern. These are corporate interest, regional, ethnic, or communal interest (in polyethnic armies), class interest, and personal interest. In the 1960s and early 1970s, scholars were mostly concerned about the *reasons* for the military takeover of civilian regimes, and much dispute took place over the respective weight to be assigned to these four motivations. It was not made better by the deep-rooted and pervasive belief that, at the end of the road, there is always a *single* cause for a major political phenomenon; a belief which, apart from any scholar's genuine pleasure in believing that he has found *the* key to the universe, derives its rationale from an absurd belief among some political scientists that they not only must but can develop their discipline to make it as exact as the natural sciences. Today, however, interest has rightly shifted from the causes of military *coups* to their consequences—what kind of regimes do they establish, and with what social and economic consequences—and, for the most part, scholars in this field have abandoned the quest for a single, key motivation to explain the decision of the military to intervene. The greatest remaining dispute centers upon the relative importance of class motivation v. corporate self-interest.

Corporate self-interest is a summary term for three particular concerns which, incidentally, are in no way mutually exclusive. The armed forces react against cuts in the military budget, or they demand increases; they react against political interference in promotions and conditions of service—i.e., they demand a high degree of internal autonomy or, if you will, self-regulation; and, finally, they bare their teeth at any paramilitary forces not under their own control—popular militias, constabularies, and the like. There is strong empirical support for the salience of this motivation to act against the government of the day. One scholar, who surveyed 229 military *coups* in order to try to identify soldiers' grievances, reports that 23 percent were motivated by "corporate positional grievances" (e.g., autonomy, the absence of rival militias, etc.), 33 percent were due to "resource grievances," and 31 percent were preemptive strikes against governments expected to restrict corporate privileges.

As to *class*-interest—or, if you will, the perception of a national interest in (perhaps subconscious) class terms—there is no reason to doubt its existence as a motive in certain regions. It is hardly existent in the states of sub-Saharan Africa, where classes in the Western sense hardly exist, but it could be witnessed in the course of events in Ethiopia (1974 onwards), where groups of army officers from a middle-sector background intervened harshly against the landowning oligarchy which made up the governing elite. The same can be said of the Middle Eastern Arab states, and those of North Africa also. It is preeminently in some of the Latin American countries, where a large and often organized working-class movement exists, that one begins to approximate the Western class analysis, and in many of the *coups* this motivation is clearly a very powerful one. In most countries today, officers no longer come from the traditional "upper class" of rural landowners or captains of industry, and neither do they come from manual laborers. They come from the multitude of occupational classes intermediate between these two. Insofar as they are governed by class perceptions, this can lead the officers into overthrowing governments of a predominantly oligarchic, landowner basis (Egypt, 1952; Syria and Iraq, post-1963 and post-1958, respectively; Ethiopia, 1974 and subsequently, for instance), and also into overthrowing governments that favored mass expectations in a populist style as in some Latin American countries (Brazil, 1974 onwards, Argentine from the Peronista post-1945 era, Chile in 1973, are examples). This is why it is not possible any longer to view military *coups* as being always "reactionary," as used to be the case when only the Latin American *coups* were considered. Nowadays, it is obviously possible for military *coups* to be also regarded as "progressive"; hence, liberal or leftist admiration for the Peruvian or Ethiopian *juntas*. Indeed, in certain Communist quarters, it has been seriously asked whether the armed forces might not be able to substitute for the "historic role" of the peasantry or proletariat by establishing a so-called "revolutionary democratic dictatorship" under their own hegemony.[3]

The view that class interest is paramount over all others has, however, been strongly expressed by a group of Western scholars who draw from it very wide and *a priori* conclusions about the necessarily modernizing role of military rule. We shall deal with this claim later.

There remain to discuss only the communal/ethnic/regional motivations on the one side, and the personal on the other. The latter is obvious, for example, in the case of Idi Amin. The importance of the communal/ethnic/regional motivations was dramatically illustrated by the first and second military *coups* in Nigeria, 1966, with Ibos pitted against Hausa-Fulani, and the ultimate secession of the Ibos to form their own independent state of Biafra. It is also illustrated by the fate of the multi-communal Lebanese army when civil warfare erupted in 1976; under the stress of the surrounding communal tensions, that army simply melted away. Africa is preeminently a region where such motivations are important. W. R. Thompson (1973:29-31), who has made a systematic study of the grievances of *coup*-makers, concludes that between 1946 and 1970 the proportion of *coups* related to this matter stood at 12 percent in Asia (without the Middle East), 19 percent in the Middle East, and no less than 27 percent in Africa.

To summarize: military intervention in politics is to be seen as the outcome of two summary variables. These are, on the one side, the *systemic* variables, i.e., those societal factors which conduce to military intervention; and on the other, the capacity of the military to intervene, allied with their motivations for doing so. Without the motivation and will to intervene, there will be no intervention. Without societal conducive factors, there is unlikely to be intervention, and if it occurs, it will not succeed. The military *coups* occur where societal factors conduce to such activity, and this includes almost all the states of the Third World, and where the military have the motivation and the mood to intervene—and this, at the moment, accounts for something like half of those states, but could, in principle, account for all of them.

THE MILITARY REGIMES

The Different Kinds of "Military Regimes"

After what has been said, it might appear easy to define a military regime: it would be a regime that is the outcome of a military *coup*. But in that case, what about regimes which take their shape and many of their orders from a military that do not use the *coup* or threat of violence against a civilian regime, but exercise a pressure which is acted on in the knowledge that the military are the first as well as the last resort of the regime against domestic violence or insurrection? The fact is that the class of "military regimes" embraces a number of distinct subtypes which merge, gradually, into civilian regimes.

It is a semantic matter where we choose to draw the line. At the "most civilian" end of the spectrum there are, for instance, regimes which are constitutional and party-competitive, but where the constitutional guarantees are suspended from time to time, often for long periods—consider, for example, Sri Lanka, where a state of emergency, under which 18,000 persons were imprisoned, lasted from 1971 to 1977. Next, there is a sizable group of countries with a constitutionally appointed chief executive or head of state who is, however, exquisitely reliant on the active support of his military forces. A large number of such states are supposedly "constitutional monarchies"; some are absolute monarchies, like the Sultanate of Oman or the Emirate of Bahrein; and at least one is the remarkable example of the Philippine Republic where President Marcos, duly reelected in 1969, introduced martial law in 1972 and, using its provisions to suspend Congress, arrest opponents, and censor the press, has governed as a personal dictator ever since, using referenda from time to time to validate his actions.

These are indubitably *civilian* regimes. To stress the military presence, however, we might called them military-supportive regimes.

We now come across another subclass of civilian regimes, with powerful and self-confident armed forces who have intervened in the past and who intervene again—temporarily only, and from time to time—when they feel it their duty or interest to "correct" the course the civilian political forces are steering. A classic illustration is the 1971 demand of the Turkish army (which had already made a *coup* in 1960), as a result of which the cabinet was forced to quit and martial law was imposed. We might call these *intermittently indirect* military regimes.

The next class of regimes is much more arguably "military." It comprises countries which, as a result of behind-the-scenes military muscle and pressure, are headed by civilians or military men no longer on the active list. Guatemala, El Salvador, and, in its own peculiar way, Nicaragua, provide examples of this kind of regime, which, with some justice, we might call the *indirect-military* regime.

It is only at this point that we reach *military regimes* proper. At the moment of writing, these number forty-two, ranging from Afghanistan to Zaïre.

The Format of the Military Regimes

There are three questions to be answered in connection with these military regimes: What is the role of the armed forces as such (as opposed, for instance, to the ruler they have installed)? What is the relationship of the government to the rest of the political system? To what depth does the government penetrate the life of the country?

The role of the military in a "military" government. The first major characteristic of these forty-two governments is that the head of state has been installed by virtue of a military *coup*—and all but two (Uruguay and Afghanistan) have military men at the top. However, the installation of a military man in the presidential office by means of a military *coup* does not necessarily imply that the armed forces as a whole, or their senior ranks, or even that group of the senior ranks who made the *coup*, will continue to play a creative part in governing the country afterwards. It is doubtful—to anticipate a later suggestion—whether the Zaïre military do, as such, play any significant part in shaping policy under General Mobutu, and a similar caution might well be raised about the Egyptian army under Sadat. We can go on, therefore, to distinguish two major groups of military regimes.

The first group, numbering twenty-four countries, installs a group of officers next to the president in what is sometimes called a "revolutionary command council" (RCC), or a "high security council," or—as is most common in Latin America—a "*junta militar*." These bodies are very small, rarely more than twelve members and sometimes consisting of only three, and it is they who exercise sovereign power. To carry on the day-to-day work of government, such councils appoint cabinets, which may be military in composition, mixed civilian-military, or wholly civilian.

The remaining states, numbering eighteen, do not possess organs like the RCC, but in three of them (Peru, Bolivia, and Burma) the cabinet is entirely military, so that the armed forces are as securely entrenched here as in the former group. Of the remaining fifteen, the (military) head of state governs through a mixed civilian-military cabinet. In these states, one might surmise that it is the president who makes policy—

with the advice and the support of the military, certainly, but by no means at their demand.

This leaves only Egypt, South Korea, Zaïre, Rwanda, and the Central African Empire. Here the military are not installed in a Command Council, nor have they any place in the cabinet, which is exclusively—or all but exclusively—civilian. These, we may surmise, are governed by the head of state, with the military in a supportive rather than a creative role.

The political system in the military regimes.   So far we have examined the *executive* power in these states, to see how far the military control it, or how far it may be said—in the person of the head of state—to control them, and we have seen that in at least twenty-seven states it may be stated that the military as such control the executive branch, and that they play an important part in another ten. The next question is: how far does the executive branch control the rest of the political system? This is indicated by the status of the political parties, of legislatures, and of civil liberties in military regimes. It may be stated right away that, except in a handful of marginal cases, military regimes either disband parties, or install their own official single-party system, or, at the most, control parties by way of licensing; that, for the most part, they suppress legislatures; and that they suspend those parts of the constitution which guarantee individual freedoms, and in many cases carry out mass arrests, practice preventive detention without charges, and establish military or "kangaroo" courts to "try" their political opponents. Military governments are all *authoritarian,* and the only question is the degree to which their authoritarianism is pushed.

Turning first to the twenty-four command council–type regimes and the three additional states with wholly military cabinets, we may remark—and then pass on—that of these twenty-seven states where the military form the supreme executive, political parties have been banned in fifteen; ten have single-party systems, four of these states having legislatures; the only two in which parties exist are Peru (where the congress stands dissolved), and the Comoros, where they are inactive, though not legally suppressed. In these military governments *stricto sensu*, then, the military rule without any civilian institutions, or *via* a party and a legislature which they themselves have fashioned for their own ends and which is an emanation of their power.

But the fifteen remaining regimes, ten with mixed cabinets and five with civil, raise the engaging problem as to where, precisely, the military fit in. The regimes with a mixed civilian-military cabinet are the ones that *prima facie* still provide an institutionalized niche for the military as such. In two cases only, however, are the military the ruling corporation—in Togo, a small country with a remarkably unified army, and in Brazil, where, despite dissidence among the top leaders, the armed forces also display strong corporate solidarity. For the rest, the best discriminators between the different types of regime are the two conjoint factors: licensed parties plus a legislature. These comprise Brazil (already noted as exceptional), and then, proceeding across a spectrum, Indonesia, Paraguay, Syria, Honduras, Egypt, and Korea. The arrangement in each one of these countries is idiosyncratic, and they can well be said to represent those on the margin of "military regimes." In each, the relationship between popular political forces, the civil bureaucracy, and the armed forces is complex, and, in each, the balance has been struck in a different way. In all of them it can be said that the effective ruler is the individual head of state—be he Suharto, Sadat, Park, Assad, and so forth—who maintains the closest ties with the armed forces, listens carefully to their grievances, balances these against other claims on his attention, and certainly regards them as the first and last source of his power. But, and this is the decisive point, as far as the military is concerned, their members play a part in policymaking that is advisory and *supportive*. They are no longer the prime movers. If these are to be regarded as military regimes, it can only be on the grounds that they have provided the head of state and can remove him, and that, as a consequence, their interests become the first charge upon the state.

The next best discriminator is simply whether the state still possesses a legislature. This yields Panama, Sudan, and Zaïre, and leaves us with only four states: Uganda, the Central African Empire, and Rwanda in Africa, and Bangladesh in Asia. All are personal dictatorships, discriminated only by the following fact: that whereas the presidents of the first three have established a firm personal control over their military forces, the Bangladesh armed forces are in mutinous disarray.

The penetration of the military in the sociopolitical system.   There remain two things to be understood about the role of the military in a ''military'' regime. These are the extent to which they move their military-professional personnel into other structures, notably the political parties and the bureaucracy; and how far, *qua* corporate body, they manage national affairs. The first may be styled military *colonization* of other institutions, where the military acts as a reservoir or *core* of personnel for the sensitive institutions of the state; it means the expansion of military personnel into the political parties, the industrial enterprises, the unions, and the bureaucracy. The military establishments in the military regimes also differ, often very sharply, in the degree to which they press their *control* of social and, particularly, of economic activities. Some simply superintend the processes of society, correcting their course as seems necessary to them, while others go further and assume the *direction* of affairs, and at least one—Burma—goes much further and even *administers* the major services.

When we consider the extent to which the military colonize institutions, on the one hand, and the degree to which they interfere with society and economy, on the other, it will be clear that, combining the one variable with the other, military regimes are likely to differ among themselves, sometimes sharply, as to their *style* of government. And unless we can differentiate them in this way, it seems, frankly, rather silly to try to estimate the social and political performance of ''military'' regimes as compared with ''civilian'' regimes. Consider, for instance, the cases of Thailand and Burma. In the first, the Thai military, who have been in power off and on since 1932, (1) rule, (2) do not act as a core, and (3) superintend—rather than direct, let alone administer—the economy. In the Burmese case, the military have been in power since 1962, and they (1) rule, (2) act as a core, and (3) administer the economy. The first have achieved a high growth rate; the Burmese military, on the other hand, have achieved a *negative* growth rate. One conclusion that may be drawn—and, indeed, frequently is drawn—is that "military regimes" have a fifty-fifty chance of success in managing the economy. But this is to equate the two regimes simply by virtue of one characteristic—the corporate rulership of the military in each—and to fail to distinguish *what* the military do and *how* they do it. From this standpoint, it might be possible to conclude that the degree of economic success one might expect from the military regime depends on *what kind of regime* we are talking about. This matter will be taken up shortly. It is mentioned here to show that the distinctions made above are not unnecessary pedantry, but, on the contrary, are essential to adjudging the claim that military regimes are more successful than their civilian counterparts.

In Nigeria, Ghana, and, as far as we can see, in most of the West African regimes if not in all of them, the military as ruler make use of the preexisting civil administration; indeed, this military-bureaucratic symbiosis is one of the most striking features in this area. Furthermore, there is evidence to suggest that the military *qua* rulers, while definitionally possessing and exercising a veto power, are often very much in the hands of their top civil servants. It has been reported that the Ghanaian military (Bebler 1962:203–4), for instance (the NLC, 1966–1972),

relied heavily on information, advice, execution and supervision provided by top civil servants, even in areas where the junta members reserved and retained a monopoly on ultimate decisions, . . . [and that, in fact,] regardless of the formal organization of power, the real impact of military rule on state administration seems to have been an increase in its autonomy. The military removed or minimized party and "political" pressures on the bureaucrats without bringing in their own system of effective control.

However, the military rulers of these countries did aspire to direct and plan the nation's affairs. The Thai style is somewhat different. The military elite is almost a "connexion" in the eighteenth-century sense, and has intermarried with the Chinese business community that is central to the economy, and with the traditional bureaucracy; indeed, it is common for leading families to place one son in the army and the other in the civil service. Political parties have intermittently been permitted, and some of these, too, have effectively been instruments of the military leadership. So organized, this group has supervised the flow of Thai business and agriculture, and has kept a close watch over political activities.

We can now turn to the three countries in the *ruler core* tradition. Burma is the most striking of these. It forms almost the mirror image of the Thai free-wheeling style. The military are a politicized army, professing and trained in Burmese socialism. Since 1962, their leading group has carried on a bitter feud with the civil service, which it regards as a relic of colonialism, and has stuffed the ministries and development agencies and nationalized sectors with its own trained junior officers. It has organized and staffed a monopolistic political party (the *Lanzin* party), which is hierarchically organized down to the rural district committee level where the local chairman is, effectively, the district commissar. It has nationalized industry, transport, internal and external trade, communications, and finance.

Brazil comes nowhere near Burma in any of these respects, but follows the same configuration, albeit at a considerable remove. Here, the military government has carried out two five-year development plans, involving massive investment in industry, energy, education, and health. This is a private enterprise economy, but "planned"—or, if one wishes, subsidized—by the national exchequer, not the socialist economy of Burma, and the military, as a core, are a small one. For all that, it is noticeable that there had been, according to an acute and well-informed observer, "extensive, direct penetration . . . by military officers."

Indonesia illustrates the military in their role of *support* core, and it is a very substantial core indeed. It has expanded its administrative functions both centrally and in the rural regions. It has created and staffed the higher echelons of its own "official" political party (*Sekber Golka*), which has found no difficulty in winning elections to the House of Representatives, and it has permeated and become the major power in economic entrepreneurship and management. The military's economic empire includes large holding companies, industrial and commercial conglomerates, trading syndicates, as well as individual firms engaged in banking, petroleum, timber, and transport.

We can end our survey by looking at a state where the style of the regime has shifted markedly over time, and that is Egypt. In June 1954, the supreme rulership was exercised by the Revolutionary Command Council, consisting of eleven officers. Under this was the cabinet, with nineteen ministers—eight of them from the RCC, who obviously dominated the remaining eleven civilian ministers. At the same time, more than one thousand officers were made ambassadors, provincial governors, managers and directors of economic agencies, and the like. By June 1974, however, the RCC no longer existed. There is now a president (an ex-officer), a vice president (also an officer), and thirty other cabinet ministers, of whom only one—the Minister of War—is an officer. Furthermore, of this cabinet, fifteen members bore the title of "Doctor", and another seven that of "Engineer." At the same time, the flow of officers outside their service has dried up. Thus, in twenty years the Egyptian military have moved from the role of a *ruler-core directorate* to that of a simple *support*.

The transit of regimes. With remarkable smugness, the left and far left repeatedly assure us that "power grows out of the barrel of a gun," but do not add that it will shrink back again unless it acquires mass popular support. The military are acutely aware of this, since they occupy the hot seat and not comfortable armchairs.

A *junta* that is acclaimed when it comes to power (and many are) will call elections or referenda to prove it. If it is unpopular, then it will *fix* elections and referenda to "prove" how popular it is. If neither avail, then it can either oppress its public with whips rather than scorpions or, alternatively, decide to hand power back to the civilians.

This exit from power is fraught with difficulties. The causes for which the soldiers made their *coup* are likely to be abandoned or destroyed. Even worse, the returning civilian politicians may wreak revenge on the soldiers who turned them out. Hence, most military establishments that have decided to turn power back to the civilians seek certain built-in guarantees against either of these gloomy possibilities. Sometimes this takes the form of a special constitutional status for the military; thus, when the Turkish army returned power to the political parties in 1962, it made sure that its own nominee and leader occupied the presidency, and that it was represented, *qua* military, in the upper house of the Turkish parliament. More usually, the military withdraw, but keep a watchful eye on the antics of the politicians. In this way, the original command-council type turns into what we have styled the "indirect" type, where the military *monitor* the government, pressurizing it on an intermittent—but sometimes continuous—basis. But such monitoring, after a time, seems inadequate, even dangerous, if the civilian government seeks to curb the military's power; and so, usually, a spell of such indirect rule is terminated by yet another *coup* and another command-council regime. The process is vividly illustrated by the entire course of Argentinian politics since 1930, when the armed forces intervened for the first time in this century—and have not ceased since.

Legitimation, quasi-legitimation, or repression. Genuine legitimation is very hard to come by. Few military establishments willingly turn their backs on power; those that do, carefully monitor their civilian successors, and very few, indeed, find these sufficiently worthy over a period of years to accept a role of political neutrality. Venezuela and Colombia are interesting examples of countries where this has apparently occurred.

For the most part, the military establishments that eschew the retreat to the barracks react in one or other of two typical ways—more severe repression, or fake legitimation. This can be illustrated by the current *va-et-vient* in the military regimes end-1976/early-1978.

First, let us note instances of genuine—if modest—relaxation and institutionalization of the regimes. Nigeria was proceeding towards the election of a constituent assembly, with a view to a return to civilian rule. Paraguay likewise was convening a constitutional convention. President Sadat of Egypt permitted the appearance of three political parties, one of which, however, is "official" (and always wins, of course); but he has recently suppressed two of them. In Indonesia, elections took place to the House of Representatives, although, as already noted, the military's official party (*Sekber Golka*) was assured of a majority. Elsewhere, we may note that the Bolivian government lifted the state of siege in July 1976, and is currently holding a general election.

Now we can see for what they are the instances of fake legitimation, or "quasi-civilianization." In Burma, where the military *junta* led by Ne Win had already put off their tunics and affected the civilian title of "U" (The Honorable)—but, for all that, still retained full powers as before—General (now U) Ne Win has been reelected as chairman of the ruling *Lanzin* party. In the Central African Republic, the former President Bokassa has proclaimed himself Emperor Bokassa, and has introduced a new constitution—which, however, vests full executive power in himself, as before (December

1976). The Council of the Revolution has been dissolved, and the emperor presides over a civilian cabinet. In Libya, President Qadhafi introduced a new constitution in March 1977. The Command Council has been replaced by a "General Secretariat" in which Colonel Qadhafi and the other four former members of the RCC will sit, retaining their power as before. In Bangladesh, General Zia, having persuaded President Ahmed to step down for him, had his assumption of the presidency confirmed in a referendum (May 1977).

So much for fake legitimation. But this can only go so far. The alternative is heightened repression, and this is much frequented. We can pass rapidly over the states of terror unleashed by the Dergue in Ethiopia and by President Amin in Uganda, since these are matters of everyday knowledge, and note, first, the Argentine military's postponement of civil rule, imposition of further penalties on trade unions, and dissolution of still more political parties in the last two years. In Chile, in March 1977, President Pinochet imposed a total ban on parties and extended the state of siege for another six months, although at the very moment of writing he has announced a complete amnesty on political prisoners. And in Peru, alongside with promises to return to civilian rule, the *junta* has made monthly extensions to the state of siege.

THE PERFORMANCE OF THE MILITARY REGIMES

It was the 1960s that saw the most extravagant claims made for government by the military, perhaps because the data were so scarce. This was due to the liberal academics' perennial triumph of hope over experience. Even to this day, nobody refers to *any* African military ruler other than President Amin as a "dictator"; this term is reserved for Latin America. The heads of state in countries like Nigeria or Pakistan are politely referred to as "the military ruler" of such and such a country.

Three claims were made for military government. The first was that the military were the most prominent—or perhaps the only—"modernizing" force in the Third World. The second was that the military were perennially middle class, and acted as the spearhead to enable middle class to take over. The third was that the military alone could bring stable political conditions to their strife-torn countries. Not a single one of these claims has turned out to be unequivocally true; in general, it can even be said that each has been falsified.

The Military as Modernizers

Two *a priori* assumptions were made here. The first was that all military regimes were alike; the second, that all military were also alike in that they and they alone were technologically specialized, were competitive with other military and thus sensitized to the need to build up their own country's economy, and, finally, had admired advanced societies when they went overseas for training. Even as it stands, these arguments ring false in most countries of the Third World. Take the claim for "technological skills" and the like: almost all the African armies are tiny infantry armies hardly running to more specialized units than a couple of signal platoons or a company of engineers. Also, if the claim were true, we should expect the navies to be more innovative and even more revolutionary than the armies, for their hardware is far more technically advanced. Instead, the navies nearly everywhere have proved conservative.

However, it is unnecessary to pursue this *a priori,* since there are enough regimes in existence to permit empirical inquiry into whether military regimes are economically more successful than civilian ones. And indeed, since 1970 there have been three inquiries of this kind on a global basis. The first, by Eric Nordlinger (1970:1131–48), took seventy-four countries, and tested the military against the civilian regimes in respect to their performance in seven fields amenable to governmental manipulation. Aggregating all these indicators to form a summary index, and making no distinction for re-

gion, Nordlinger concluded that the political strength of the
military in a country's polity was correlated to success in all
seven fields to the extent of only 0.04. This is statistically
negligeable, and the only inference is that the performance of
a country was, statistically, the same, whether the military
were in charge or were not. Finally, even these correlations
alter when the seventy-four states are broken into their component regions. It then turns out that only in Africa was military rule positively correlated to the growth of GNP (0.45), to
industrial growth (0.42), to agricultural growth (0.60), and to
educational expansion (0.34). As for the other regions—
Latin America, the Middle East and North Africa, and
Asia—with three statistically insignificant exceptions, there
was a *negative* correlation between military rule and each
single field of endeavor. In short, the military made matters
worse, not better. And when we turn back to the exception
noted in Africa, it turns out that the basis of the calculation is
a mere *six* military regimes in which the military are said to
have been "influential," and only *one* in which they were
actually in office.[4]

A second inquiry using aggregate data was mounted by
Messrs. McKinley and Cohan in 1974 (1974; 1976:850–64).
This drew on a more ambitious universe—all the independent
states in the world over the decade of the 1960s, excluding
only the communist states, for which data were not available.
They summarized their major finding thus: "While the civilian regimes (less than $900) have a higher export growth rate
and a lower cost of living rate than either military regimes or
regimes that had previously experienced military rule, none
of these differences is significant."

This result clearly differs from that of Nordlinger, who as-
serts that in four regions—Africa being the exception—the
military actually make things worse. However, in 1976
Nordlinger's results were reanalyzed by R. W. Jackman
(1976:1078–97). His method was significantly different from
Nordlinger's and, in addition, Jackman introduced new and
more reliable data concerning sixty independent states of the

Third World in the 1960s. His results contradict Nordlinger's and, in their general conclusions, bear out the rather agnostic conclusions of McKinley and Cohan: "Military governments have no unique effects on social change, regardless of level of economic development. . . . Blanket statements portraying military governments in the Third World as either progressive or reactionary are without empirical foundation."

This very important finding receives powerful support from a splendidly conceived piece of analysis of Latin America by Philippe Schmitter (1971:493–94). He reports:

In summary, no regime-type seems to be exclusively responsible for "developmental success" in Latin America. Competition, and with it, less coercion and more participation and voluntary compliance, seems in the long run to have promoted a greater "publicization" of the development process and greater equality in the distribution of its benefits, but with certain "overhead" costs in terms of wider and more rapid policy fluctuations and higher rates of inflation and budgetary imbalance. Military regimes have occasionally been more spectacularly successful in altering the established, and usually stagnant pattern of policy, but their longer-term effect has often been ephemeral—with a marked propensity for systems to return to some pre-established level after "demagogic" excesses. More often than not the military themselves have promoted this return to normality.

We shall conclude: so far no evidence has been deployed to show that, as a class, military regimes modernize or develop their countries any better than civilian regimes as a class. But we ought also to add that this is what we might well have expected to be shown, in view of the analysis of military regimes presented earlier. For we have argued that the "class" of military regimes is not homogeneous and, in particular, that even in its subclasses—as, for example, in the "ruler"-type subclass—the extent of military penetration and control of society differs very sharply. To a Burma we can juxtapose a Thailand; to an Argentina, a Brazil. Therefore, *prima facie*, there is no reason to suppose that the military "class" of regimes will substantively differ from the civilian type in their economic performance, even if, as a final assumption, we altogether discount the importance of the natural resources of the countries in question. And finally, it must be seen that these closely argued statistical conclusions correspond to one's impression. Brazil and South Korea have achieved spectacular growth under military rule; Burma and Argentina have done spectacularly badly.

The Military as Spearhead of a Modernizing Middle Class

This argument has taken three forms. José Nun (1970:66–118), basing himself on the Latin American experience, propounded the view that since officers are nowadays drawn from the middle class, the Latin American *coup* is a device "for protecting the middle class." Manfred Halpern (1962:278–79; 1963:Chapters 4, 13), basing himself on the Arab states, draws the opposite conclusion, waxing lyrical over the middle-class Arab officers as spearheading the arrival in politics of an Arab middle class viewed by him as impelled, "out of self-concern, to establish modern integrating institutions which can mobilize the spirit and resources of the entire nation." Finally, Huntington (1969:Chapter 4) has synthesized these opposite viewpoints by maintaining that— since the officer corps of all armies is, nowadays, middle class in origin—it will react against mass politics in Latin America and so play a reactionary role there, while opening the way for radical middle-class and anti-latifundist regimes in the Middle East, as well as promoting middle-class values in advance of the traditionalism of the masses in the African states. All three standpoints are vulnerable, in that the middle class of which they speak is a vast conglomerate consisting of all who are not ranchers or great landowners, on the one side, or manual workers and peasants, on the other. But the hypothesis has been empirically confounded by the statistical exercises discussed in the preceding section.

The Military as Stabilizers

One of the most immediate causes of the military's intervention is political disorder—as, for instance, in Turkey in 1971 or in Pakistan in 1977—and its accession to power is usually followed by a period of iron reaction in which constitutional guarantees are suppressed and order is restored. For this reason, one of the most commonplace claims for military intervention is that it is a stabilizing force. Once one moves beyond the acknowledgedly successful bout of repression which follows the *coup*, however, military intervention appears in the medium term to be a powerful *de*-stabilizer. In the first place, the suspension or abrogation of the previous constitution and the imposition of a stern authoritarianism invites counter-*coups* or civilian insurgency. As Edmund Burke said, "a constitution without the means of change is a constitution without the means of self-preservation." It was Nasser who argued that in Egypt, in 1952, constitutional change by the people was an impossibility, and, therefore, if the army did not bring it about, who would? What he said is perfectly correct; but *a fortiori* it applies to the military regimes themselves. Hence, the duration of military regimes is considerably shorter than that of most civilian ones. Nearly half last only two years, 31 percent last between two and five years, and only 21 percent last longer than five years. Nearly half are terminated by violence—in 30 percent of the cases by a counter-*coup*, in another 18 percent, by some kind of rising.

The third reason for rejecting the military's claim to act as stabilizers has so far attracted no attention, but is perhaps the most significant of all. The case rests on supposing that society is pulverized into hostile factions, whereas the military are united. But suppose that the military are themselves disunited? In that case, the fractionalization of society is paralleled by a fractionalization of the military. Both interact. One military faction reaches outside its ranks to pick up civilian allies against its rivals, who also turn to civilian factions to meet this challenge. So the factions of this society find themselves spearheaded by rival gangs of armed men, and their struggle becomes more murderous than before. This is no imaginary scenario. It aptly describes the sequence of events in Nigeria between the two *coups* of 1966 and the final crushing of Biafra, the course of events in Argentina ever since the overthrow of Peron, and, even more vividly, the anarchy, bloodshed, and confusion in Bangladesh and Ethiopia at the moment of writing.

THE FUTURE OF MILITARY INTERVENTION

Let us pull together some of the trends discussed in the earlier pages. First, the average number of *coups*—successful and unsuccessful—per annum shows no signs of abating. Next, the number of "first-time" states has decreased in the last decade compared with the previous one, but is still very positive. Third, the number of military regimes—according to our highly conservative definition, which excludes "indirect" and "military supportive" regimes—is almost double that of a decade ago, and four times the number existing twenty years ago. Taken as a whole, these indicators suggest that the trend is still towards more *coups* and more military regimes in the Third World.

On the other hand, certain civilian regimes whose socioeconomic divisions would suggest *prima facie* that they were candidates for military intervention have survived, even if by the imposition of emergency regulations—notably, India, Sri Lanka, and the Philippine Republic—while other states whose past history has been a chronicle of nothing but military intervention, like Mexico and Venezuela, have reverted to civilian regimes which have persisted. Such facts must make us more than ordinarily wary of simply extrapolating the trends mentioned in the preceding paragraph.

For all that, it is our view that in the foreseeable future there will be more of the same, much of it in the states that have experienced military intervention already, but with significant extensions to states hitherto unaffected. Most military regimes are handed back to civilians by the decision of the military themselves. The reason that the military so often leave the barracks and seize power again is that such forces continue to nurture the same motivations and to be possessed by the same corporate self-interest that originally compelled them to intervene. Such forces have not become politically *neutral* after they have quit government; simply *disengaged*. Yet, to ensure that they will no longer intervene requires that they be the former; and this is far harder to bring about than the usually temporary disengagement that is the condition in most of the ex-military regimes—and a large number of civilian, but military-supportive, states—in the Third World.

For the military to become neutral requires two conditions: in the first place, that the military do not fear their civilian successors, and, in the second, that these civilian successors do not need the military to keep themselves in power. The first is much easier to meet than the second. These civilian successors would have to be careful to respect the corporate autonomy of the armed forces, spend perhaps exorbitant sums on salaries and matériel, and take active and persuasive measures to ensure broad agreement between their priorities and those of the leaders of the armed forces. Given enough money (and states like Venezuela or Libya or Nigeria or Algeria have become oil-rich), this is not impossible. It certainly implies a powerful—and perhaps a major—role for the armed forces as such in the counsels of state; but this is merely to respect a role which is already traditional in Latin America and the Middle East and in much of Asia, and is novel, perhaps, only in sub-Saharan Africa. In any case, these military have come to stay, and to treat them in this way is to face a fact of life.

It is the second condition that is the problematical one. For, as argued earlier, a very high proportion of the Third World states are in latent but chronic crisis: opinion is feebly organized, often self-divided, and a sense of legitimacy is correspondingly weak or even negative. Precisely because of this, all such states require a strong executive—a requirement the "single party" was reputedly designed to meet, though it has not done so, and which accounts for the frequent use of emergency powers and the suspension of constitutional guarantees in the "civilian" governments of the Third World. To this extent, then, all such states are those with governments that are abnormally dependent on their armed forces. And, indeed, this is precisely why they experienced military intervention. For, the more dependent on the military, the more a government must comply with their demands.

Until and unless these conditions alter, as *has* happened in Mexico and seems to be happening in Venezuela, the most a state can hope for is the *contingent* disengagement of its armed forces. Which is as much as to say that they are likely, given the necessary motivations, to reenter the political arena.

But the creation of political community is a long and extremely delicate process. The history of the European states shows what a mixture of diplomacy and coercion—sustained over decades and, in most cases, centuries—was required to create the firm-rooted national communities of today. In the Third World, quick returns should not be looked for. Some exceptional states may, over the quarter of a decade, lay the foundations for political community, on the one side, and military neutrality, on the other; but, for the most part, the outlook for a majority of the states is the gloomy one of a first military regime to be succeeded by a second one, with the interval filled in by alternative bouts of indirect rule, monopartism, or feebly functioning competitive party systems backed up by martial law or states of siege.

6

PETER T. BAUER

BASIL S. YAMEY

The Third World
and the West:
An Economic Perspective

The stereotype of Third World nations—a misconception. The relation between natural resources, population, land, and economic development. The importance of commercial contact with the West. The effect of demographic change on economic standards. Fertility and birthrate ratios—lack of correspondence. The effect of Third World government policy on national development. Free market v. planned economies. Tension-provoking government controls. The immense diversity of the Third World—its origin, its needs, and reality.

I

What would you say about a Third World country with the following features? It is one of the most densely populated countries in the world; its population is growing rapidly; it is without natural resources and has to import most of its water and all of its oil. Its government does not engage in economic planning, and there is not even exchange control; it receives no foreign aid; the inflow of large numbers of refugees imposes heavy burdens on the country and onerous tasks on its government. Its exports are restricted by protection in the West. And, to cap it all, it is one of the few remaining Western colonies. You would have to say that this country must be poor, stagnating, and without hope—that is, you would have to say this if you followed the most influential stereotype of Third World economics. According to this model, it is doomed to failure. Yet in this country real income and real wages have risen rapidly and dramatically since the second world war, and its inflation rate is low. It is Hong Kong. It gives the lie to the stereotype. The experience of many other countries does the same.

The principal components of the stereotype are the following. Natural resources—especially land—and capital are the primary determinants of economic performance. The Third World is poor in both. The supply of natural resources, notably, of land, is fixed. Accumulation of capital is obstructed or prevented by poverty itself. The effects of paucity of resources and capital are exacerbated, and poverty is perpetuated, by rapid population growth and by Western exploitation of the Third World.[1] These adverse forces are outside the control of Third World countries. Because these forces are ubiquitous, the Third World constitutes a broadly uniform collectivity or entity.

This stereotype, as well as each of its elements, is false and misleading. It provides no sound basis for policy, neither in the Third World nor in the West.

II

Lack of capital is not a barrier to escape from Third World poverty. The misconception that it is a practically insurmountable barrier underlies the much-canvassed notion of the vicious circle of poverty, according to which a low level of income by itself prevents the capital formation necessary for higher incomes. This notion is often adduced in support both of foreign aid and of confiscation of incomes in Third World countries, referred to as resource mobilization (for explicit formulations of the vicious circle, see Bauer 1976:32–33).

If this notion were valid, countless individuals, groups, and societies could not have risen from poverty to prosperity as they have done all over the world. Today's developed countries could not have progressed either, as they all began poor. And over the last hundred years many poor countries have progressed rapidly without external donations. On the strict interpretation of the vicious circle, there could not have been any development in the world: in the beginning the world was underdeveloped, and it received no resources from outside.

The notion is thus a misconception. It is so on several grounds. First, even very poor individuals and societies can generate, and often have generated, capital. For instance, they have sacrificed leisure for work, including the clearing and improvement of land. In many erstwhile poor areas, people have transferred labor and land to more productive uses, as, for instance, by replacing subsistence production with cash crops. Again, initially penniless traders have often accumulated capital in the process of opening up local markets, and thereby also made new opportunities available to the people there.

Nor does material progress depend on large investible funds. The establishment and improvement of agricultural properties, the building up of traders' inventories, or the establishment of workshops and small factories requires little finance. Conversely, some of the most expensive types of capital formation, especially buildings, are more akin to durable consumer goods than to instruments of production. In all, capital formation is better seen as a concomitant of economic advance than as its precondition.

When the conditions for economic advance are present, capital will be generated locally or will be supplied from external sources in the expectation of an economic return.

Paucity of natural resources, especially land, is not a constraint on development.

Most of Africa and Latin America, and much of Asia, are very sparsely populated. Some of the poorest groups live in such largely empty spaces (even where the land is not particularly infertile) as, for instance, Borneo, Sumatra, and much of Latin America. The aborigines in Southeast Asia, Central Africa, and the Amazon region have very large areas—sometimes immense areas—at their disposal. Even in India and Bangladesh there is much uncultivated land recognized in official publications as cultivable. Over vast areas of the Third World, land is freely available to all prepared to develop and cultivate it.

Extreme material poverty amidst unlimited land should not come as a surprise. The Indians before Columbus were wretchedly poor amidst abundant land and natural resources, at a time when much of Europe, with far less land and higher population densities, was already rich and had developed a high culture.

The small size and low productivity of farms in much of the Third World reflect the want, not of land, but of ambition, energy, and skill, which also explains the low level of productive capital.

Sustained prosperity owes little or nothing to natural resources—witness, in the past, Venice, a wealthy world power built on a few mud flats; Holland, much of it drained from the sea by the seventeenth century; and now West Germany, Switzerland, Japan, Singapore, Hong Kong, and Taiwan, to cite only some of the more obvious instances of prosperous countries short of land and natural resources, but evidently not short of human resources.

The relation between natural resources, population, and economic development cannot be discussed sensibly without taking cognizance of personal and group differences in economic performance. There are very wide differences in economic achievement, and hence in income, among persons of different ethnic and cultural groups within the same Third World country or region and with access to the same physical resources. For instance, in Malaysia, the poor, uneducated, Chinese immigrant laborers who entered the country before the second world war, largely barred from owning land, soon outdistanced economically both the Malays and the immigrant Indians.[2] This is only one instance of such wide differences among ethnic and religious groups in the Third World: Asians and Africans in East Africa; Ibo and others in Nigeria; Jews, Armenians, Greeks, and Arabs in the Levant; Greeks and Turks in Cyprus; and Chinese, Lebanese, and West Indians in the Caribbean.

The Caribbean islands are supposed to be heavily overpopulated. In the 1950s there was a substantial stream of emigration from the West Indian islands to North America and Britain. At the same time, many Chinese and Lebanese wished to emigrate to these islands, and most of the few who were admitted prospered; some developed substantial businesses. In India, too, there are substantial differences in economic performance between some of the smaller groups—like the Parsees and the Jains on the one hand, and the rest of the population on the other hand—and perhaps less prominent differences between some much larger groups, such as the Sikhs and Punjabis on the one hand, and the Bengalis and the Telugu on the other.

Such group differences in economic performance are pronounced, and pertinent to discussions on economic development. They are hardly ever mentioned in the contemporary literature on development or on population problems, and more rarely in popular or political discussions.

Throughout the Third World, the most prosperous regions are those with the most extensive commercial contacts with the West. This is evident in Southeast Asia, West Africa, and Latin America. In the last hundred years, the conditions of existence there have been largely transformed over vast areas under the impact of Western contacts and the local response to them. Here are a few instances. In the early years of the nineteenth century, Hong Kong and Singapore were empty—respectively, a barren rock and a swamp. Today they prosper, with large populations. Rubber and tin converted Malaya from a sparsely populated region of poor hamlets and fishing villages to one of the most prosperous Third World countries, with a large population enjoying a longer expectation of life and a higher standard of living. Somewhat analogous developments occurred in extensive regions in West Africa through the massive production by Africans of cocoa, groundnuts, cotton, and palm products in response to the opportunities opened up largely by the activities of Western traders and shipowners.

Over most of the Third World, economic achievement declines as we move further from the impact of the Western economic contact. The extreme poverty and backwardness of countries and groups without commercial contact with the West are limiting cases—witness countries such as Tibet and Sikkim, and groups such as aborigines and pygmies. External commercial contacts expand people's choices and opportunities, and provide outlets for their produce and sources of supply for goods they want and for which they are prepared to work and save. They serve as channels for human and material resources, skills, and capital. When these contacts are with more advanced societies, they serve as vehicles for new ideas, and for knowledge of new methods, crops, and wants; they often first suggest to the local population the idea of change and of economic improvement; and they have often led to uncoerced erosion of attitudes and mores unpropitious to economic achievement. The very idea of economic progress is of Western origin.

Over the last hundred years or so, commercial contacts between the West and the Third World have offered much greater opportunities than in the more distant past. All this applies with even greater force today, because these contacts now offer access to scientific and technical advances developed elsewhere, as well as to large markets for exports, and to extensive and diverse sources of imports.

The idea that the West has caused and perpetuates Third World poverty reflects in part the ancient fallacy that the incomes of the relatively prosperous must have been taken from those less well off, and that they are not earned or produced. The rise of Marxist-Leninist ideology and the play of political forces have added momentum to the appeal of the idea. Nevertheless, it misconceives the nature of economic activity, and is mistaken in treating total income as given. The idea is indeed the opposite of the truth, because the material prosperity of some conduces to the material advance of others.

In addressing an American audience, it is necessary to take note of the Atlantic slave trade. But horrible and destructive as this trade was, it cannot legitimately be claimed as a cause of African backwardness. The slave trade to what is now the Middle East began before the Atlantic slave trade, and far outlasted it. And, as it happens, the most backward parts of the continent—such as the interior of Central and Southern Africa and most of East Africa—were relatively untouched by Western slavery, while the currently most advanced areas, notably West Africa, were much involved in it. Asia, of course, was altogether untouched by it.

III

Since the second world war, population has increased very rapidly in most less-developed countries. Currently, the natural increase for the Third World as a whole is about 2.5 percent per annum, compounded. This rapid population growth has come about as a result of a sharp decline in mortality without any substantial reduction in birthrates (either crude or age-specific rates).

Population growth is now increasingly regarded as a major constraint on Third World material progress. The so-called population explosion is much deplored. The need for policies of population control in the Third World is widely canvassed in the West as well as in the Third World.

The relations between population growth, per capita incomes, and living standards are often complex, and we cannot examine them fully here. We confine ourselves to some elements in these relationships which bear directly on Third World performance, prospects, and policies.

In the past, as well as more recently, incomes and living standards have risen with both rapid and slow rates of population growth. In recent decades, in many Third World countries in the Far East, Southeast Asia, Africa, and Latin America, incomes have increased substantially with rapid growth in population. This also often happened in the West in the past, as in the United States, Britain, and Germany at various times during the last two hundred years.

Conversely, there have also been instances of substantial increases in per capita incomes simultaneous with a decline in birthrates. But the increase in incomes could not possibly have been brought about by the decline in the birthrate: a decline in the birthrate by itself can lead to higher incomes only after several decades at the earliest. This is because changes in birthrates denote changes in the rates of change of population, and these can affect the level of income appreciably only after such a long time span. Even drastic policies of population control would not be able to achieve the favorable effects claimed for them within the time horizon of interest to national and international politicians.

A rapid natural rate of population increase in the short run necessarily reduces national income per head as this is conventionally measured. This is so because there are more children: what applies to a family applies also to an aggregation of families. The birth of a child immediately reduces income per head within the family; and the same applies in the nation. But do the parents of the family feel worse off? Conversely, would they feel better off if they could not have children, or if some of theirs died young?

The so-called population explosion is the result of a sharp fall in mortality, unaccompanied by a corresponding decline in birthrate. It is usually deplored, because of the resulting decline in per capita income. Yet what it means is that people and their children live longer, and therefore it represents a manifest and pronounced improvement in the standard of living of those who have survived and whose children live longer. This improvement is omitted from the conventional national income statistics which ignore improved health, longer life expectation, and the survival of children as positive components of income and living standards.

Per capita income, as conventionally measured, is in no way a surrogate for economic well-being. If it were, then an increase in the death rate of the poor in a country would have to be regarded as an economic improvement. Paradoxically, the birth of a calf shows up in these statistics as an improvement, because it is registered as an increase in total—and hence also in per capita—income, while the birth of a child shows up as a deterioration, because, by itself, it causes a fall in per capita income. Conventional interpretation of per capita national income figures, and obsession with differences and changes in these figures (for countries or collectivities), can result in a perversity, such as the assertion by Gunnar

Myrdal that "for mankind as a whole there has actually been no progress at all" in the twentieth century.[3]

People in the Third World typically see children as a boon and not as a burden. Children give pleasure; they often contribute significantly to family income; they serve as a source of security or a form of insurance for old age; they are outlets for affection; they sometimes bring prestige and influence; and they enable people to project themselves into the future.

Parents in the Third World do not have children simply because they are irresponsible or cannot help it. Fertility rates are well below fecundity rates. It is often said that people in the Third World have such large families because they have no access to Western-type modern contraceptives. But this poses the question why these contraceptives are not marketed on a large scale in countries where cheap consumer goods, both imported and of local production, are readily available, and where transistor radios, watches, and mechanized transport are widely familiar. The answer is that the demand is not sufficient. Most people still prefer to have large families— large, that is, by Western standards—even when they know about modern as well as traditional methods of fertility control.[4]

Since about the middle 1960s it has come to be argued increasingly and insistently that birth control is indispensable for Third World development. We have seen that this argument is defective on several grounds. It relies on misleading statistics; it misunderstands the determinants of economic progress; it misinterprets the causalities in changes in fertility and changes in income; it greatly exaggerates the potentialities of a reduction in the rate of population growth on the level of income in the foreseeable future; and it envisages children exclusively as burdens. The practical effects of this package of misdiagnoses are enhanced by the implicit but clear assumption that a large proportion of the population of the Third World procreates, heedless of consequences. Faulty analysis and superficial observation are adduced to justify policies to propagandize, induce, or even force people to reduce birthrates.

Pressures for population control in the Third World largely emanate from the West. For example, the World Bank supports population programs in several Third World countries, including India. These pressures and their sources were evident in India, where a sustained and mounting pressure for birth control culminated in the compulsory mass sterilization campaign of 1975–1977 in which the number of people sterilized against their will, often in brutal and insanitary conditions, is reported to have run into hundreds of thousands or even more (Hanlon and Agarwal 1977:268–70).[5]

Fears of a Third World population explosion are generally based on projections of recent demographic trends. Similar population projections made in other contexts, or simple predictions based on observed trends, have often turned out to be seriously defective. Changes in fertility rates in the Third World may well occur with economic and social change, Western contacts, and the spread of education, so that the fears may prove to be grossly exaggerated. In any case, even drastic policies of population control will not be able to achieve the favorable effects claimed for them within the foreseeable future, certainly not within the time horizon of interest to national and international politicians. On the other hand, population policies which involve open or disguised coercion, or which in other ways are repugnant to the people concerned, will rapidly produce anguish, anxiety, and tension, with serious effects on personal and social well-being and economic performance. Indeed, those who seek urgent solutions to a problem they claim to have discovered are apt to propose or prescribe policies which generate, for the people directly affected, difficulties and problems far more acute than those they would otherwise experience.

IV

Assertions that Third World poverty is caused by the West diverts attention from crucial domestic factors affecting economic performance. Thus, they distract attention from the policies of Third World governments and their effects. They also spuriously justify Third World government restrictions on external contacts, which governments favor for their own sake.

Especially when they want to be heard in the West, Third World governments insist that they wish to promote economic development and improve the lot of the poor. These protestations are rarely borne out by their actual policies. The policies of most Third World governments, in fact, adversely affect both current and prospective incomes compared to what they would have been otherwise.

These policies range from support of patently uneconomic activities and enterprises to the expulsion of economically productive groups such as traders, or members of unpopular tribes or ethnic groups—even to the condoning of massacre. Chinese in Southeast Asia, Indians in Burma, Asians in Africa, and the Ibo in Nigeria have been victims of severe persecution or repression, to name some significant examples.

The spectrum between the extremes includes such diverse and widespread policies as the creation and entrenchment of state enterprise in industry, finance, and trade; state monopolies in the purchase of farm produce or in the conduct of foreign trade; extensive restrictive licensing of major trade, transport, and industrial activities, often on a discriminatory basis penalizing minority groups and foreign as well as efficient local enterprises; suppression of private trade and industry; heavy protection of uneconomic manufacturing activities; restrictions on the inflow of private foreign capital; wholesale confiscation; and penal taxation of producers of cash crops. This is not a comprehensive catalogue.

Some of these policies, as, for instance, the expulsion or repression of productive groups with above-average incomes, promptly reduce per capita income and also retard its growth. Thus they impoverish these countries, and widen the current and prospective difference between Western incomes and Third World incomes. While prosperous groups like traders and landowners and ethnic or tribal minorities are most directly affected by such policies, they also cause far-reaching harm to the majority of the local people, including the urban poor and the rural population, whose access to cheap consumer goods and to markets for their labor and produce is gravely impaired, even denied. The destruction or severe weakening of efficient private trading and transport networks resulting from such policies has contributed to regional food shortages and at times to famine in parts of Burma, Ethiopia, Tanzania, and Zaïre.

Several of these policies are, at times, regarded as components of comprehensive development planning, which in turn is widely regarded as necessary for Third World progress. In current terminology, comprehensive planning usually denotes actual or attempted state control of most economic activity, to mobilize local resources, and consciously to organize their more efficient deployment. At times, yet more far-reaching purposes are advocated or envisaged, including attempts to remold man and remake society. Here is Professor Myrdal (1968:115–16, 109) on Asian development:

The bigger and more rapid change ordinarily must be attained by resolutely altering the institutions within which people live and work. . . . But institutions can ordinarily be changed only by resort to what in the region is called compulsion—putting obligations on people and supporting them by force.

He wonders

whether people will change in the way development requires: and whether all these things will happen rapidly enough, without a deliberate reformation of popular religion that would drive out superstitious beliefs and elevate in their place the cherished rites, philosophical thoughts, and general moral precepts accepted by most of the intellectuals.

Development experts like Nobel laureate Myrdal assert that comprehensive planning is essential for development. This is not so. Comprehensive planning obstructs economic development. It does not augment resources. It only concentrates and increases power in the sense of the control of governments over their own people.

The more strictly economic effects of large-scale planning in the Third World have been adverse, as has been frequently noted. Professor Myint, a prominent student of economic development and a leading authority on Southeast Asia, has drawn attention to the contrast between the rapid rate of economic advance in Thailand, the Philippines, and Malaysia, and the economic stagnation of Burma and Indonesia. Myint (1971:33–34) attributes the failure of the latter countries primarily to the fact that they leant "heavily on economic planning and large-scale state intervention in economic life combined with an inward-looking and even hostile attitude towards foreign trade and enterprise."[6] Another recent study (Görgens 1976:214) finds that "the average growth rates are distinctly higher in those developing countries that are more oriented towards a free market economy . . . than in the countries more oriented to a planned economy." This comparison, moreover, does not allow for the fact that planned economies typically include relatively larger sectors whose outputs do not serve to raise living standards. Indeed, visitors to the cities of more intensively planned economies are frequently impressed by the unavailability of simple, everyday, consumer goods, including food.

Apart from the directly harmful economic repercussions—and even brutal results—of policies pursued by many Third World governments, the ensuing extensive politicization of life (inseparable from close state control of economic activity) provokes tensions. The tensions provoke conflict, sometimes extending to civil war, and they divert energies and ambition from economic activity to politics and its offshoots. It becomes crucial who has the government. Such economically counterproductive or exceedingly damaging policies are widely adopted, because they help governments to maintain or extend their power over their subjects, both directly, and by placating their supporters and undermining actual or potential opponents. All this affects the deployment of people's activities, and this in turn is fundamental to the economic position and prospects of any society.

These policies and their results are rarely and reluctantly noted in the West, chiefly because their recognition by a wider Western public would harm the powerful political, financial, and emotional interests which support foreign aid, the international organizations, and the extension of state-controlled economies in the Third World. Indeed, some of the specific policies, as well as the general policy orientation, are advocated and promoted by influential Western groups and the international organizations. Western ideas and resources have greatly influenced these policies of Third World governments. Western personnel and money have at times been indispensable in sustaining governments which pursued damaging, coercive, or even brutal policies. Thus, large-scale support from the World Bank was indispensable for the survival of the government of Tanzania over a period in which wholesale coercive collectivization of farmers was the cornerstone of its policies.

V

To reflect on the prospects of the Third World is to reflect on the future of the majority of mankind. The Third World comprises some two-thirds of mankind, and yet at the same time it is a residual category. It is mankind, except the West or the Westernized world.

Extensive speculation on the future of this extremely diverse majority of mankind would be unrewarding. Social studies are littered with miscarried forecasts, including those based on apparently sophisticated methods. Instead, we make some suggestions about what the West can do to help, or at least not hinder, the material advance of the peoples of the Third World. In doing so, we shall remember—and we also wish to remind the reader again—that the material progress of the numerous societies of the Third World depends largely on domestic factors, notably official policies, and on the attributes and motivations of the people at large.

We have already noted that there are wide group differences in economic performance in many Third World countries. This accords with expectations, because groups and individuals differ in all sorts of ways, including their economic aptitudes, attitudes, values, and mores, which evidently affect their economic position and prospects. They differ in such matters as the value attached to leisure, reflection, or innovation, or their attitude to women's work outside the home, their readiness to take animal life, or generally to harness nature to their own ends. Most people like to have higher incomes, more of the good things of life. But both individuals and societies differ greatly in what they are prepared to give up for them.

We know very little about the biological, historical, cultural, or other reasons for personal or group differences in economic performance, or about their likely persistence. For instance, we cannot tell how deeply people are attached to their mores and modes of conduct. But speculation on these important matters is not required for the choice of policies. Liberal economic policies, and extensive, varied, and widely dispersed external contacts, promote uncoerced modification of attitudes, mores, motivation, and conduct uncongenial to material progress. They allow people, to the extent of their abilities, to change their ways to achieve higher incomes *if that is what they want*. But such policies and contacts do not force people to do so.[7]

In some parts of the Third World, attitudes and mores have changed little or slowly. A revival of Islamic orthodoxy and explicit rejection of Western habits are evident in countries such as Iran. Conversely, in some parts of Africa, change has been rapid after contact with the West. Peru provides an example of long-term change in economic attitudes and abilities. When the commercial exploitation of its guano islands was undertaken in the first half of the last century, entrepreneurship, capital, and labor all came from abroad, as local supplies were not forthcoming. A century or so later, after the second world war, the fishmeal industry was established and rapidly developed largely by Peruvian entrepreneurs, using local finance, locally produced equipment, and labor attracted from all over the country.

All this greatly complicates the assessment of the economic prospects of individual Third World countries, let alone of the Third World as a whole.

Much the most effective way in which the West can help Third World countries is to reduce its trade barriers against their exports. These barriers are severe, and take the form of import taxes, direct subsidies to domestic producers, and import quotas often imposed or intensified at short notice. The extent and severity of these restrictions can be expected to increase under the impact of two sets of influences. The first is the increasing range of Third World products which are competitive in Western markets. These products now include ships, electronics, and engineering products, besides the familiar textiles, garments, and footwear. South Korea, the new Japan, has become a world force in shipbuilding, and has successfully invaded the markets of the heavily subsidized shipyards of Japan and Western Europe. The second is that Western economies are exhibiting a pronounced and possibly increasing inflexibility, a reluctance or inability to undertake structural changes to accommodate the increased volume of competitive imports.

Western protectionism inhibits material progress in the Third World, reduces long-run real incomes in the West, and provides substantial grounds for criticism of Western policies *vis-à-vis* the Third World. What can be done to reduce Western protectionism, or to prevent its increase? Probably very little, given the play of political forces. To resist the pressure for import restrictions, it might be worth while to try to compensate specific groups damaged by imports coming from the Third World by deploying part of the large funds now going into official aid. Such a system would entail serious drawbacks. It would be asked why some groups should be singled out for compensation for the effects of economic change or of changes in official policy, or why beneficiaries of such changes were not taxed. Such objections are formidable. But before concluding that such a scheme is altogether impractical, one might examine its feasibility on a limited and clearly defined scale, using aid funds for this purpose. Without some such measure, we seem to be saddled with Western protectionism, probably coupled with increasing aid to the Third World, a sort of conscience money.

What about Western aid to the Third World?[8] We think that aid ought to be terminated as soon as existing commitments are discharged. As we have dealt with major aspects of the effects of aid in greater detail in accessible publications (Bauer and Yamey 1977),[9] we limit our discussion here.

Official aid is neither necessary nor sufficient for the economic development of Third World countries. Many nations have experienced sustained economic development without aid; many have received aid, have not developed, and are unable even to repay loans received interest-free or on subsidized terms. The favorable effects of aid are in any case limited, since governments and businesses in recipient countries with good growth prospects can generally borrow capital through the market. The unfavorable effects have been serious in many countries. Aid must bear a heavy share of responsibility for the adoption and pursuit of detrimental economic policies in many Third World countries. The transfer of aid resources to a recipient government increases its economic power *vis-à-vis* its subjects, enables it more readily and extensively to carry out its chosen policies, however unfavorable their effects may be, and makes it easier for it to mask or conceal their ill effects, at least for a time. Moreover, some of the policies detrimental to economic advance, such as economic planning, have been advocated by those responsible for the distribution of aid. Aid has also discouraged the prudent conduct of economic affairs in that, for instance, the emergence of balance-of-payments difficulties could itself be used as an argument for further aid.[10]

But the vested interests behind official aid are now so strong, and its advocacy so influential, that it is impossible to finish it in the foreseeable future. The second-best solution is to see how it can be confined and improved.

Aid should take the form of cash payments to recipient governments, for this makes it far easier to identify the amounts involved than, say, with commodity agreements or debt cancellation, which are also open to other major objections. The cash payments should take the form of grants rather than of subsidized loans, for otherwise handouts are confused with investments. The grants should not be tied as regards their spending, to make clear that it is the recipient governments and not the export industries of the donors which are being subsidized. They should be bilateral, to maintain some vestige of control by the elected representatives of the donors—i.e., the taxpayers—which, among other advantages, may somewhat retard the use of development aid for such objectives as global equalization of incomes and living standards which lie behind much advocacy of multinational aid. The grants should be for specific and limited periods. They should be treated explicitly as *ex gratia* donations, and should not be coupled with international or other declarations implying Western guilt and restitution. They should not be linked to the achievement of specified rates of growth or levels of income in recipient countries, as this implies open-ended commitments, since the attainment of these objectives depends primarily and predominantly on domestic factors.

But above all, aid should be given only to countries where humane leadership, effective administration, and personal freedom enable people to deploy their activities as they think best, which is also likely to be most conducive to economic advance. This means giving aid only to governments which, within the constraints of their human, financial, and administrative resources, set out to perform the primary tasks of government and not to impose state-controlled economies on their people; that is, to governments interested in developing the framework within which people can improve their living standards, if that is what they want and are willing and able to do. In the conditions of most Third World countries, the adequate performance of the extensive and complex primary tasks of government, which individuals cannot perform for themselves, would fully stretch their resources.[11]

That implementation of this suggested prescription for aid programs would involve immense changes from the present aid regime should be evident. Nevertheless, even if aid programs were in future to conform more closely to our suggestions, the beneficial results would be more in discouraging harmful policies and promoting favorable policies in Third World countries than in any active contribution to growth of the transferred resources themselves. This is so because, to repeat, development depends primarily on people's attributes and on government policies.

VI

We began with a concrete example of a Third World country: Hong Kong. We finish with an abstraction: the Third World—previously known as the underdeveloped world, the less-developed world, and now becoming known as the South.

What is there is common between, say, Nepal and Argentina, Hong Kong and the Maldives, Botswana and Chile, Afghanistan and Ecuador, Egypt and Cambodia, and Chad and Brazil? Very little. As we have shown, it is certainly not that they or other Third World countries are components of an economic collectivity at the mercy of the unpropitious forces depicted in the usual stereotype. It is not even that they are unified in poverty. There are very wide differences in incomes and other economic variables within the Third World, the constituent societies of which range from aborigines to commercially sophisticated and materially advanced groups and societies.[12] Average incomes in the richest Third World countries are in any case not very different from average incomes in the poorest developed countries.

Many individual Third World countries are themselves extremely diverse, and include substantial groups and societies with materially different average incomes. They are so different ethnically and culturally that these countries are best regarded as collections of different societies rather than as single countries or nations. This internal diversity applies to many Asian and African countries, and to some extent also to the larger Latin American countries such as Brazil.

In most of the Third World countries, the great majority of people do not even know of the existence of other Third World countries. Some are in uneasy truce with their neighbors, as are India and Pakistan as well as many African states. Others are engaged in intermittent hostilities, as are Algeria and Morocco; yet others have recently been in deadly combat, as were Ethiopia and Somalia.

The profound diversity of the Third World inevitably raises the question of the concept itself. Its use and its superficial plausibility have helped to provide a spurious veneer of uniformity and homogeneity to what is a vast aggregate of radically different and sometimes mutually antagonistic components.

The Third World did not exist before the second world war. The concept was forged after the war, largely under United Nations auspices and leadership. But it is an abstract concept with a very concrete purpose. From its inception, the unifying characteristic of the Third World has been that its constituents—with the odd exceptions—demand and receive aid from Western governments. The specific and, potentially, extremely important purpose of promoting and organizing the flow of aid from Western governments provides the essential and enduring bond.

But the pursuit of the common purpose sets up tensions at times. Tensions arise because interests conflict over the sources and forms of such aid, and over the distribution of the aid among recipients.

In a perceptive and illuminating article, Professor Martin Bronfenbrenner (1976:829) has characterized as follows the declaration of the New International Economic Order, a recent expression of Third World demands:

The unifying idea behind all these things is the desire to increase the bargaining power of ldcs [less developed countries] against mdcs [more developed countries] over a broad range of international issues relative to trade, to aid, and to the international transfers of both capital and technology.

What seems to have developed is a collection of self-serving ldc theories of international economic relations, summarized under the glittering head of "A New International Economic Order". Of this collection, . . . UNCTAD (in concert with other ldc-dominated U.N. agencies) has become the leading world spokesman.[13]

The basic purpose of the concept of the Third World as an instrument for securing wealth transfers from the West, as well as the uneasy unity within the Third World, is a major theme of a recent, well-received book by Dr. Mahbub ul Haq, *The Poverty Curtain: Choices for the Third World*. The author holds the key post of Director of the Policy Planning Department of the World Bank. He writes (Ul Haq 1976:181–82):

A major part of the bargaining strength of the Third World lies in its political unity. This unity is going to be even more important in the struggle ahead and far more difficult to keep as the ranks of the Third World may be divided by the lure of short-term gains and separate deals with the rich nations. If that happens, the Third World would deserve the perpetuation of an inequitable economic order as it would have demonstrated that it is not yet ready to challenge the existing balance of power.

VII

If Western governments wish to promote the interests of the peoples of Third World countries as well as those of their own, they must learn to distinguish between myth and reality in the analysis and assessment of Third World demands. To do this, they must rid themselves of the false notion that the Third World is a homogeneous collectivity whose economic fate and fortune are outside its control. They must learn that policies which serve the interests of Third World governments need not serve the interests of Third World people. They must learn that even appropriate policies towards Third World countries will not be enough to ensure rapid or pervasive economic development in many of them.

Persistent and increasing pressure for large-scale transfers of aid can be expected from Third World governments, the United Nations network, and their supporters. Unless Western governments resist this pressure, the forces making for global egalitarianism may well become uncontainable. And they will not resist effectively unless they rid themselves of unwarranted feelings of guilt for Third World poverty: for guilt feelings inspire policies shaped more to relieve such feelings than to achieve their ostensible object.

Attempts to move substantially towards global egalitarianism will require extensive political coercion in face of the manifold and deep-seated differences in economic performance among and within groups and societies. Such attempts would therefore require not only some form of world government, but world government with totalitarian power.

7

SEYMOUR MARTIN LIPSET

Racial and Ethnic Tensions in the Third World

The problems of ethnic diversity. Prejudice and intolerance in historical records. Skin color and status. Latin American racism. Heterogeneity, tolerance, and intolerance in South Asia. The conflict of languages in India, Pakistan, and Sri Lanka. Africa—ethnic superiority due to race, culture, occupation, religion, and tribe. The increased tension in industrial and urban areas. Second-class citizens in the Middle East. The assimilationist program in the USSR and China. Antidiscrimination measures and ethnic pluralism.

To understand the politics of Third World countries, it is necessary to move beyond problems related to their low levels of economic development, their highly stratified social systems, and their lack of education, which have concerned much social science literature. Most of these states, particularly the new nations of Africa and Asia, face the fact that they are multiethnic, often multilinguistic societies, many of which do not even have one numerically dominant ethnic group. Tensions stemming from this situation add considerably to the task of creating and maintaining democratic, or at least noncoercive, politics. For—in addition to seeking to allocate resources, to foster policies which may be seen as equitable by diverse social strata—they must find ways of securing the loyalty of ethnic groupings, which constitute sub- or embryonic nations whose initial loyalties and sense of group consciousness, of "we versus them," is to themselves rather than to the nation-state. And since their economic resources are low, it is not surprising that ethnic conflict often bodes well to tear the countries asunder, to produce outcomes in which dominant groups, sometimes minorities, discriminate against others in access to political power and economic and social advantages.

The problems which ethnic diversity pose for efforts at nation-building have—as Walker Conner (1972:320) has pointed out in a brilliant article—been largely ignored by social scientists concerned with the topic. It is not, as he notes, a minor phenomenon, nor is it limited to Third World countries.

The remarkable lack of coincidence that exists between ethnic and political borders is indicated by the following statistics. Of a total of 132 contemporary states, only 12 (9.1 per cent) can be described as essentially homogeneous from an ethnic viewpoint. An additional 25 states (18.9 per cent of the sample) contain an ethnic group accounting for more than 90 per cent of the state's total population, and in still another 25 states the largest element accounts for between 75 and 89 per cent of the population. But in 31 states (23.5 per cent of the total), the largest ethnic element represents only 50 to 74 per cent of the population, and in 39 cases (29.5 per cent of all states) the largest group fails to account for even half of the state's population. Moreover, this portrait of ethnic diversity becomes vivid when the number of distinct ethnic groups within states is considered. In some instances, the number of groups within a state runs into the hundreds, and in 53 states (40.2 per cent of the total), the population is divided into more than *five* significant groups.

In this chapter, I seek to deal with the problematic consequences of such ethnic variation for the task of nation-building and social solidarity both in the past and present.

THE HISTORICAL RECORD

Unfortunately, both the historical and contemporary comparative records indicate that ethnic interaction has almost invariably been accompanied by intolerance and conflict. President Kennedy noted in 1963 that the phenomenon "is as old as the scriptures." The Bible, of course, reports the basic elements of anti-Semitism and racism in the story of the first Exodus, both in the way the Egyptians reacted to the Israelites, who had worked harder than they and waxed wealthy, and in the way the Israelites treated the various peoples of Canaan as they took it over.

The dominant peoples of the ancient world justified their superior position by negative judgments of others, which some explained as derivative from geographical factors. Five centuries before the birth of Christ, Aristotle wrote that the people living in northern Europe were brave, but not as intelligent as Mediterraneans. To Aristotle, northern Europeans were unfitted for tasks which required organizational and leadership abilities. To the Roman Vitrius, southern Europeans exposed to a humid and warmer climate were more intelligent than northern Europeans, who were exposed to a cold and therefore dulling atmosphere (Santa Cruz 1971:1).

The historical record is sufficiently full of intolerance that A. N. Sherwin-White saw fit to deliver the Gray Memorial Lectures at Cambridge University in 1965–1966 on the subject of "Racial Prejudice in Imperial Rome." The Romans, he notes (Sherwin-White 1967:18), justified their conquests of alien peoples and the subsequent annihilation of their cultures by using invidious stereotypes; according to Caesar, for example, the Germans "were savages characterized by *arrogantia, iracundia, termeritas, crudelitas* and *perfidia*." Roman literature is also replete with anti-Greek references. In the Greek areas of the empire, "Greek disliked Jew, and Jew disliked Greek." Diodorus writes of the Jewish "lack of human feeling," "dislike of strangers," and "hostility towards the human race" (Sherwin-White 1967:71–87).

The awful story of medieval Christian anti-Semitism need not be detailed here, but a word is perhaps in order about the Arabs, who purport to have been much better than the Christians and to have allowed non-Moslem believers in God to live undisturbed lives. Their writings emphasize that "Jews and Muslims and every heterodox Christian were subject to constant persecution in Christian Europe." While there is little doubt that the Arabs dealt with non-Islamic minorities better than Christians treated Jews during the Middle Ages, the Arab record is far from good. The Arabist Gustave von Grunebaum (1946:177–84) details the situation of Jews and Christians in medieval Islam: "Their personal safety and their personal property were guaranteed them at the price of permanent inequality." Bernard Lewis (1958:93–94) describes them as "second-class citizens," who paid much higher taxes than Moslems, and who were, on occasion, subject to open persecution.

In spite of various myths to the contrary, Lewis (1970:23, 28–29) documents conclusively that Moslem Arabs long despised Negroes. As early as the eighth century, assorted poems and writings described blackness as inferior. Writing in the ninth century, Jahiz of Basra said, "We know that the Negroes are the least intelligent and the least discerning of mankind." Although Arabs held both white and black slaves, the great majority were black, and the word *abd*, first used for slaves of all races, ceased, according to Lewis, "to be used of any slaves but black ones and eventually, in many Arabic dialects, simply came to mean a black man irrespective of whether he was a slave or not.''

Christians also rationalized their maltreatment of the black in religious terms, justifying the slave trade, for example, by the ''heathenism'' of the Africans. Since blacks could convert, slavery required enduring legitimation, which the white Christian masters found in a Biblical event which also appealed to Moslems: ''they claimed black skin was a punishment from God. They evoked the curse . . . upon Ham, son of Noah, who had found his drunken father naked in a tent'' (Bastide 1968:36).

Prejudice against dark skin is not restricted to white Europeans or Arabs. In fact, color-linked prejudice seems to have appeared long before the white man needed a justification for exploitation of the Negro. Theories about the negative and positive qualities of color, Hugh Tinker (1969:223) explains, are also found among dark-skinned peoples. Among non-Westerners there is

an anthropomorphic association of darkness with dread and mystery, and lightness with everything admirable and good. Presumably this is a residual folk memory from the dawn of mankind when the hours of darkness were a time of constant danger; while during daylight hours man's puny physical strength was compensated by his superior cunning.

The explanation for preference for light skin color in some nonwhite societies prior to contact with whites may lie in the fact that the privileged strata could be lighter than others by staying out of the sun and avoiding tanning themselves, while peasants and laborers forced to work out of doors in agrarian societies were invariably darker. To be able to have light skin color was, in effect, a form of conspicuous consumption for the elite. In Hawaii, prior to the arrival of Captain Cook who was hailed as a god because his skin was white, ''fair skin was valued as a sign of nobility,'' for, according to Edwin Burrows (1947:18–19), a student of Hawaiian culture, ''those who sit in the shade and receive tribute are lighter-

hued than those who have to work for a living out in the sun.''
Japanese also have tried to avoid suntans. Their values emphasized '''white skin' as beautiful and deprecated 'black
skin' as ugly''—long before contact with Europeans.
Japanese described their own skin color as ''white,'' as distinct from Southeast Asians, whom they saw as dark-skinned
(Wagatsuma 1968). Hugh Tinker (1969:223) notes that the
''dark-fair antithesis continues [from India] through Southeast
Asia into East Asia, though the color pattern changes somewhat. The fair (or rather, the pale) is still the color of virtue.''

More surprising is the fact that the same pattern has existed
among some black African tribes, seemingly before close
contact with or rule by whites. ''Within Ibo culture the col-
ours and textures grouped under *ocha* [white] are admired.''
That this preference has deep roots may be seen in traditional
ritual patterns, such as the fact that ''priests of Amadi Oha,
the lightening deity, had to be of yellowish complexion and
most still are'' (Ardener 1954:71–73).

LATIN AMERICA

The two great civilizations that existed at the time the Spanish
arrived in America, the Aztecs and Incas, like the Hawaiians,
had as a central myth a belief in white-skinned gods or
semi-gods. The privileged strata among the Indians in these
cultures purportedly were somewhat lighter in color than the
average Indian (Segrera 1974:62). Peru was dominated by a
supposedly lighter-skinned elite, largely composed of the descendants of an endogamous single family (Ferguson
1961:8). Similarly, the ruling tribes of Mexico came from
northern regions, and also were reported to be lighter in skin
texture. When the Spaniards came to Mexico, Moctezuma
tried to identify with this superior group by emphasizing his
supposed lightness, and, of course, helped the Spaniards take

over (Segrera 1974:56, 62, 64). The Spaniards were able to easily conquer these complex and well-organized societies, in large part because racism, ethnic imperialism, and tribal warfare and conquest existed long before the Europeans set foot in the Western world (Parkes 1960:51). Paintings and myths testify to the presence of a pre-Columbian racism. Both the Aztecs and Incas cruelly treated the inferior tribes who formed the majority of their populations.

The mixed-blood and Creole (native-born whites) middle and upper strata of the Spanish colonies created a racist society, which emphasized the superiority of white European ancestry. Such views were not challenged by the revolutionary movements which eliminated Spanish rule at the beginning of the nineteenth century. Simon Bolivar spoke of ''the threat of the dark skinned'' (Segrera 1974:167). He feared the ''invasion of the Africans.''

Throughout the nineteenth and early twentieth centuries, the Creole elites of Latin America, even the liberals among them, sought to attract ''real whites'' from Europe to populate their lands. In Argentina, the liberal president D. F. Sarmiento repeatedly spoke of the need to attract Europeans as a means ''to secure racial balance, thus correcting the backwardness of the Indian race'' (Segrera 1974:218). Peru tried to ''promote the immigration of similar races,'' i.e., whites, totally ignoring the fact that the country was overwhelmingly Indian. In Mexico, European immigration was sought as an ''active tonic to raise the Indian to a civilized life'' (Segrera 1974:221). Brazil also sought to attract white settlers. Immigration laws in Venezuela have prohibited the entry of blacks.

The current situation in Latin America varies considerably from country to country. Yet in spite of racial and ethnic pluralism, stratification correlates with racial ancestry in almost all of the nations. That is, the privileged classes are largely of white background and/or are lighter skin–colored than the less affluent strata. ''Money whitens'' in these societies, in that those darker-skinned persons who manage to succeed economically do not face overt social discrimination, and they and their offspring frequently marry whites. This fact enables Latin Americans to argue that their societies are not racist or caste systems. Yet little is done in most of them to integrate the nonwhite groups or to give any special assistance to those of Indian or African ancestry who are to be found in considerably disproportionate numbers in the rural and economically less-developed portions of their countries. Urbanization and industrialization have done little to improve the situation. The class structure of most racially heterogeneous cities is closely correlated with color.

The Caribbean nations, all of which are former European colonies, reveal an even greater emphasis on color and race than elsewhere. Whites and/or mulattoes occupy the dominant positions, even in predominantly black societies such as Haiti and Jamaica. There is a "high value placed on color—the 'white bias' to use Henrique's phrase—in all these societies," and the dominant Creole population has largely imitated the style and behavior of the European whites. Although some of these societies are now ruled by political parties dedicated to ʾequalitarian and even socialist objectives, "their economies are not expanding at the rate sufficient to allow for significant group mobility among the mass of the black lower classes" (Patterson 1965:317–19). The tension between the promise of greater opportunity and equality and the fact of a continuing racially stratified society has intensified color consciousness among the lower strata and resulted in increased signs of militancy among them.

SOUTH ASIA

Caste Systems

The Indian caste system, while not racist in the full sense, probably represents the most complete effort to institutionalize blood or ancestral purity. Indian caste is not color bound but, as Gerald Berreman (1972:395) points out, "few would deny that colour consciousness is an important part of the ideology and metaphor of caste in India." And Pierre van den Berghe (1967:14–15) observes, "*Varna* (the broad division into four groups of castes: Brahman, Kshatriya, Vaisya and Sudra) literally means 'color'; Hinduism uses the same kind of color symbolism as the Judeo-Christian tradition, associating evil with black and good with white."

The supposed origins of that system are similar to those in other societies, with militarily or economically stronger races having imposed their own attributes, such as lighter skin color, as morally superior to those of the people they ruled or owned (Suyin 1971:3). Not surprisingly, as André Béteille (1968:174) emphasizes, Indian stereotypes

dwell on the physical features of the different castes, the upper castes being always represented as fair and the lower castes as dark. Further, a reversal of the assumed correlation is viewed as not only unusual, but sinister. A Kannada proverb says, "Trust not a dark Brahman or a fair Holeya"; a North Indian proverb maintains, "A dark Brahman, a fair Chuhra, a woman with a beard—these three are contrary to nature."

Since independence, India has formally outlawed "all forms of discrimination against any group of people," and has promoted "the adoption of positive measures to put an end to Untouchability." Nevertheless, "the power and activity of caste has increased in proportion as political power passed" from the British to the Indians (Srinivas 1962:23). Political party conflicts, in large measure, reflect caste differences. And economic development and urbanization do not appear to have reduced the emphasis on caste (Sebring 1972:587–600).

Moslems in the Indian subcontinent, though members of a religion which contains no theological reference to caste or *jatis* (lineage groups), have followed a loose version of the Hindu caste system. David Mandelbaum (1972:546–47) notes that "Muslims in all regions of India classify themselves into endogamous hereditary groups which are ranked in relation to each other. . . . Where Muslim untouchables exist, they are so treated by both Hindus and Muslims.''

The Importance of Language

Caste, of course, is not the only source of ancestrally derived group division or conflict in South Asia. The peoples of Pakistan, India, and Sri Lanka are also separated along language lines, typically linked to different regions. These lines of linguistic variations usually are associated to differences in economic status and political power (Morris-Jones 1967:51–66). Almost invariably, minority or less affluent language groups see themselves as oppressed by their more powerful co-citizens who speak an alien tongue, and respond by demands for greater autonomy, sometimes independence. Thus, after the Bengali speakers of East Pakistan broke off from Pakistan to form Bangladesh, various of West Pakistan's language groups, Sindhi, Baluchi, and Pasto, ''staged their own movements of autonomy,'' attacking the position of the largest linguistic group in the truncated country, the Punjabi. In India, where the most commonly spoken tongue, Hindi, is used for national government activities, almost all the other major language groups during the 1950s and 1960s demanded and obtained their own states. These victories did not mean the end of linguistic politics, for subminorities within many of the states have waged battles for equal rights usually ''directed to securing facilities of instruction in their own language'' (Das Gupta 1974:67, 71). The same is also true in Sri Lanka (Kearney 1978:521).

Comparable problems and tensions have occurred with varying outcomes in many other new states in Asia and Africa. Given borders—in most cases carryovers from the colonial division of these continents—almost all include people of diverse language cultures, not infrequently with no one language group constituting a majority. The Indian federal solution has been rejected in many countries such as In-

donesia and the Philippines. Where lines of language variation correspond to major ethnic divisions as in Nigeria, the
tension may lead to efforts to secede and to civil war (see
Fishman, Ferguson, Das Gupta 1968). Still, Das Gupta
(1974:71) notes:

Language demands, especially in developing nations, can not be
inferred from the nature of language groups. These groups tend to
make demands only when social mobilization offers competitive
opportunities and values. In this sense language demands are a
function of economic, social and political development.

Southeast Asia, Milton Esman (1965:391) emphasizes, is
"ethnically the most heterogeneous of the world's regions,"
but hardly the most tolerant. Intercommunal rivalries and bit-
terness have occasioned civil wars and efforts at secession in
Burma, Indonesia, Malaysia and Singapore, Laos, Cambodia, Vietnam and the Philippines. Struggles over the power
of the central government, linguistic and regional autonomy,
and religious differences continue to bedevil these societies.
Esman (1965:410–11) concludes that the communal group,
which dominates the political center of each state—usually
the largest, but not necessarily the majority—will "continue
the process of consolidating control over their 'national' territories and peoples. . . . This is the inevitable consequence
of economic and administrative development and is abetted
by current international practice which distributes economic,
technical, and military assistance exclusively through central
governments." As in other parts of the Third World,

urbanization which has been regarded as a modernizing phenomenon, in which traditional, particularistic, communal loyalties become irrelevant, is having the opposite effect. Rapid urbanization
tends to aggravate communal antagonisms in close-quartered competition for scarce jobs, housing, educational opportunities, and political influence. (Esman 1965:417)

Chinese minorities, sometimes described as the "Jews" of
the region, have played important economic roles as business
people in Thailand, Indonesia, Malaysia, the Philippines, and
Vietnam. They have been "both aggressive *agents* of

changes emanating from western commercial expansion and aggressive *retainers* of traditional Chinese social practices,'' behaviors which created considerable hostility from the indigenous population. As a result, strong opposition to Chinese rights has developed in most of these countries (Hamilton 1977: 346, 348; Purcell 1965), ranging from a persecution verging on genocide in Indonesia in 1965–1966 to the recent emigration of virtually all Chinese from Vietnam.

AFRICA

Racism, as well as assorted forms of tribal and ethnic domination, has characterized many black African cultures. Slavery, involving the seizure of members of one tribe or people by another for service or for export, inherently gave rise to, or sustained, strong feelings of ethnic superiority. So little did Africans think of other tribes that, according to Irving Markovitz (1977:143, 123–28), they sold more than fifteen million people over a period of two millenia, first to Arab traders and later, of course, to Europeans. Slavery continued into the present century in African cultures like Ethiopia, Swahili society in East Africa, and various emirates in northern Nigeria, and the descendants of slaves remain lower caste in some societies.

Cultural and occupational differences produce racist reactions among the peoples of Africa, as elsewhere. Opinion studies indicate considerable consensus about ethnic rankings. Thus, stock-raising tribes look down on fishing ones. Groups which were once dominant militarily in given areas see themselves as far superior to the peoples they once ruled. In Uganda and nearby states, the Ganda, who were headed by a royal family and aristocracy in the large state of Buganda, fill "the high-status categories" which others respect (Southall 1961a:228).

The Kanuri of northern Nigeria rank various ethnic groups in three status categories, with themselves at the top. Cohen reports that the "degree of status consensus applied to ethnic status is quite high." The Kanuri look down, for example, on pagan Cameroon tribes such as the Banana and Gwozz peoples, whom they historically took as slaves. They "comment that such groups have no shame, no religion, indeed several informants went further and remarked that they were akin to animals" (Cohen 1970:240–44).

Although most ethnic forms of status discrimination in Africa occur among people who are seen by others as black, racist attitudes and behavior exist in black Africa as in other parts of the world. Having long been ruled by whites, it is to be expected that white skin and European mannerisms should be associated with prestige among blacks, although, as noted earlier, some tribes seemingly exhibited this preference before colonialism. A study of intergroup attitudes among thirty African tribal groups in East Africa, conducted in 1965 (Brewer and Campbell 1976:115), found that "perceptions of skin color, cleanliness, and beauty were frequently associated with the relative progressiveness of ethnic groups."

Anthropologist M. G. Smith (1971:133–36) describes the situation in northern Nigeria, where the Fulani conquered the Hausa in the beginning of the nineteenth century:

In Zaria, also, social significance is given to color distinctions, value is placed on lightness of skin as an attribute of beauty, and as a racial character, and a host of qualitative terms reflect this interest such as *ja-jawur* (light copper skin), *baki* (dark), *baki kirim,* or *baki wal* (real black) and so forth. The Fulani rulers of Zaria distinguish on racial grounds between themselves and their Hausa subjects, stressing such features as skin color, hair, and facial form, and also make similar distinctions among themselves, since past miscegenation has produced wide physical differences among them.

Ronald Cohen (1970:242) reports that among the Nigerian Kanuri, who are Moslems, "Arab facial features, skin color, and general appearance are regarded as the most pleasing physical features."

Ethnic-based antagonisms severely disrupt many African polities today, and have contributed to civil wars and *coups d'état* in nations like Nigeria, Zaïre, Ethiopia, and the Sudan. Ethnic particularism still accounts for tensions in every black African state, save Somalia—between the Agni and the Bete in the Ivory Coast, the Wolof, Serer, Diola, and Fulani in Senegal, and the Ewe and the Ashanti in Ghana.

Industrialization and urbanization, which bring together people from diverse tribal backgrounds, have generally served to heighten rather than reduce ethnic consciousness and tensions in various African states (see Hanna and Hanna 1969). Almost invariably there is considerable variation in the

ethnic allocation of preferred wage employment, socially prestigious roles, or key political positions. Such disproportions are among the major causes of civil strife in developing African nations; herein lie the roots of the bitter "tribalism" with which many African political leaders must contend. . . . A key point to bear in mind is that while the traditional "tribalism" is predominantly rural-based, modern "tribalism" is at least as urban as it is rural. . . .

[A]s we have seen, the process of industrialization may increase ethnicity in a given polyethnic society, despite the presumed ameliorative effects of education, increased "social communication" and sophistication, and other concomitants of industrialization: Ethnicity, therefore, can hardly be regarded simply as a relic of a pre-industrial age. (Duran 1974:45–46, 63)

THE MIDDLE EAST

Finally, to this dreary story of tribal, ethnic, religious, and racial conflict in the Third World must be added the Middle East. As noted earlier, non-Moslems always suffered some form of discrimination, of inferior status in the Islamic world. The multinational, multireligious Turkish empire, however, allowed non-Turkish communities—Christian, Jewish, and others—to live in self-governing communities in which their religious laws and authorities prevailed, the so-called *millet* system.

The rise of Turkish and Arab nationalism in the twentieth century undermined the position of the minorities. The first modern holocaust, the killing of over a half million Armenians by the Turks during World War I, attested to the tension between nationalism and minority rights. More recently, Arab nationalists in Iraq have turned on their minorities, the Assyrians, Jews, and Kurds. The latter, fully one-third of the population, "have never been allowed to use their own language or to study their own culture in the schools and they have never been allowed to exploit their natural resources, particularly petroleum, for their own local development" (Moutafakis 1977:70–72). Their demand for autonomy led to a civil war in which they were crushed. Radical military regimes turned on the Greek minority in Egypt and on the Armenians in Syria, treating them much like the Jews had been earlier.

Essentially, most forms of Arab nationalism from Algeria to Iraq have identified non-Arab, non-Islamic minorities as groups to be submerged, assimilated, or driven into exile. And as a result, Jewish and Christian groups have emigrated in large numbers. Those who remain do so as second-class citizens.

COMMUNIST SYSTEMS

The suppression of ethnic and tribal groups within the context of authoritarian societies in the Third World has led to the recognition that nationalism can lead to the denial of basic human rights. French historian Jacques Julliard has written in the left-wing *Nouvel Observateur* (1978:3): "The time has come to realize that the right of peoples—the right of 'self-determination'—is now the principal instrument of the suppression of human rights." As he notes, nationalism not only has lost its role as a democratic ideology in the First World, it is used to justify authoritarianism and minority rule in the Third.

Ironically, however, it may be argued that the efforts to suppress ethnic and tribal minorities by "radical" Third World and communist countries may correspond to the teachings of the founding fathers of Marxism, Karl Marx and Friedrich Engels. In the original Marxist theory of historical necessity, ethnic minorities were considered an unnecessary distraction, if not inhibitors of economic and political progress. Classic Marxist reasoning gave unlimited historical justification to racial discrimination because it performs an historically useful mission: that of reducing non–class related conflict to its lowest denominator—class—accelerating the final confrontation between the capitalist and the proletarian. As Carlos Moore (1974–1975:125–56) points out, Marx's systematic condemnation of "inferior races" stemmed from his belief that their liberation movements could easily become obstacles in the way of progress in Western industrial societies. To Marx and Engels, the plight of the then politically oppressed blacks, Asians, Slavs, and Latins was a distraction from the "real" issues of class struggle.

Marx and Engels lashed out against Bohemia and Croatia for seeking freedom from German (Austrian) imperialism. In writing of the situation in the Austro-Hungarian Empire, Engels recognized three of its peoples as destined for a progressive role: the Germans, the Poles, and the Magyars. Then, in an unfortunate turn of phrase, he emphasized (d'Encausse and Schram 1969:10), "The chief vocation of all the other races and peoples, great and small, is to perish in the revolutionary holocaust." Marx wrote of the Mexican Indians as "the last of men" deliberately delaying the United States' "imperialist adventure," thus prolonging "the waste" of California in the hands of "lazy Mexicans." Marx's recommendation was to accelerate progress by handing all of Mexico over to the "industrious Americans" (Moore 1974–1975:135).

Writing in 1888, Engels (1953:204) also favored American annexation of Canada, where

one imagines that one is in Europe again, and then one thinks that one is in a positively retrogressing and decaying country. Here one sees how necessary the feverish speculative spirit of the Americans is for the rapid development of a new country . . . ; in ten years this sleepy Canada will be ripe for annexation . . . and they may tug and resist as much as they like, the economic necessity of an infusion of Yankee blood will have its way and abolish this ridiculous boundary line.

Just as Mexican resistance worked "against the interests of development," so did the Algerian revolution retard the historical process. To Engels (1848), the "conquest of Algeria [was] an important and fortunate fact for the progress of civilization." India, too, should submit to the "superior" English. Marx (1960:77) wrote approvingly of the British role. "England has to fulfill a double mission in India: one destructive, the other regenerating—the annihilation of the old [reactionary] Asiatic society, and the laying of the material foundations of Western society in Asia." As Carlos Moore (1974–1975:150) documents in detail: "For the dark-skinned majority of mankind . . . colonization, oppression and slavery became 'regenerating,' 'civilizing,' and 'revolutionary agents.'"

On a formal ideological level, the communist regimes which have come to power since 1917 have rejected Marx's and Engels's insistence that minority and backward peoples must be absorbed into the cultures of more advanced societies. Lenin proposed that national minorities in the Soviet Union should have as much autonomy as possible, and the right to secede. In practice, as the totalitarian regime emerged in that country, the numerous ethnic minorities were brought under the control of the centralized Communist Party. Although most of the minority nationalities, except for the Jews, have been allowed to maintain their own language and culture, "the Soviet authorities . . . for many years have been advancing a theory of gradual *sblizhenie* (rapprochement) of the various nationalities inhabiting the country, ultimately leading to the creation of a common 'Soviet' nation" (Pipes 1965:459). This assimilationist program, though stimulated by the economic and social advantages involved in learning and using the Russian language, has been a failure. Most minority peoples insist on retaining their mother tongue, and resist efforts to Russify them. In 1978, Georgians and Armenians demonstrated against proposals to eliminate their language rights, and the central regime gave in.

Yet the spread of Russians into the minority areas, where they usually occupy a disproportionate number of the better jobs and housing, has been an effective method of unifying the country at the expense of the minorities. Not surprisingly, there is considerable evidence that such migration is strongly resented by the indigenous population. The Soviet Census of 1970, which reported on linguistic knowledge, provides insight on the effective treatment of minorities.

In 1970, 29 million Russians lived in areas set aside for national minorities. . . . Of this 29 million at the very most 870,000 bothered to learn the language of the population among whom they regularly resided. This figure is a better commentary on the attitude of Russians toward non-Russians than any dozen treatises on Soviet nationality policy. (Pipes 1965:464)

Although ethnic minorities in China form only 6 percent of the population, much less than in the Soviet Union, these 50 million or more people constitute fully 90 percent of the population in the border regions (Pye 1965:500). This fact undoubtedly affects the efforts of the Chinese Communists to change the character of these areas. As in the Soviet Union, the majority Chinese (Han) were mobilized to move into minority areas. Thus, migration into Sinkiang "raised the Han proportion from 5.5 percent in 1945 to 20.5 percent in 1962 and 45 percent in 1966" (Pye 1965:497). Similar developments have occurred in Mongolia and Tibet.

With the Great Leap forward in 1957, the Communist Party officially abandoned its commitment to the Leninist principle of minority autonomous rights. The change was presented as a return to "true" Marxism. Internationalism was once more stressed, and tolerance toward minority nationalities' languages, customs, and life-styles abruptly ended. Minorities such as the Kazakhs were once more required to "learn Han Chinese, adopt Han cultural forms and give up various 'decadent customs'" (Dreyer 1977:160). At the same time (and presumably as a measure to encourage assimilation and allegiance to Han China), Han residents received preferential treatment in the allocation of food and other rationed commodities. Ironically, the pressure on minorities to study Han seemed to be a reversal of policies to those used by China prior to communist rule. The regime clearly is desperately eager to "Hanize" the minority border areas (Dreyer 1977:169).

In China, the media show almost frenetic joy at each new archeological find in Sinkiang that links the province with China proper. A rally is held, with banners and headlines proclaiming, for example, that "T'ang [Dynasty] Relics Prove Sinkiang Historically Part of China." Rally leaders dutifully reiterate the most recent twist in the party line, and explain that these latest discoveries will give the lie to nationalistically minded internal "splittists" and to the Soviet revisionists who wish to separate Sinkiang from the ancestral land.

These assimilationist policies are likely to exascerbate rather than reduce ethnic conflict in China. As Lucien Pye (1965:510–11) emphasizes,

the leveling of cultural differences can lead to greater ethnic tensions as economic and political power considerations are elevated to relative importance. In China we are not seeing the cultural leveling between Han and non-Han because of industrialization but rather as the result of a combination of ideological commitment and national security concerns on the part of the government. Therefore China may shortly be confronted with the types of ethnic divisions typical of advanced industrial societies while remaining in a pre-industrial state and lacking the material resources that more affluent countries may have for ameliorating their ethnic divisions.

CONCLUSION

That no nation in the world is free from some form of violation of human rights in the form of ethnic, religious, or racial discrimination, unless it is totally homogeneous in these terms, is by now a well-known fact. Third World countries, though past victims of racial domination, are, in the main, also guilty of such behavior. What steps do they take to solve the problem?

Many countries have attempted to outlaw various specific forms of discrimination. Brazilian law establishes the penalty of imprisonment and a fine for whoever "through racial or color prejudice" refuses in "a commercial or educational establishment of any kind to house, serve, attend or receive a client, customer or pupil." Similar antidiscriminatory legislation exists in many countries. In Mexico, where a minority of light-skinned European descendants are clearly privileged, the crime of "genocide" has been entered in the law (Santa Cruz 1971:34). A recently incorporated paragraph in the Argentine Penal Code stipulates that it is a "criminal offense to participate in organizations or to support propaganda based on ideas of the superiority of a group of persons of one color or ethnic origin" (Santa Cruz 1976:58). India, which is formally dedicated to eliminating discriminatory practices linked to caste, has outlawed discrimination against the large group of "untouchables." Going beyond antidiscriminatory legislation, it has specified employment quotas in the public service for this depressed group.

Third World nations vary with respect to their degree of acceptance of ethnic pluralism. Federalism, advocated as a means of allowing minorities autonomy, works out quite differently in India and Nigeria. In India, a federal system gives control over cultural, educational, and linguistic policies to state governments whose boundary lines are largely drawn to correspond to ethnic variations in response, as noted earlier, to collective protest. In India, this division appears to have sharply reduced linguistic-based political conflicts. In

Nigeria, on the other hand, the original division of the state in 1960 into three tribally distinctive regions with their own "parliament, police force, university and budget derived from local revenues" failed to prevent serious tribal conflict. The Ibo dominant in the eastern region attempted to secede and form their own state of Biafra. Following the two-year-long bloody civil war, the victorious federal government divided the country into twelve states, with the Ibo concentrated in a new East Central state. This, however, was now "one out of twelve instead of one out of three." By so doing, the national rulers hoped that the smaller states would "offer little resistance to central authority." The new federal constitution gives the central government control over many of the policies once in the hands of the pre–civil war large states (Enloe 1973:89–93).

Other countries seeking to downgrade ethnic differences as a source of political conflict and power have emphasized the goal of creating one people out of diverse minorities. In Peru, where the "progressive" military government seeks to eliminate cultural and socioeconomic differences linked to race, the constitution "specifically forbids the establishment of special schools for indigenous persons." Every possible measure has been taken in an attempt to de-emphasize differences between Spanish and Indian groups, including that of playing down the importance of group heritage. A similar policy of assimilation was introduced in certain African countries after independence. Rather than asserting the culture of black Africans as separate and distinct from that of the Europeans, Kenya opted for "Europeanizing" Africans through an integrated educational system in which European schools were required to accept blacks in their student bodies. Rather than an all-black syllabus for post-independence schooling, "common syllabuses" were introduced.* By 1966, the proportion of Africans at European and Asian schools had risen to 30 percent, and a year later the figure rose to 50 percent (Ministry of Education [Kenya] 1967:2).

*Some former French colonies follow similar policies.

Another example of an attempt by an African government to discourage indigenous practices is that of the Ivory Coast, where "tattooing, scarring or other means whereby the human body is marked for reasons of ethnic identification are prohibited under the Penal Code" (Santa Cruz 1971:34). According to the 1977 *United Nations Report on Racial Discrimination,* most Third World countries which have minority populations do not give them any special status under the law.

Clearly, there is no agreed upon strategy to resolve the problem of racial discrimination. While an autonomous cultural life, including separate systems of education, is encouraged in some countries, in others this policy is viewed as a return to colonial policy of racial discrimination, and is therefore strictly forbidden.

Pride in ethnic heritage groups may be considered simultaneously as "progressive" and "regressive." Some middle-of-the-road countries have attempted to combine a right to an autonomous life with a right to integration in the dominant culture. In some countries, this compromise policy favors under-privileged groups, while in other countries it favors privileged minorities.

The right to equal, organized, political participation by different ethnic/religious groups is by no means clear cut. The right of citizens to unite in organizations based on nationality or race is restricted in some Third World countries on the grounds that it would create conflict.

It is impossible to evaluate the varying success of different measures to deal with discrimination in various Third World countries. It is evident, however, that, for the most part, they have as yet had little impact. Given the fact that most people in these nations live in rural areas, that systems of communication are relatively inefficient, that central government control is also generally weak, legislative enactments in the capital cannot be expected to have much effect on social practices which are deeply rooted in traditional values and in variations in personal and group resources.

The less-developed nations vary greatly in their pace of development. Where the rate is low, little social change in custom or patterns of inequality is to be expected. But, as we have seen, where it is high it often exascerbates the competition among diverse groups and may, in fact, make for greater rather than less inequality, since those groups who are more advantaged with respect to wealth, education, skills, or achievement motivation are able to benefit from new opportunities much more than the less advantaged. François Bourricard's (1965:382) description of Peruvian developments is probably typical for such societies.

From the beginning of the 1950s until 1967, the development of Peruvian society was remarkable in the classic sense of the word: rapid urbanization, growing national product, average income, and exports (copper, fish meal), and expanding public services, such as education. This of course aggravated regional disparities and social inequality, sharply affecting the relations between Indians, metis, creoles, cholos.

In India, sociologists point to the ways in which development and greater emphasis on social mobility have disproportionately benefited the traditional higher castes, such as the Brahmans. With their superior education, social and organizational skills, they have been able to take over the new higher positions in Indian society, although a job quota system for "untouchables" does benefit this very depressed group.

Still, it is necessary to recognize that in the low-income Third World countries the long-run reduction of group tensions is inevitably bound up with economic development, even though in most cases such growth will increase tensions in the short run. As Imitiaz Ahmed (1971:26) puts it, writing of India, but in terms also applicable to many other less-developed nations:

Political analysts must recognize that in a country which is characterized by glaring inequalities, appalling poverty, a highly vitiated social and political climate, wherein traditional loyalties are critical and where the political system has encouraged the jockeying for power caste by caste and community by community, the political secularization of minority communities cannot take place at a rate faster than that of the whole society.

Race and ethnicity provide the most striking example of a general failure among experts to anticipate social developments in varying types of societies. Until recently, both Marxist and non-Marxist scholars agreed that ethnicity reflected the conditions of traditional society, in which people lived in small communities isolated from one another, and in which mass communications and transportation were limited. Most scholars expected that industrialization, urbanization, and the spread of education would reduce ethnic consciousness, that universalism would replace particularism. Marxists were certain that socialism would mean the end of the ethnic tension and consciousness that existed in pre-socialist societies. Non-Marxist sociologists in Western countries assumed that industrialization and modernization would do the same. Assimilation of minorities into a larger integrated whole was viewed as the inevitable future. Nathan Glazer and Daniel P. Moynihan (1965:6–7) note that it was generally believed that

divisions of culture, religion, language, [and race] . . . would inevitably lose their weight and sharpness in modern and modernizing societies, that there would be increasing emphasis on achievement rather than ascription, that common systems of education and communication would level differences, that nationally uniform economic and political systems would have the same effect. Under these circumstances the "primordial" (or in any case antecedent) difference between groups would be expected to become of lesser significance. The "liberal expectancy" flows into the "radical expectancy"—that class circumstances would become the main line of division between people, erasing the earlier lines of tribe, language, religion, national origin, and that thereafter these *class* divisions would themselves, after revolution, disappear. Thus Karl Marx and his followers reacted with impatience to the heritage of the past, as they saw it, in the form of ethnic attachments.

As we all know, the opposite has occurred in both the Western and communist worlds, and in the less-developed world as well. The Achilles heel of communism has turned out to be nationalism and ethnicity, the consciousness not only of Poles and Czechs vis-à-vis the Soviet Union, but of the various national groupings within the Soviet Union and Yugoslavia as well. Most of the multilingual, binational, or bireligious states that have persisted for many decades, if not centuries, have faced turmoil in recent years. Canada, Belgium, Malaysia, and Lebanon all face crises of national existence, pressed by minorities for autonomy, if not independence. Pakistan and Cyprus have divided. Nigeria has suppressed a massive ethnic rebellion. In the classic case of Switzerland, tension has risen within multilinguistic cantons. France faces difficulties with its Basques, Bretons, and Corsicans. In Spain, Basques and Catalans demand linguistic rights and greater autonomy.

The sorry fact must be faced: the racism and ethnic tension that have been potent aspects of human experience from ancient days down to the present continue to be as strong or stronger than ever. People still resist and resent those who differ from themselves in race, culture, and religion. Many have sought to institutionalize privileges for members of their groups. In modern times, both rulers and the masses have turned to virulent expressions of bigotry in response to social tensions, to threats to those in power, and to insecurity stemming from economic or status anxiety. The most extreme racist effort, the Holocaust of European Jewry, occurred in modern times. Racism remains the policy of communist states which, like Poland, make themselves *Juden rein* or, like the Soviet Union, restrict the rights of Jewish citizens. Racism still prevails in many African states where the politics of ethnicity continue to determine who rules, and in others which, like Uganda, seek to eliminate East Indian minorities, among others. The white-dominated societies of South Africa and Rhodesia continue segregation policies against their majority black populations. In Asian states like India or Japan, which have outlawed discrimination against untouchable lower castes, one finds that practice largely ignores the law. Ethnic divisions have severely undermined or destroyed the apparent unity of countries as diverse as Belgium, Canada, the United Kingdom, Cyprus, Pakistan, Malaysia, Lebanon, Nigeria, and Zaïre.

Most of the tensions which have erupted into overt conflicts have, of course, long predated current controversies. Ironically, what has exascerbated them in many cases is political or economic progress, which upset traditional relationships among peoples now occupying the same national space. Independence for former colonies raised the issue of the relative power and status of indigenous populations. Economic development inherently has been an unequal process, with some ethnic groups benefiting much more than others. And the accompanying processes of urbanization and geographic mobility have brought groups of diverse cultural background and economic resources into direct competitive contact with each other. No part of the world has been spared these developments. But it must be noted that Third World nations, once viewed solely as victims of racism, have now joined as independent states the ranks of those in which people of varying ancestry, culture, religion, race, or language hate, oppose, and oppress each other.

8

DANIEL J. ELAZAR

Federalism, Governance, and Development in the Third World

The extent of federalism in the Third World, and the need for accommodation. Characteristic failures. Successful federations, and their explanation. The advantages of federalism to developing nations—diversity, economic decentralization, use of resources, power-sharing. Need for reorientation of Western support.

THE RECORD OF FEDERALISM IN THE THIRD WORLD

Virtually all of the ninety-two new states created since World War II are considered part of the Third World. Federal arrangements have or had a role to play in the case of forty-six, or precisely half of these. Eleven were ordained by their colonial rulers to be federations or parts of a larger federation. and their struggle for independence was related to their rejection of some federal arrangement. Twenty came into existence as federal polities. Fifteen were involved in federal or confederal linkages with other states, ranging from full federation to common-market style arrangements. In three, their original political systems were subsequently reconstituted on a quasi-federal basis to accommodate particular needs. (Since a few of the new states were actually involved in more than one of the foregoing, the total is more than forty-six.)

At this writing, six states have remained federal systems, fourteen continue to be involved in more or less meaningful federal arrangements, and five are involved in arrangements that continue to exist on paper but have become essentially meaningless. The federations alone contain a population of some 750 million, or a quarter of a total Third World population of some three billion. It is evident that federalism, in one or another of its forms, has been widely tried in the Third World. While the results have been mixed, it remains a reality for many people in Asia and Africa.

Why has federalism in its various forms been attractive at one point or another to so many Third World peoples and polities? Why has it so often failed? Under what circumstances has it been successful? What benefits and costs have federalism brought in its wake? What uses can federal arrangements have in the context of Third World political life and what prospects are there for the further use of such arrangements? This chapter will attempt to answer these questions in a preliminary way.

By and large, federal arrangements for the internal structuring of the new states have reflected the felt need to accommodate ethnic, religious, or linguistic diversity, or some combination of these, while efforts to create transstate or multistate linkages have been directed toward the achievement of economies of scale or, in the case of the Arab world, the effort to implement a vision of national unity. While we are all of us discovering how ethnically heterogeneous the whole world is, nowhere is there greater undiluted ethnic heterogeneity than in the Third World, where religious, tribal, and ethnic divisions exist in almost a pristine state, unmodified by overlays of modernization or new national identities tied to the newly emergent state system. With very few exceptions, these ethnic divisions are the basic and enduring ones while the newly formed states are still struggling to acquire the loyalties and attachments of the people within their boundaries. Thus, all questions of federalism, like all questions of state-building, modernization, development, and the like in the Third World are dealt with, of necessity, within the context of the realities of ethnic diversity and heterogeneity.

Why Federations Failed

While every failed federation is a case study in and of itself, there are some commonalities that stand out clearly, five of which are striking.

(1) The federal arrangement was imposed from outside without ever having any serious internal support. Thus, the Cameroon federation was brought into existence as the only acceptable way to unify a country that had been divided into British and French colonies. It was a device developed by the two colonialist powers, principally to allow the French to claim that French Cameroon would preserve its Gallic personality (to the extent that one had been established there). Despite the anticipated supports for federation flowing from the fact that one of the constituent units was British in its "Western" character and the other French, in neither case had Westernization sunk in very deeply, and in neither was there strong popular support for maintaining federalism. Thus, when a strong centralizer came to power, he was able to eliminate the federal system without difficulty.

Ghana and Uganda represent other cases where the colonialist power attempted to impose a federal solution to accommodate very real ethnic claims which it perceived to be important, but in which those solutions were rejected by the time of independence or immediately thereafter.

(2) The ascendancy of a strong man has been a major factor in terminating federal structures. In the very nature of things, a strong man seeking to impose dictatorial rule is not interested in fostering the dispersion of power, even in a nominal way. Since federal arrangements rest upon the constitutional dispersion of power, they must necessarily conflict with strong-man rule. If the strong man survives, the federation is likely to be terminated. The strength of Kwame Nkrumah was undoubtedly a factor in aborting the proposed federal structure for Ghana before independence. In Libya, King Idris gutted that country's federal institutions as he grew in strength; with his overthrow, the *junta* put the formal finishing touches on its dismantling. On the other hand, we shall see in Nigeria, where federalism has shown itself to be very much a part of the scene, that the effort of a strong man to eliminate that country's federal system led to his downfall, a lesson learned by subsequent military rulers who have fostered federalism—at least in some respectable way, rather than attempting to confront it at great political risk.

In some cases, attempts to link newly independent states into larger federations have failed because of the competing interests of strong men in each. Thus, the East African Community, which began as a common market and joint service entity that went beyond the kind of economic confederation represented by the European Economic Community, has since collapsed, in no small measure because of the competition between Jomo Kenyatta of Kenya, Julius Nyerere of Tanzania, and Idi Amin of Uganda.

(3) Ethnic conflict has been another cause of the break-up of federal systems. It has had this effect when the conflict was too intense to be managed by the federal structures and arrangements. In some cases, the conflict may not be objec-

tively more intense than it is in other circumstances where federalism has survived, but it is so structured that it falls along the basic cleavages around which the system is built. Thus, the Central African Federation collapsed because of the white-black conflict, and the ability of the blacks of two of the three constituent units to force the dissolution because they were in power in those units. In the third unit, Rhodesia (then Southern Rhodesia), the white minority was so dominant that its blacks had to resort to other means in their struggle for self-determination, a struggle easily won by Malawi and Zambia on the basis of the break-up of the federation.

In Burma, the overwhelming Burmese majority soon put to rest the quasi-federal institutions left by the British to guarantee the rights of ethnic minorities in that country, although it should be noted that while the institutions no longer survive, the conflict does, and Burma suffers from a perpetual, if low-key, interethnic civil war.

(4) A fourth factor is lack of resources. In one sense, this is a minor consideration that bears only indirectly on the proximate reasons for the failure of federal arrangements in the Third World. That is to say, it is not at all clear that even Third World countries *per se* lack either the human or the monetary resources to maintain federal systems. If they really had to maintain full-blown welfare states on the Western model, and also support the redundancies inherent in federalism, then perhaps this argument would be more significant. But, considering the limited government that actually prevails in such countries, it is entirely conceivable that if local elites were mobilized to handle tasks of governance, those countries would be fully capable of fielding as complete a set of governors at an affordable cost as was the case in early nineteenth-century United States or pre-industrial Switzerland or nineteenth-century Latin America.

Given the orientation against such local involvement in political life, it is possible to speak of a lack of resources, not in terms of budget or manpower in the statistical sense, but in terms of psychospiritual resources. Contrast India with any of the failed federations. Certainly in material resources India is in no better a position than they and, indeed, is poorer than many of them. Nor is India's manpower ratio that much superior; although it should be noted that India may have more formally schooled manpower, which results not in greater efficiency, but in larger bureaucracies. Yet federalism has been maintained in India in a workable condition, because India has the orientation required for mobilizing human resources to maintain diffused governmental institutions, power-sharing, and the like.

(5) A fifth factor is the absence of a federally inclined political culture. This dimension is one that has been explored least, although perhaps written about most, by analysts of federalism. Increasingly, those analysts have come to the conclusion that the successful federal polities are those that have a political culture that is either federalist in orientation or open to the absorption of federal principles. Conversely, the analysts agree, absence of a federal political culture, or one open to it, makes the maintenance of federal arrangements very problematic indeed.

(6) Lack of sufficient common interests is a sixth factor that has contributed to the failure of federations, particularly efforts at linking established states to one another. The Mali Federation was founded on the basis of putative shared economic interests that proved to be insufficient. The secession of Bangladesh from Pakistan and Singapore from Malaysia reflect the lack of sufficient common interests within established federations. Conflicting interests led to the gutting of the East African Community.

(7) Unbalanced federal arrangements also rarely succeed. Two-unit federations are particularly vulnerable, since they do not offer sufficient opportunities for tension-reducing coalitions. Nor are federal arrangements likely to work where one entity is clearly dominant. The Ethiopian-Eritrean federation suffered from both of these defects, although other factors, such as the absolutism of Haile Selassie and the lack of an interest in power-sharing, were more important factors.

Why Federations Succeed

What, then, of the successful uses of federal principles or arrangements in the Third World? How are they to be explained? In most respects, by the very obverse of the reasons for the failures.

(1) Federal systems have worked where they have served to manage ethnic or intercommunal conflict. In India, the commitment to managing ethnic conflict through federal arrangements—that is to say, constitutionally protected diversity on a federal basis—led the Indian government, however reluctantly, to change state boundaries, and even to create new states to accommodate linguistic (and in one case, religious) diversity when it became apparent that this was the greatest desire of the Indian public. By making these changes, Indian federalism managed to defuse conflicts that had already reached the violent stage, demonstrating the effectiveness of federalism in the management of such conflict, and reinforcing its importance in the minds of the people who benefited from the changes.

Nigeria has also used federalism as a successful device for ethnic conflict management, although the issue there was briefly in doubt during the Biafra war. It has already been suggested that the one effort to abolish federalism in Nigeria led to the overthrow of the strong man who initiated it. Beyond that, once Biafran resistance was ended, the Nigerian government utilized federal principles to restore amity, restoring to the Ibo their state government, even if in a smaller state, and allowing them to resume positions of influence through the federal structure. Moreover, the Nigerian government has undertaken two reorganizations of the federal structure, both increasing the number of states in the Nigerian federation so as to better accommodate the country's great ethnic diversity (Nigeria has over one hundred different tribal or ethnic groups, more than all of Europe). Beyond that, Nigeria has applied federal principles in the local arena as well, by encouraging the organization of the internal polities of the states in such a way as to accommodate tribal and ethnic groups too small to acquire states of their own. Thus, many of the Nigerian local authorities, more or less equivalent to American counties, are so structured as to provide smaller tribes and ethnic groups with what are, in effect, autonomous regional governments.

In yet another way, the Sudanese reorganization to grant regional autonomy to the southern part of the country and its inhabitants represents another, if more limited, application of federal principles to manage interethnic conflict, which also seems to be having a real measure of success.

(2) A second element leading to the successful adaptation of federal principles and arrangements is the substitution of government by an elite in place of government by a single strong man. It has been suggested that strong-man government, by its nature, is inimicable to federalism. While elite government may not be as fully democratic as some would like, a properly structured elite does make possible the application of federal principles. In successful federal systems, the existence of such a properly structured elite is almost a *sine qua non*. Malaysia, for example, has been successful as a federation because of the existence of the sultans of its states, who find federalism a useful way for sharing power among more or less equals. The one successful (to date) federal experiment in the Arab world, the United Arab Emirates (UAE), is based on a similar principle. The emirs of the Persian Gulf sheikhdoms that have federated together form an elite which is able to share power.

In Nigeria, the elite is less oligarchical and formally structured. Nevertheless, military rule there is clearly rule by a group rather than a single strong man, a group which includes representatives of the major ethnic groups and their states. India, the most democratic of the Third World countries, has a far more amorphous elite, one spread more fully among the country's total population, and perhaps more closely approximating the kinds of elites found in the West in the sense that it is more representative. All this is reflected in the strength of Indian federalism. Even Indira Ghandi, in the period during which she exercised dictatorial rule, did relatively little to interfere with the prerogatives of the states.

(3) Similarly, the availability of resources, both human and material, is an important dimension in the successful application of federal principles and arrangements in the Third World. Both India and Nigeria are countries of very large populations, and India especially has a substantial educated group available to man the machinery of government—although matters are not so simple, since it is that same educated group seeking positions that leads to the multiplication of bureaucracy beyond any necessary proportions. More important than the numbers of people available is the cultural predisposition of people to work within shared power systems, something which not all Third World countries share by any means. The very fact that India is not rich, yet quite successfully federal, and that many countries richer than the federal ones in the Third World have been unable to utilize federal mechanisms even when they have tried, reinforces the view that it is not economic so much as human resources that are important here.

(4) This brings us back to the question of political culture once again. What seems to be characteristic of successful federal systems in the Third World as elsewhere is the existence of a political culture that is at least predisposed toward federalism, if not federalist in orientation—a political culture that rests upon some basic commitment to power-sharing, some notion of political self-restraint, and some orientation towards the involvement of larger numbers of people in the governing process.

(5) Successful federal arrangements have not been imposed from the outside, but have developed indigenously in ways that suit the entities involved. The Moslem world's tendency to federate rulers other than populations is well reflected in the more successful Malaysian and UAE esperiences, as contrasted to the less successful Pakistani effort. The still-working autonomy agreement in the Sudan was developed

indigenously, while the three-unit Libyan federation that failed was imposed by the United Nations.

(6) The existence of common interests, especially economic and seniority interests, is a necessary if not sufficient factor reinforcing successful federal efforts, although alone they can serve to encourage consolidation as well.

(7) Multi-unit federal arrangements have a far better chance of success than those of only a few units. India, Nigeria, and Malaysia have over ten states each; the UAE has seven, while Pakistan has five.

If any such generalization were in order, overall, Asia has proved to be more hospitable to federalism than Africa, apparently for political-cultural reasons. While neither continent is known for fostering the kind of liberality that is a prerequisite for federalism to flourish, Africa has even fewer breaks on the centralization of power in the hands of strong men. Asia, on the other hand, tends to foster rule by elites which is less incompatible with federal arrangements. Also, Asia has long since developed institutionalized modes of accommodating communal differences that are more compatible with the demands of modern statehood.

THE USES OF FEDERALISM IN THE THIRD WORLD

From the foregoing discussion, it should be possible to draw some conclusions about the uses of federalism in the Third World countries.

Accommodating Diversity

Most immediately, federalism has proved useful in accommodating diversity. Indeed, once there is a commitment to the accommodation of diversity, then federal solutions are likely to follow as a matter of course. Most of the resistance to federal solutions has come precisely from those who do not wish to accommodate diversity, but to eliminate it. Perhaps enough has been said about this theme already, but it should be recalled that it has more than one dimension. That is to say, it is not only a question of particular rulers opposing diversity, but of particular tribal, ethnic, or religious communities within the polity opposing it as well—some of whom are victims of discrimination and persecution because they are minorities, but who would not behave differently if they were to acquire power.

Thus, it is hard to say that Zaïre, which abandoned a proposed federal, or at least quasi-federal, arrangement upon achieving independence from Belgium—and which, as a result, has been plagued by periodic efforts on the part of Katanga, now Shaba, to secede—would have become more federal had the Katangese won. When Moïse Tshombe, the original leader of the Katangese secession movement, briefly became president of all of Zaïre, he was no more friendly to diversity than were those who opposed him originally and ultimately had him assassinated. In short, the peoples of Zaïre, whatever their tribal, ethnic, or regional background, seem to be interested in promoting the exclusive rule of their particular group, not in finding some *modus vivendi* through power-sharing.

In Nigeria, on the other hand, the Ibo, from all accounts, have a political culture which is either ''federalist'' or quite open to federalism. The Yoruba have a political culture which, while not federalist in orientation like that of the Ibo, has built within it the notion of power dispersed among elites, so that it can absorb federal principles relatively easily and certainly learn to live with federal arrangements. On the other hand, the Hausa of the north have a strong tradition of centralized power—a tradition reinforced by their Islamic faith—which renders federal solutions foreign to them. It requires constant efforts on the part of the other two major partners in the Nigerian federation plus the many minor ones to accommodate Hausa demands, which are not only substantively great, but structurally difficult as well. The rule of the Nigerian military *junta,* whatever its other drawbacks, may indeed be for the moment the most reasonable way of preventing Hausa dominance or secession, and thereby preserving the federal structure as a means of accommodating diversity.

In those situations where federalism rests upon some structured elite, as in Malaysia or the United Arab Emirates, the elite has a strong commitment to maintaining the diversity it represents. Since the elites are so dominant in both cases, it is difficult to analyze what would happen without them, although in both cases such diversity as exists among the population is not strictly along the lines of the federal territorial divisions. Malays representing the major force, if not the majority of all the states of Malaysia, have antipathy toward the Chinese who form a minority everywhere. Only in Singapore do the Chinese represent a majority, which is one of the reasons why Singapore seceded from Malaysia—and was, indeed, allowed and even encouraged to do so by the other members of the federation. In the UAE, some tribal groupings cross emirate boundaries, others do not; but apparently there is not an intense problem of diversity among the population.

Pakistan, on the other hand, is a country founded ostensibly on the principle of unity—in this case, Islamic unity, a principle which did not give appropriate recognition to ethnic differences within the Islamic whole. Consequently, each successive ruler of Pakistan has attempted to centralize power in strong-man fashion, while at the same time the population insists on the diffusion of power to accommodate the country's ethnic diversity. Federalism survives in Pakistan on paper and, to a greater or lesser extent, diffusion of power survives in practice, principally because of the weakness of the central government vis-à-vis the provincial and subprovincial groups rather than out of any desire on the part of the former to make federalism work.

The essentially abortive Philippine effort to grant some measure of autonomy to the Moros of Mindanao and other southern Philippine islands has failed to date because, despite a certain lip service to the accommodation of diversity, neither side was particularly interested in such an accommodation. President Marcos enjoys a sufficient monopoly of power in the center to prevent implementation from that side, while the Moros possess sufficient power to maintain the guerrilla war which they are conducting on behalf of their revolution. The result is a stalemate actively reflected in continuing military operations rather than a quasi-federal accommodation. Since it seems rather clear that neither side can achieve its exclusive goals, that rather violent stalemate is likely to continue indefinitely unless an agreement of some kind along federal or quasi-federal lines is reached.

Diversity is not likely to disappear in the Third World, no more than it has in the First or Second, even, in some cases, after centuries of concerted effort at national integration through homogenization. Only massacre or expulsion of minorities can change that situation. In most of the Third World countries, the number and diffusion of tribal, ethnic, religious, or linguistic groups is such that even those ugly options can achieve the desired result of homogeneity in only a few cases. Consequently, federal arrangements can offer a useful way to deal with diversity in more than a few cases.

Strengthening Liberty

In the Third World, as elsewhere, federalism is a means for strengthening liberty. This, too, is one of the reasons that failures are more numerous than successes in that segment of the world. Very few of the Third World regimes are interested in strengthening liberty. Their commitment to independence and nation-building does not necessarily include a commitment to freedom for the people involved. Often, quite to the contrary, every argument is used to justify the restriction of freedom, and even the elimination of those traditional liberties that do exist, such as tribal and customary liberties, in the name of national independence and national development. In such cases, federalism—which is, almost by its very nature, a constant goad in the direction of the maintenance of liberty, and a certain reminder of its importance in a polity striving toward democracy—is at best an embarrassment and at worst a real hindrance. Again, the successful examples all testify to the importance of federalism for strengthening liberty, whether in the case of India, which has clear democratic aspirations, or in the cases of Malaysia and the UAE, which at least wish to preserve the liberties of the constituent rulers.

Spreading Economic Development

The importance of federalism in spreading economic development and its benefits has been almost entirely overlooked. By and large, what has passed for national development in the Third World is not national at all, but rather concentrated in a single metropolitan area, usually that of the capital. This area not only has monopolized the infusion of new resources into the country, but has managed to drain the countryside of a major share of such resources as did exist there prior to independence. The resultant impoverishment of the countryside without appreciable progress in the metropolis has become a feature of Third World national economies which reflects a vicious circle. As the countryside becomes impoverished, its people migrate to the metropolis in search of opportunity, or in most cases, sheer survival. In their masses, they overwhelm the metropolis and transform it into what has come to be known as the Calcutta syndrome. The metropolis absorbs all wealth-generating capacity; people rush to the center, so that the new capacity is lost in the magnitude of the problems created. The only ones to benefit from this are the ruling class, whose members are able to siphon off a substantial share of the development funds for their own personal use or for their Swiss bank accounts.

Development in federal countries suffers from some of these Third World problems. But, because of the existence of federalism, the new resources are inevitably spread over a number of centers. At the very least, the capital of every federated state has some claim on the national resources, and together they work to prevent the single metropolis syndrome. This means that more people have a chance to benefit from development efforts. At best, it means that some of the worst excesses of resource concentration are eliminated, and a basis for truly national development begins to emerge.

India and Nigeria are prime examples of this. While Calcutta and, of late, Bombay and Lagos suffer from the worst aspects of the rural-urban migration, in both countries one does not have to live in Calcutta, Bombay, or Lagos to gain benefit from economic development. Rather, development efforts have been spread throughout the country, if not uniformly, at least in significant ways. Many people who have stayed home or migrated to less prominent centers have managed to improve their lot, if not sufficiently, at least more so than their peers in more centralized states. This phenomenon deserves to be studied in detail.

What is clear is that, as always, politics has its influence on economics as well as vice versa, particularly in the contemporary world, where state intervention is once again crucial in the economic realm. The way in which politics is structured affects the economic future of every inhabitant of any particular polity. Thus, while economic measures which do not differentiate between segments of the polity may reveal one thing, the realities of economic resource use and development may be quite different. The politics of federalism offers a means for extending economic benefits more widely than has otherwise been the case in the Third World.

THE POSSIBILITIES OF FEDERALISM IN THE THIRD WORLD

At first glance, the possibilities of federalism in the Third World would seem limited indeed. While presently existing

federal systems do not seem likely to lose their formally federal character, changes in regime could move them away
from the realities of federal power-sharing, even if the forms
are preserved. At the same time, there is no evidence that
nonfederal polities are likely to embrace federal principles,
much less transform themselves into federal systems, even if
objective conditions might recommend such solutions to their
problems. So much for the short run. In the long run, however, federalism should not be written off as a means of coming to grips with Third World problems. In the first place—
with one possible exception—historically, throughout the
world, no country which has embraced federalism as its form
of government has ever abandoned federalism out of its own
choice if it has survived as a federal system for at least fifteen
years. In a few cases, outside intervention has put an end to a
country's federal character—but that, of course, has not been
as a result of domestic choice. Thus, if historical precedent is
to hold, there is some reason to believe that those systems
presently constituted as federal ones in the Third World will
continue to exist and will have to come to grips with their
federal structures in one way or another.

Beyond that, it is unlikely that the problems of diversity
which have stimulated and suggested federal solutions will
significantly diminish in most Third World countries. There
may be periodic successes through massacre, as in Uganda,
or expulsion, as is presently being tried in Burma, but these
cannot be counted upon for countries like the Philippines or
most of Africa. Thus, some means of accommodating diversity will have to be found, and it is unlikely that any better
means will emerge. Moreover, since there are many possible
ways to implement federal principles through numerous different federal arrangements, some possibility should exist for
almost every situation, although the will to implement them
may not.

The use of federal principles in building new interstate arrangements may be hardly more promising. Nevertheless, at
least one example of an incipient regional confederation has

emerged rather suddenly and even unexpectedly. The Association of Southeast Asian Nations (ASEAN), which combines the Philippines, Malaysia, Indonesia, Singapore, and Thailand to create a regional community of over 200 million people, has moved from a paper body to a league which is presently trying to build a common sense of political unity, a common economic policy, and even a common market. Four of the five states involved are highly centralized internally, but all seem to have a very strong commitment to building ASEAN as a joint enterprise, even emphasizing the political dimension above all. These kinds of regional arrangements offer another opportunity to utilize federal principles for mutual advantage.

Elsewhere, this writer has described the variety of federal arrangements. All of these arrangements have already been tried in the Third World, some with success, others with less. When all these arrangements are taken into consideration, the impact of federalism is seen to be far greater than is usually perceived.

There is no reason to believe that federal solutions are appropriate for every Third World state or regional grouping of states, but there is every reason to believe that they are appropriate for more states than have successfully applied them to date. It is especially difficult to recommend immediate practical steps toward the internal application of federal principles in Third World countries. It is hardly helpful to make gratuitous suggestions about the elimination of strong men as long as the countries involved are what they are. One can simply hope that over the course of time they will develop in another direction. Perhaps from time to time outsiders may be able to extend incremental help to those forces moving them in another direction, but even that is dubious at this particular stage.

What the West can do is to provide special support at every opportunity for those Third World countries which have adopted federal or quasi-federal solutions to the problems of governance, development, and political integration; to recognize them as moving down the road toward a polity of dispersed powers that is a prerequisite for liberty and truly free government. Among other things, this would require a reorientation of the State Department and other Western foreign offices, whose basic predisposition and outlook is to seek the ''sovereign center'' of every polity, and to treat every state as if it were unitary. Western cultural exchanges and technical assistance programs, oriented towards strengthening the constituent as well as overarching governments within Third World federal systems, could be very helpful indeed. A theory of technical assistance that recognized the potentialities for dispersal of economic development inherent in federal arrangements would be very much in place.

Finally, a worldwide association of federated states, parallel to the International Union of Local Authorities, would encourage Third World countries to adopt federal systems. It would also create another set of links between the various ''worlds'' that comprise our increasingly interdependent planet.

III

International Affairs

9

EDWARD N. LUTTWAK

The Strategy of Inaction

Soviet offensive in Africa. The failure of U.S. counterintervention policy due to lack of tenacity. The politics of economics v. power accumulation. The legacy of colonial boundaries. The propaganda conflict—Soviet and Western. The Russian advantage to African ambitions—weapons, technological personnel. The sociological explanation of Soviet activities. The military threat to the West. Recent change in U.S. policy toward the USSR. The need to restore a global military balance.

In international politics, the Third World has loomed large in recent years. Many strategists indeed argue that contests therein may surpass such critical areas as the Central European front in importance to the West or as potential flash points of world war. Despite Soviet advances throughout much of the Third World, American policy there, and particularly in Africa, has apparently derived from different concerns.

Whatever else may be said about the Carter administration, its spokesmen certainly cannot be faulted for lacking ingenuity in devising excuses for inaction in the face of Soviet activism in Africa. Action is sufficiently justified by its results, but passivity in the face of danger needs many excuses.

There is, first of all, the denial in form simple: "The USSR is a second-rate power that has little ability to influence events beyond its borders. They can bring the nuclear holocaust or do nothing at all, with very little in between."* Thus a member of the State Department's Policy Planning Staff, in denying that the Soviet offensive in Africa is a threat to the United States. The form or consequences of the threat are not examined; instead, its very feasibility is denied, absurdly enough *ex post facto*. And yet the most ominous lesson of the Angolan and Ethiopian wars is precisely that the Soviet Union has developed a highly flexible and low-cost ability to "influence events beyond its borders." Cuban troops, Soviet weapons of 1950s' design vintage—all the more suitable for being relatively unsophisticated—a Soviet naval presence to raise the risk of any Western counterintervention, long-range air transport, and small numbers of Soviet technicians and field commanders have all been skillfully combined into a highly effective instrument of intervention, which in fact has a global reach. As a *political* tool, the combination has now acquired all the power of persuasion that two victories in a row may confer.

The first excuse is obviously nothing more than a case of cognitive dissonance. The second, the denial of *lasting* consequences, is not so transparently inane. In the words of a State Department Africa specialist: "Have the Soviets done all that well? Their successes have been modest and ephemeral. In many countries, including Egypt, Sudan, Ghana and

---

*I am indebted to my former student Mark Katz for conducting the interviews from which the quotations herein were taken.

Somalia, all Soviet gains have been lost.'' In this context, much is made of Soviet ''heavy-handedness.'' Episodes of bitter contention between Soviet instructors and Egyptian officers are invoked, and inevitably we are reminded yet again of those legendary Soviet tractors which were sent to Equatorial Africa fitted out with closed cabs and permanent heating.

There is no doubt that Soviet policy has failed in many places. So has the American—and at far greater cost. Both Russians and Americans have been guilty of grotesque errors, but there is a fundamental difference: Soviet policy has a tenacity which the American altogether lacks. Tenacity is not a virtue that our culture values greatly. Certainly we all admire creativity much more. But tenacity is the one quality that makes empires, and the greatest empire in our own cultural experience was precisely the Roman, the achievement of a people equally remarkable for their secular tenacity and for their feeble creativity. As these lines are written, congressmen are being told that if the United States were to deny combat aircraft to Egypt, sooner or later the Russians will be invited to return as that country's military patrons. The Russians were expelled from Egypt in 1972, as the Americans were later ejected from Indochina; but the Russians are willing to try again—and again.

It is not the skill or even the military power-base of Soviet policy that should worry us, but rather its sheer persistence. It took the Romans two centuries to suppress guerrilla war in Spain, Roman forces being defeated again and again. But by 19 BC the job was done, and thereafter the Spanish provinces paid taxes quietly for four centuries; to this day the language spoken south of the Pyrenees (and south of the Rio Grande) is a late version of Roman army slang. The Russians may not be Romans, but they do have the imperial instinct, and the one imperial quality. Failure in any one country does not lead with them to an abandonment of effort, as in the American case. Failure is merely a prelude to another try, and the next time, at least some errors will be avoided.

The third excuse for inaction rests not on mere precedent, but on a theory—specifically, an inverted political economy, unconsciously Marxist—in which the economic is to dictate the political, and not *vice versa* as in the common experience of mankind. The version of a senior official: "The fundamental needs of the developing nations are economic. Basic U.S. influence is economic, while the Soviets do not have this. Even after Angola, the U.S. still retains influence with Luanda due to their economic needs. The Soviets do not have the capability to maintain influence."

On its face, the argument is plausible. It is, after all, a fact that the Soviet Union as an economic power is a very secondary second to the United States. More important, as a *trading* power it is very much less than that: though its GNP is just over half that of the United States, the Soviet capacity to pay for imports, or to supply desirable exports, or to lend or give away capital, is very much smaller than the GNP figures may suggest. One-half of the theory regarding Soviet economics is therefore quite solid. Unfortunately, the other half rests on an implicit assumption about African politics which is simply wrong. This is the quaint hope that the foreign policy of African states will be dominated by the priorities of economic development, so that even if the Russians successfully promote a regime in warfare, this will turn to the United States as soon as a (Soviet) peace is established. There is by now a reasonably substantial record of postcolonial African politics; whatever else it may be, clearly it is not a Western-style politics of prosperity, but rather the politics of power-accumulation.

Endowed with colonial boundaries that enforce the intimacy of diverse (and often bitterly hostile) peoples, provided with the instrumentalities of statecraft but not with the social relations that give them substance, the small cliques and single dictators that rule most of Africa do so in a state of deep and chronic insecurity. The pursuit of economic development, the *deus ex machina* which is to promote good relations with the United States, is not the first priority of these rulers, or even the second; it is, at most, a poor third. First must come the preservation of the power of the dictator or ruling clique. And in this respect the Russians have much more to offer than the United States.

Their clients can count on the broad support of Soviet propaganda, which will ceaselessly proclaim their virtues, no matter what their barbaric exactions may be. So long as they remain friendly to the Kremlin, African rulers can retain their credentials as "progressives," and inevitably this will commend them to Leftist opinion, especially in Europe—still the major point of reference for African elites—even if they revive cannibalism, or have a weakness for executing people at random. By contrast, dictators of cliques friendly to the United States will have no such support from our side. Instead, they may expect the visitations of critical newsmen, who operate with the equation *pro-Western = corrupt* firmly in mind. Being relatively free to travel through the country, they will report the poverty as an accusation rather than a predicament, and the extortions of petty officials as willed by the regime, rather than as the natural result of European centralism without European bureaucrats. And the great wealth of the privileged as compared to the mass will be presented as an outrage, instead of being explained as the inevitable concomitant of the superficial development that has taken place in Africa since independence.* At the same time, pro-Western regimes will be under constant attack by the Soviet propaganda machine, which will often do its work by quoting Western accounts.

Aside from propaganda support, rulers friendly to Moscow can also expect other, more direct, forms of political support. Complete teams of East European security experts have been

---

*Very different are the stories filed by American newsmen from countries unfriendly to the United States, where the visits of newsmen are few and tightly regulated. Instead of *exposés*, we then get expositions—of development plans, of reforms achieved or to come, as well as detailed paraphrases of official handouts. Inevitably, newsmen who have travelled far must write *something,* and if real observation is denied, reportage of conducted tours will have to do instead.

active in Africa, and a bodyguard of Cubans may be becoming the latest status symbol. As elsewhere, Soviet intelligence will be as active as possible (and much more active than any but bureaucratic urges could explain), and friendly rulers may expect to receive due warning of any military *coups* or palace revolts that the Russians hear about.

For all these reasons, it is the Soviet Union and not the United States that is the more desirable patron as far as the preservation of personal or elite power is concerned, and this is naturally the first priority of policy. The second priority is the extension of state power, so that its reach can begin to approximate the dimensions of boundaries drawn long ago by neat British or French civil servants who liked straight lines. This calls for large military forces, and a commensurate police strength. Here again, it is the Russians who have the advantage; it is they who have large disposable stocks of weapons, released by the constant renewal of Soviet military inventories. Moreover, the Russians will supply weapons to their friends promptly, and by the shipload, while U.S. weapon deliveries were agonizingly slow, even before the Carter administration instituted arms transfer practices that often preclude any deliveries at all.

The Russians, moreover, can supply quite readily all the instructors and technicians that African armies still need to absorb any weapons but the very simplest. The Russians can procure the services of East Germans or Bulgarians as well as Cubans, and they have an inherent advantage in disposing of the personnel: an American (or a Frenchman) will not willingly serve in some bleak up-country military base, while Russians and even East Europeans are seemingly very happy to go anywhere abroad, since virtually everywhere they can enjoy all manner of things denied to them at home. Thus, the Russians have the men, and the guns, and the willingness to supply large numbers of both.

Therefore, the undoubted superiority of the United States as an *economic* patron is often of little consequence: the *peoples* of Africa undoubtedly need economic development, but their rulers are much more interested in security and armed power--after all, *they* already live very nicely.

What, then, is one to make of the official's claim that the United States has already gained influence in countries organized under the *Pax Sovietica*? ("The United States still retains influence with Luanda.") The explanation is seemingly quite simple: the word is highly elastic. In relations between a country with all the attributes of the United States, and those feeble structures of power that nowadays claim most of Africa, "influence" should mean a great deal. At the very least, the rulers in place should deem it prudent to consult with the U.S. ambassador before undertaking any initiative in foreign affairs that might affect American interests. But clearly that is not the extent of the "influence" that the United States "retains in Luanda." Apparently what is meant is merely access, and a very limited access at that. Specifically, American oil companies are allowed to lift crude from the fields they have developed—paying the full premium entailed by the OPEC (Organization of Petroleum Exporting Countries) price for the privilege. The supposed influence which we "retain" in Angola did not suffice to prevent the judicial murder (by retroactive law) of the American ex-soldier captured in the service of the NFLA, nor does it suffice, as of this writing, to dissuade the Luanda regime from supporting the Southwest African People's Organization (SWAPO), an organization whose goal is to disrupt the American-supported settlement in Southwest Africa.

So much, then, for the third excuse, the theory of African "economic politics." The whole record of human history reveals that rulers will systematically subordinate the economic welfare of the people they rule to their own accumulation of power, and it is downright bizarre to expect that African rulers will be any different.

The fourth excuse emanates from a particular group within the administration, a group which has much influence on its policies towards the Soviet Union. The argument in this case cannot be defined with full clarity, but the following quotations begin to suggest its substance:

Influence is not a zero-sum game; an increase in Soviet influence is not necessarily a decrease in our own. It would be good to engage the Soviets in positively approaching the problems of the world, and to do this, the Soviets must get into the problem. How, then, should we meet the political competition while directing it into positive channels?

and

A certain amount of increased Soviet influence is not harmful, but serves as a socialization process. They are not always going after politico-military influence. One must look at what the various Soviet bureaucratic interests are after. Sometimes there is an accidental spread of influence.

Since the complex of ideas (and attitudes) here revealed is, of course, influential in the wider realm of U.S.–Soviet relations, it is worthwhile to examine them in some detail. This requires some elucidation of what are merely suggestive statements, and in the process there is the danger of misrepresenting the view as more coherent than it is.

The central notion is clearly suggested by the word "socialization" used by the second official quoted above. Several connotations come to mind, but it is fairly clear that the right one derives from educational sociology: the Soviet Union is a child to be "socialized." Its behavior is that of the robust infant just old enough to enter nursery school; a trifle unruly perhaps (a sign of good health), but essentially a good boy. What the child needs is some regulation of his habits, and then sound teaching, so that he will be able to make himself useful in turn when he grows up (i.e., "to engage the Soviets in positively approaching the problems of the world"). The child may break a toy or two in his first days, but certainly one should not punish him for that. Above all, we must of course admit him into the nursery school. To keep him out (as the "Cold Warriors" want to exclude the Soviet Union from Africa) would merely prevent the child from being "socialized," and would delay the moment when he will begin to make a "positive" contribution. Worse, if we succeed too well in a preclusive policy, the child will grow up unlettered and resentful as well as undisciplined, probably becoming a delinquent who might do real harm.

The implicit assumptions open to decisive objection are several. First, the Soviet Union is not a child, or at least has long ago exhausted the license of childhood. The United States only began to focus seriously on the Third World during the later 1950s, with 1956 being as good a year as any for the beginning. By then the Soviet Union had been active very seriously and on a large scale for at least two years (Syrian arms deal), while its first steps went back a full generation before that. If it is a question of "directing [the competition] into positive channels," we can see that the Russian child was already at the college level in 1956, for certainly Soviet officialdom could not know then that the Aswan Dam would finally emerge as a dubious investment for Egypt—as well as for the Soviet Union.

Second, there is the larger assumption about the fundamental character of the child. Is he a healthy, normal boy who does no harm but for inadvertence ("Sometimes there is an accidental [*sic*] spread of influence")? Or is he autistic, or perhaps merely a congenital wrecker, *à la* Hitler? Or perhaps is he not a child at all, but rather a would-be teacher, who wants to take over the nursery school and run it for his own profit? One way of separating out the possibilities is to examine the record.

Has there been "learning"? Hardly. Soviet policy has not become more "positive"; rather, the reverse is true. For example, twenty years ago economic aid loomed large in Soviet relations with the Third World. Today, we have military intervention. Twenty years ago, Soviet sensibilities were sometimes still sufficiently alert, if always selective, so that a Nasser would be exposed to occasional censure for having thrown communists into jail. Today, *Pravda* will not convey an ill word on Idi Amin, whose killings no doubt comprise the odd communist. Not much wisdom may be extracted from the close scrutiny of unwise pronouncements. But the beginning of a real explanation begins to emerge.

What we have here is a case of perceptual transmutation, not so much malevolent as self-indulgent. The sociological explanation has the great virtue of diverting attention from the harsh realities of power, and the emergence of an unprecedently powerful Soviet Union, to the hopeful vision of a "positive" Soviet Union, which seeks to participate in the system for much the same reasons as the United States is active in the system. In fact, the denial of a fundamental difference between the ultimate purposes of Soviet and American policy is quite basic to the argument. (Notice the reference to Soviet bureaucratic politics in the second quote: we have bureaucracies, they have bureaucracies.)

The Soviet Union is not, of course, presented as a replica of the United States. But in this view, it is not a fundamentally different creature either. "Having been invaded so often," it is naturally much more protective of its military security, and indeed "needs" more military power than we do, being surrounded by enemies. (Why this should be so is not an interesting question for those who hold this view.) And the Russians are somewhat rough in their policy and diplomacy. But they are not systems-wreckers, as the Nazis were. They merely seek a commensurate influence. We must not try to deny them influence everywhere ("a certain amount of Soviet influence is not harmful"), because it is precisely through access to the outside world and activity beyond its borders that the Soviet Union will become a constructive force in the Third World. Of course, the Russians are still at the stage where the pursuit of anti-Western goals dominates their "system-building" goals, but we are well on our way to that happier state. When that point is reached, the Soviet Union will have become the co-responsible superpower. Those who hold this view regard the simpler theory of Soviet expansionism as hopelessly vulgar and simplistic ("Influence is not a zero-sum game"). Much is made of the fact that the span of Soviet control has been delimited to date by territorial contiguity, whether in actual physical expansion (the post-1945 annexations) or in the client-state system of Eastern Europe, Cuba being, of course, an irrelevant exception.

It is not surprising that those who believe in the "socialization" theory do not recognize the recent pattern of Soviet conduct as a classic imperial phenomenon. For one thing, they are apt to confuse what the United States tried to do in Vietnam with actual imperialism ("Will Angola become their Vietnam?"), and this precludes any realistic conception of the genuine article. Moreover, those who advocate this view are intellectually far removed from the study of military power and of its consequences, so that in any case it would be very difficult for them to recognize Soviet imperialism as a consequence of the shift in the balance of military power, as any imperialism rampant must be. In fact, they are intellectually and politically committed to the view that military power does not matter much in the affairs of mankind anyway, except when and where war is actually imminent. Finally, one cannot expect the true objects of a phenomenon to recognize its lineaments.

For that is precisely the case. The more important consequence of the change in the global balance of military power that is taking place is not that the Soviet Union is acquiring certain discrete "options"—whether to destroy the bulk of the *Minuteman* force, or to intervene militarily in Africa with X troops, Y aircraft, and Z warships—but rather that general conceptions of the scope of permissible, acceptable Soviet action are being tacitly redefined. Ten years ago—and certainly, fifteen years ago—American opinion, including the officials quoted above, would have regarded the Angolan expedition as a gross and intolerable excess on the part of the Soviet Union. The leaders of the Soviet Union, on their side, would not have conceived the intervention scheme in the first place. In the world that was, characterized by sharp American (or all-Western) military superiorities in every dimension of capability except land warfare, the leaders of the Soviet Union could not have allowed themselves to contemplate the possibility that they might brutally impose their chosen regime in Angola. Already then, they had control of Cuba and of its soldiers; already then, they had spare second-string weapons and assorted warships to station off the Angolan coastline, as well as transport aircraft to provide quick-reaction logistics. But what they did not have was of much greater consequence: they still lacked the license to *use* these capabilities in a place as far removed from the natural sphere of Russian action as Angola then was.

The military balance is manifest precisely in defining the limits of each country's natural sphere, and in shaping general conceptions of what is normal and acceptable conduct. Clearly, Africa is now moving into the Soviet Union's natural sphere of action, and by common—if tacit—agreement. And once this happens through the appropriate adjustment in attitudes on all sides, it is easy enough to provide *ex post facto* a formal legitimization. Is the Soviet Union conducting a full-scale war in Ethiopia? Why, what the Russians are doing is perfectly legitimate: they are helping a sovereign state, at the invitation of its established government, to defend internationally recognized boundaries against an external aggression. Thus, Soviet action may be seen as not only legitimate, but even conservative—"systems maintenance" at its best. Some officials in the Carter administration have described the Soviet role in the Horn of Africa as that of "regional peacekeepers." Others have suggested that the Soviet motivation was "a feeling of responsibility," since it was, after all, the Soviet Union which had armed the Somalis in the first place.

And what if the Russians had supported Somalia to conquer the Ogaden, instead of switching sides as they did? Why, it is perfectly legitimate. Do we believe in self-determination or do we not? The Ogaden is inhabited by Somalis, and in helping the Somalis on both sides the Soviet Union is following a Wilsonian policy, and why should the United States object? One can readily visualize the outcry if the United States had remained on good terms with Ethiopia, and if it had helped that country to regain control of the Ogaden. Once again, we would have been depicted as being on the wrong side, helping an anachronistic ethnic domination to resist the strongest political force of our day, nationalism aroused.

Once the realities of power become manifest in the outlook of all concerned, action becomes feasible, and if it is *Soviet* action, a perfectly plausible justification will soon be forthcoming also. (It is all too easy to devise the appropriate legitimization of the next moves that the Russians might make, this time with Rhodesia as the target.)

But not only the objects are changed by the change in the balance of power; the protagonist is changed also. In this case we may well be witnessing the classic transition from a territorially delimited Soviet imperialism to the would-be global variety, which has no natural geographic limit at all, but can only be limited by countervailing power, *directly* applied. Having chosen to allow the global military balance to deteriorate under the aegis of a general curtailment of activism, particularly in the case of the Third World and especially Africa, the United States, ironically enough, will be faced with the need to intervene more often and more widely than ever before. If a wide margin of military superiority obtains globally, this will inhibit hostile action globally also, by a latent but powerful deterrence. If the margin of advantage is lost, the general deterrence of hostile action is correspondingly eroded, and then each threat must be confronted individually, where and when it emerges.

This is, of course, an entirely natural sequence, since, after all, there are only two laws of strategy that are truly universal in applicability: each move has its costs and risks, and no participant may choose to leave the game. He may turn his back; he may even proclaim his principled opposition to playing the game; but he must still pay his dues at each round, and the refusal to play merely means that he can lose but not win. Hence the profound irrelevance of the objection that the United States is at a disadvantage *vis-à-vis* the Soviet Union in contending with the more plausible African contingencies.

It is not *in* Africa that the major action should take place, even if one focuses on African problems and African solutions. The problem of Soviet imperialism must be confronted at its source, and not in its outward manifestations; only a rehabilitation of American power can deal with the threat. Attempts to preclude the opportunities of Soviet action by opportunistically siding with the most radical party in each conflict will not solve the problem. Whatever moral reservations we suppress, whatever interests we neglect in the eager courtship of the most radical guerrillas we can find, we can be sure that Moscow will find (or create) a faction more radical still. Whatever settlements we may contrive to negotiate in conflict areas, Moscow will still be able to find those it can back in opposing the settlement, so long as anything at all in it conforms to our interests.

It is possible that by the summer of 1978, as this is being written, the Carter administration has finally come to recognize that its policy of courting guerrillas was futile all along. But it may yet be too early for the deeper realization that the activism of the Soviet Union must be contained in the only manner that our circumstances allow, at the level of the global military balance.

10

DANIEL PIPES

The Third World Peoples of Soviet Central Asia

Russian conquest of the Central Asian peoples. Tsarist and Soviet governing policy. The five national republics— Kazakhstan, Kirghizia, Tajikistan, Turkmenistan, Uzbekistan. Political, economic, and cultural aspects of the relationship between Moscow and Central Asia. Russian control of internal affairs. Suggested U.S. policy.

Most of the more than thirty million Third World peoples of the Soviet Union live in Central Asia, a large area north of Iran and east of the Caspian Sea.* These are Muslims (Turks

---

*If, strictly speaking, the Third World is defined as those developing areas under the aegis of neither the United States nor the Soviet Union, then all peoples of the Soviet Union are in the Second World. We might say, however, that they are potentially Third World peoples.

and Iranians) who fell under Russian rule over a century ago. In striking contrast to other Third World peoples, who had been ruled by Europeans and who by now have gained independence, the Central Asians are still governed from Moscow. The fact that so many Third World peoples are in the Soviet Union under Russian dominion raises many questions about their relation to the Soviet Union and their potential restlessness for independence. Since Central Asia is very little known, we shall first present some introductory facts.

HISTORICAL BACKGROUND

During the past several centuries, as West Europeans sailed around the world conquering territories and establishing colonies, the Russians followed a similar pattern by a different process. They, too, conquered territories and established colonies, but rather than sail, they marched.

Russians expanded into Asia in three stages.[1] In the first, they crossed the Ural Mountains from the 1580s on, and continued east through Siberia all the way to the Pacific. Although they traversed immense distances, they encountered only sparse populations of primitive peoples, and reached the Pacific in 1638 without serious opposition. The non-Russian peoples of this vast area concern us little, because they are still few and primitive.

The second wave took about a hundred and fifty years, from 1711 until 1855. During this period the Russians conquered the Caucasus region and present-day Kazakhstan. Although both of these areas had larger and more developed populations than Siberia, they, too, did not include any centers of power or culture.

The third and final wave went more rapidly. Between 1864 and 1884, the Russians took control of all the important cities of Central Asia—Bukhara, Samarqand, Khiva, Khokand, and Merv—which, surprisingly, fell almost without a struggle. And thus the Russians found themselves suddenly wielding power over some five million persons of an alien civilization, many of them educated.

The vast majority of Central Asians were Muslims. For a millenium they had actively participated in Islamic civilization, producing many of its great dynasties and cultural achievements. Accordingly, the population was heavily oriented to Muslim areas of the south and east. Most of the population spoke Turkic, but some spoke Iranian, and Iran had a predominant cultural influence; in important ways, Central Asia was virtually a part of Iran. The Central Asians did not constitute national groups in the Western sense. Divided politically and linguistically, they had almost no sense of territorial loyalty. Rather, they considered themselves primarily as Muslims. Since the area had only fleeting and antagonistic contacts with a distant but expanding Russia, the Russians as conquerors appeared completely alien to the indigenous peoples.

Although the Russians had reached Central Asia by land, they acquired and ruled the region as a colony, with their land empire closely resembling the sea empires of the British, French, Dutch, Spanish, Portuguese, Italians, Germans, and Belgians of the time. The Tsarist government was unabashedly imperialistic in its expansion. Like other colonial masters, it believed in the overwhelming superiority of its own culture. The Russians insisted on using their own language, despised local customs and culture, and they especially scorned Islam, attitudes which were characteristic of all European colonizers in the Third World. In this way, Russian settlement in Central Asia was similar to that of the French in Algeria, the British in Rhodesia, and the Portuguese in Angola.

The Tsarist government also exploited its colonies for strategic and economic benefit, much as did the other European powers. Central Asia served the Russians in stopping a British advance north from India. The government built a railroad connection to Russia, encouraged the planting of cash crops such as cotton, and set high tariff levels for foreign goods in order to keep Central Asia as a captive market for Russian industrial products. Russians settled Central Asia not only in towns, but also on farms, especially growing grain on the Kazakh plain.[2]

Before 1917, Russian communists unambiguously condemned every instance of European imperialism, including the Tsarist presence in Central Asia. On coming to power, the Bolsheviks promised a new era, and spoke of the cultural—and even political—autonomy of the old colonies. Yet despite these intentions, more than sixty years later those areas are still part of the Soviet Union. How and why did this occur?

It occurred because the communists found it much easier to give away the Tsar's possessions than their own. Once in power, they resisted every effort to break up the empire— indeed, they reconquered a number of non-Russian regions that had set up local rule. Finally, in 1924, with the turmoil of the revolution and the subsequent civil war behind them, the Soviet government began implementing a "nationalities policy." Rather than release the non-Russian peoples from Soviet rule, this policy provided them with national republics within the Soviet Union. In Central Asia, this meant dividing the region into five republics which, with minor adjustments, survive to the present: Kazakhstan, Kirghizia, Tajikistan, Turkmenistan, and Uzbekistan.

The boundaries of these republics were drawn with scrupulous attention to the minor linguistic variations in Turkic dialects (this explains the extremely odd shape of Uzbekistan). The republics did not reflect national groups, however, for there was no national consciousness along linguistic or any other lines in Central Asia. The creation of national republics introduced a new political concept: suddenly, on orders from Moscow, the Central Asians became five distinct peoples.

Imposing national republics on the Central Asians served the Soviet government in two important ways: it broke the unity of the region, and thus reduced the likelihood of all Central Asians acting together in concert against the Russians. Secondly, by providing the Central Asians with their own political structures, if only in form, the Bolsheviks technically ended the colonial nature of their rule in Central Asia without allowing a fundamental shift in power. The latter point was very significant.

The establishment of national republics justified permanent Bolshevik rule over non-Russians by allowing a breathtakingly simple change in ideology. Unlike imperial regimes, which subsume the interests of the colonies to those of the ruling peoples, the Soviet leaders could claim fraternal ties and mutually beneficial relationships with the non-Russian peoples who purportedly had joined the Soviet Union of their own volition. Since the Soviet Union claims to be a revolutionary government, all its peoples benefit by federating with the progressive forces in Russia. Therefore, by definition, attempts to break away are counterrevolutionary; they represent the repressive interests of the bourgeois class. In short, the Bolsheviks devised an ideology which established that non-Russian peoples gained by remaining under Russian rule. Overnight the colonized peoples found themselves transformed from oppressed masses into "younger brothers" in the struggle for peace and equality. Since Marxist-Leninism was by nature anti-imperialistic, the Soviet Union could not—in theory—have colonies. As it would so often in years to come, the doctrine of Marxist-Leninism showed itself flexible enough to buttress any argument.

Did Central Asia really cease to be a Russian colony after 1924? Or did the creation of national republics mask a fundamental continuity between Tsarist and Soviet rule? The USSR claims that Central Asia is no longer a colony, but an independent republic; others might doubt this.

CENTRAL ASIA A RUSSIAN COLONY?

"Colony" here means a region subjugated to an alien people who rule it for their own benefit. If the experience of Central Asia since 1924 has resembled those of the West European overseas colonies such as India or Algeria, we may call Central Asia a colony. Although in many ways different from West European colonies of the past, Central Asia does share enough with them to justify calling the area a colony.

The argument against the colonial nature of Central Asia emphasizes how much better off it has been than a typical colony. The Central Asian peoples have benefited from their own political structures, from dramatic economic gains, and from great advances in education. Most striking is the fact that, in important ways, they have fared better under Soviet rule than have the Russians themselves. They have suffered less terror, dislocation, bureaucracy, religious persecution, and economic mismanagement than have the Russians. A relatively favorable experience argues against their colonial status.

But, the counterargument goes, a relatively favorable experience has nothing to do with colonialism; colonial relationships are defined by power. A colony need not be badly off, but it must be ruled by aliens. In this light, Central Asia is indeed a colony of Russia. To analyze this matter in more detail, we shall look at various aspects of life there: political, economic, and cultural. Within each topic, the noncolonial features will first be discussed, followed by the colonial features.

Political Aspect

The political situation of Central Asia differs from that of a typical colony in several ways. Its lack of power is a consequence of centralized Soviet rule, not of inequity between Russians and non-Russians. A totalitarian government such as that of the Soviet Union requires centralization; Moscow controls innumerable details in the lives of all Soviet citizens, including the Russians. Thus, the absence of power in Central Asia can be explained without reference to its predominantly non-Russian population; it would have hardly any self-rule, no matter who lived there.

Given the nature of the Soviet government, even the distance of Central Asia from Moscow has benefits, for it slightly relieves the people of the region from the heavy hand of the state. Living far from the center of power, their actions are less subject to the intense scrutiny of the government; of all Soviet peoples, the Central Asians experienced the least terror during Stalin's rule and less interference since. In an important way, then, these Third World peoples enjoy a better quality of life than the Russians.

In two other ways, too, Central Asians do not fit the status of a colonial people. First, they enjoy complete legal equality with the Russians. This does not mean that they suffer no discrimination, for they do, but that it is illegal. Central Asians are full-fledged citizens of the Soviet Union. Second, the Soviet army conscripts all citizens, without regard to regional or ethnic origin. Central Asians serve just as Russians do. Once in the army, no distinction is paid to origin, and all nationalities are freely mixed. This participation contravenes the usual colonial pattern.

Yet, granting these differences, Central Asia still shares vital characteristics with other colonies. Like many others, it has the trappings of power without its substance. Like the maharajas of India, who retained formal authority while the British ran their affairs, the republics of Central Asia are independent and sovereign. Indeed, they not only have their own foreign and defense ministries, but even the constitutional right to secede from the Soviet Union. Two of the Soviet republics (though not Central Asian ones) are full members of the United Nations. All this is a sham, however; the republics have neither their own foreign policy nor much influence on the decisions made in Moscow; their foreign and defense ministries are hollow showpieces, and the UN presence fools no one. All power to deal with the outside world is in Moscow.

Moscow's power is not limited to foreign policy; in internal affairs, too, it has the last word. While the republics make numerous local decisions, Moscow can always reverse them. There can be no rivalry between Moscow and the republics; the latter have no forces to array against the center. The instruments of power are all in Soviet—not the republic's—hands. The army and the secret police are controlled by Moscow; vital economic matters are directly supervised from there, and so on. Whatever power the republics or local authorities have, they enjoy it at Moscow's pleasure. One need not look far for indications of Moscow's power in running the republics; it can order the outcome of court cases, set censorship guidelines, discipline party members, or reverse any locally made policy.

The republics retain some little power, largely for propaganda purposes. The outside world generally, and foreign visitors specifically, must find that Central Asians have at least some self-government. If it were not for foreign opinion, the republics might have even less authority than they do at present.

Centralization of power need not in itself imply Russian control over Central Asia; if Central Asians participated in government in proportion to their population, they would no longer be under Russian control and the region would not be a colony. As in other respects, some effort is made to show that they participate, but a closer look reveals this, too, to be otherwise, for Russians dominate every decision-making body. The minorities have only token representation, and have almost no part in the deliberations which decide their fate. A decision from Moscow is a decision by Russians, and all decisions are ultimately made (or affirmed) in Moscow.

Russians not only dominate, but the whole Soviet regime is bound inextricably with their nationalism. Far from representing an internationalist ideology, as it originally intended to do, the Soviet government represents Russian interest; it is a fitting successor to the Russian empire. This has the important psychological effect of limiting the patriotic feeling of Central Asians for the regime. They generally view it less as their own than as a Russian government.

Russian power extends even within the Central Asian republics, where Russians hold many key positions. Normally, Muslims hold the top positions and ceremonial posts, while Russians fill key second-level jobs to keep a close watch on local developments. Russians also double up with Muslims in many positions. They are appointed directly by Moscow, and they maintain tight control over the local political apparatus. Tashkent will never experience a spring like Prague's.

The presence of many Russian settlers in all the Central Asian republics makes it possible to keep all political positions in local hands and still include many Russians. Moscow need not send Russians out to the provinces, for so many of them are already there. While technically keeping power in the hands of residents, the capital can give real authority to the Russians among them.

In sum, the Russians allow the Soviet Third World peoples little more power than did any colonial masters. But whereas earlier European empires made no efforts to hide this fact, the Russians have elaborated political structures and an ideology to disguise it. Ironically, the Soviet Union has both contributed to making the present an anti-imperialist age by attacking all forms of colonialism, and it has done the most to refine the colonial relationship by shedding its overt features. A "fraternal tie" looks better, but in real terms it means the same thing—the control of one people by another. Economic and cultural affairs clearly reflect this power relationship.

Economic Aspect

In some ways, again, Central Asia defies classic colonial patterns. Central Asia had barely any industry in 1917, but it has developed considerably since then. Dramatic improvements in industrial productivity and standard of living have taken place, often greater than those of the Soviet Union as a whole.

The government has made substantial efforts to accelerate growth by investing heavily in Central Asia. Moscow has apparently put more money into the region than it has extracted (Nove and Newth 1967:97, 125). If true, this defies all colonial precedents, for no metropolitan power intentionally invested more in a colony than it derived from it. Close analysis also shows that much of this investment could have brought larger returns elsewhere in the Soviet Union (Nove and Newth 1967:45); one may, therefore, conclude that it was put into Central Asia to improve its standard of living.

The Russian connection has thus brought Central Asia economic benefits, lifting the region to a prosperity which the local peoples on their own could not have attained. Comparison between the Central Asians and their nearest kinsmen in independent countries—Afghanistan, Iran, and Turkey— bears this out. Regardless which index one looks at—per capita income, mortality rates, medical services, electric power—in all respects, Soviet Third World peoples are far ahead of their independent neighbors. In part, this may be due to the more stable government in Central Asia; none of its neighbors has had the same government since 1920.

Central Asia compares favorably not only with the Third World countries to its south, but also with other regions of the Soviet Union. It experienced a smoother development under Soviet rule than most other regions. Aside from the catastrophic collectivization efforts in the 1930s, the Central Asians have almost escaped the economic excesses and reversals which have so severely afflicted the rest of the Soviet Union. In contrast to other regions, Central Asia has received enough money for agricultural investment; as a result, it is the only region in the country with a successful agriculture (Shorish 1975:412).

In all, an economic picture emerges which compares favorably with both Central Asia's independent neighbors and other regions of the Soviet Union; this latter point especially turns the usual colonial relationship on its head. Can one yet maintain that Central Asia is economically a colony of Russia's? Yes, because the power relationship implies that Moscow holds nearly total control over Central Asia's economy; whatever Central Asia enjoys, it has at Moscow's pleasure.

To begin with, the centralized policy of the Soviet government implies that Moscow makes economic as well as political decisions—right down to the trivial level. Distant bureaucrats fix factory schedules, farm productivity, and worker payment. Khrushchev himself once lectured the Uzbeks on the best type of sheep for them to raise. Moscow exercises a detailed tyranny over Central Asian economic life. Beyond this, it directly controls the most sensitive industries (e.g., gold, military production), to the total exclusion of the local authorities.

Along with internal control, Moscow determines foreign trade to and from Central Asia. The people and governments of the area do not dispose of the hard currency they earn. Instead, their profits go directly to Moscow, which usually allows them only a fraction of those funds for their own use.

Central Asia serves the classic colonial purpose of providing Russia with cheap raw materials and then importing its industrial goods (India, for instance, filled this role for Britain). All the cotton in the Soviet Union is grown in Central Asia, but in 1964 only 9 percent of it was processed locally, the rest sent out of the region (Nove and Newth 1967:138–39). In return, the Russians cut Central Asia off from direct foreign trade, and exploit it as a captive market for their inferior industrial goods.

Typical colonial relations exist not only between Central Asia and Moscow, but also between the Muslims and Russians living in Central Asia itself. The Russians there tend to have the better land and the better jobs (like the French in Algeria). The region presents a model case of ethnic stratification, wherein one group, the Russians, commonly enjoys economic advantages which few from other groups share (Lewis 1975:293–94). Even if this situation can be explained by differences in skills, motivation, and education, it still reminds the Muslims of who runs things.

Without underestimating the economic advantages that Central Asian Third World peoples have over their independent brethren to the south, it is true that in the present age of nationalism this matters very little. The economic benefits of colonial rule have been apparent in many regions, yet this almost never influences a people (unless its numbers are very small) to prefer remaining a colony. While the blacks in South Africa are richer than their compatriots anywhere else in Africa, this does not make them content; they do not compare themselves with poorer blacks in distant countries, but with the richer whites in their midst. Given the choice, all peoples choose independence, regardless of economic consequences; surely this applies also to the Muslims of Central Asia.

Cultural Aspect

Here, too, Central Asia differs in some ways from the typical Third World colony. Education has made tremendous strides since 1917. The Tsarist government before then had done nothing to encourage education, so until 1917 the literacy rate in Central Asia was minuscule; currently, nearly everyone can read. This extraordinary change came about as a result of the heavy Soviet emphasis on education, and the willingness of the government to spend on it. All children must attend school; numerous technical programs prepare them for skilled jobs; and there are now several universities in the region. These advances in education distinguish Central Asia from a typical colony, where the Third World people suffer from the European power's unwillingness to spend money on their education. In many cases, too (including the Tsarist one), the colonial power prefers an uneducated colony, expecting it to cause less trouble.

In an odd way, the Soviet treatment of religion argues again for Central Asia's relatively favorable experience. On principle, the Soviet authorities discourage religion, yet Islam has fared better than Christianity. Having Christian origins themselves, the communist leaders have persecuted Christianity with particular venom; they care less about Islam, however, so in this way the Muslims of Central Asia have a slight advantage over the Russians. If mosques were turned into post offices, Russian Orthodox churches were used as barns.

Granting the real educational advances in Central Asia and the small advantage of Islam over Christianity in the Soviet Union, Russian attitudes toward Central Asian culture, and Russian control of it, betray a colonial relationship. Both the Russian settlers in Central Asia and the Soviet regime disrespect the Islamic civilization of Central Asia. Russians are convinced of their own cultural superiority, and maintain an attitude of aversion and suspicion toward the alien culture of the region. This attitude exactly resembles that of other European colonial rulers.

In Tsarist times, the Russians viewed Islam as a sinister force; they did not understand it, and made few efforts to come to terms with it. The communists added an atheistic ideology to that mistrust. True, their atheism challenged all religions, but it had two special consequences in Central Asia. First, since the atheistic doctrines came from men of Christian origin, Muslims could not but see them as a covert Christian attack on Islam. The Russians had always fought Islam—earlier in the name of Christianity, now in the name of atheism. The results were similar, and Muslims responded badly to both types of attack. Second, since Islam is tied to every aspect of a Muslim's life, an attack on the religion also denigrates his whole way of life and his culture. Thus, by assailing Islam, the Russians malign much more than the Central Asians' religion.

Soviet policy toward the Turkic and Iranian languages of Central Asia indicates most clearly the power Russians wield in cultural matters. The government has played havoc with the local languages by changing their scripts and word meanings (Menges 1967:79–82). When the Soviet government ordered that the Central Asian languages drop the Arabic script, starting in 1922, it did this to isolate the Muslims of the Soviet Union both from their Islamic heritage and from Turkic and Iranian writings originating outside the country. Those who learned to read the Latin script could not easily handle written matter from before 1917; this gave the Soviet authorities greater control over their reading matter. Also, by abandoning the Arabic script, the Soviets made it difficult for Muslims in the Soviet Union to communicate in writing with Turkic and Iranian speakers elsewhere. The intention to isolate was proven by the Soviet reaction to Ataturk's reforms. When, in 1928, he required the Turks in Turkey to adopt the Latin alphabet, the Soviets ordered a second change in script, from Latin to Cyrillic. Cyrillic letters remain in use until this day.

The change from Latin to Cyrillic letters involved another change too. Whereas the Latin alphabets for the many dialects of Turkic had represented each sound by the same letter, the Cyrillic alphabets for the many dialects assigned different letters for the same sound. The intent behind this needless complication is clear; the different letters place obstacles in the way of communication between nationalities. In this manner, alphabet policy reduces the chance of unified action by Turkic speakers against the Russians. Again, Russian interests dominate.

The redefinition of words in the Turkic and Iranian languages also indicates Russian power. While the Soviet government has eliminated meanings of Russian words related to religion and traditional culture, it is one thing when Russians tamper with their own language and quite another when they do so with that of others. Disregarding the sentiments of those who speak these languages, the Russians have shuffled word meanings around to suit their purposes (Bodrogligeti 1975:475–91). This is blatant cultural imperialism. Russians are convinced they know the truth, and so impose their ideas on a non-European people. It matters little whether their truth be Christianity or communism; the Russians have the means and the desire to force their will on other peoples.

In the final analysis, Central Asia does appear to be a colony of Russia. Its economic progress and relative well-being notwithstanding, the complete and arbitrary power that Russians exercise over its indigenous peoples argues this. Russian control of distant alien lands makes those areas Russian colonies. Shrill anticolonialist rhetoric to the contrary, the Soviet Union retains the classic relationship of European ruler and Third World colony. Of all European peoples, the Russians alone retain a large colonial empire.[3] The other great empires have been reduced to disjointed bits: Macao, Belize, Gibraltar, Réunion, St. Helena, etc. (South Africa and Rhodesia are no longer colonies of Europe, but independent countries.) Only the Russians are left.[4] Why is the world so little aware of the Russian empire? How have the Russians maintained strict colonial control without anyone noticing?

The Russian empire has kept out of view, thanks to two features: the land connection, and the creation of republics. Regardless how far the Russians went, they stayed on land, so their colonies lacked the obviously colonial qualities of a sea empire. Although Central Asia lies much further from Moscow than does Algeria from Paris, the sea constitutes an insurmountable barrier to making Algeria part of France, while the land tie between Russia and Central Asia facilitates this. It obscures the equally alien quality of Russian rule in Central Asia.

The establishment of republics has also served to make the Russian empire invisible. Powerless local governments allow the Russians to maintain control while giving the appearance of autonomy. Although Russians rule, this becomes apparent only upon closer inspection. The establishment of controlled local governments in colonies has been a major Russian contribution to the refinement of colonialism.

PROSPECTS AND UNITED STATES POLICY

Central Asia's invisibility is coming to an end with its population explosion and its heightened political awareness. As the region gains importance, the United States will need to formulate a policy towards it, especially as the situation in Central Asia offers a momentous opportunity for checking Soviet aggressiveness and power.

Central Asia has undergone a demographic surge which is transforming its role within the USSR. In the years between the last two censuses (1959 and 1970), the major nationalities of Central Asia increased in population as shown in Table 1 (see Wixman 1973:82).

On the average, the Central Asian nationalities increased by half in slightly more than a decade; this comes to about 3.8 percent per annum, a figure which approaches the biological maximum. The Muslim population of Central Asia numbered some 13 million in 1959, 20 million in 1970, and projections see them increasing to 35 million in 1985, and to as many as 80 or 100 million in the year 2000 (Rywkin 1975:277). In contrast, the Russian population is growing at an ever-slower rate. Central Asian Muslims will thus constitute a much larger proportion of the Soviet population in the coming decades. As the region grows in numbers, its concerns will demand more attention from both the Russian authorities and from the West.

The surge in the Muslim population is already beginning to transform the Soviet work force and army, as they constitute an ever-increasing proportion of youths. Young Muslims of Central Asia are coming of working age in vast numbers just when the Soviet economy needs many more low-skill manual workers. Since they usually lack technical skills, the timing of their entry into the job market might be just right. Like the Mediterranean area workers who are working in North Europe, the Muslims of Central Asia could go north to jobs in Siberia and Western Russia. The difficulty lies in marrying

Table 1

Population Increases in Central Asia, 1959 to 1970
(by nationality)

Nationality	Percentage Increase
Kazakh	46
Kirghiz	50
Tajik	53
Turkmen	52
Uzbek	53

Source: Wixman 1973:22

the workers to the jobs, for Central Asians are reluctant to leave their region, and most of the new jobs cannot be relocated in Central Asia. Will they migrate; will the jobs come to them; both, or neither? Soviet and Western analysts are debating this issue;[5] and it does bear attention, for if Central Asian workers and the jobs are not brought together, the Soviet economy will suffer and Central Asians will be restlessly underemployed.

Central Asians in the army are another worry for the Russians. If universal conscription is continued, Central Asians will constitute a third of future recruits. This could have a profound effect on Soviet military policy. Not only are most Central Asians ignorant of Russian, less educated, and less skilled, but their loyalty to the Soviet Union and their motivation to fight for it are open to question.

Politically, too, Central Asia promises to become more troublesome. As its isolation breaks down, the Muslims have begun to enjoy increased contacts with the outside world. These have made them increasingly aware of the world order

FIGURE 1
"A slower growth of comrades in Russia . . ."*

Average Annual Percent Change in the Work Force in Each Plan Period 1971-2000

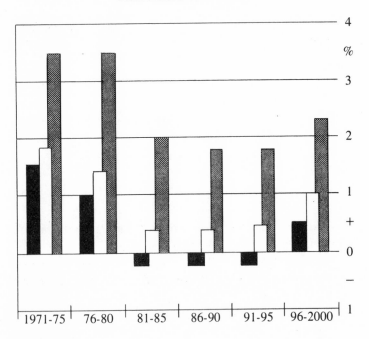

Source: Foreign Demographic Analysis Division, U.S. Department of Commerce (quoted in *The Economist*, 24 June 1978).

*Males: 16-59; females: 16-54.

Key: ☐ USSR total

■ Russian Soviet Federated Socialist Republic

▨ Central Asia, Kazakhstan, and Transcaucasia

and of their own anomalous position. In a world divided into sovereign nations, why are they one of the few peoples still not independent? Why are they yet under the thumb of a distant city?

Until now, Central Asian nationalism has been muted, but in the long run it is inevitable that these peoples, like all others, will demand independence. Eventually (though when is a matter of great disagreement), the Uzbeks, Tajiks, et al., will become stubbornly nationalistic, and the Soviet regime will face unprecedented internal troubles. The articulated discontent of Central Asian Muslims will cause not only domestic unrest, but it could severely damage the Soviet Union's cultivated anti-imperialist image and sabotage its standing in the Third World.

Recognizing the potential importance of Central Asia—and, indeed, all the non-Russian areas of the USSR—the United States government needs a policy. To date it has had none, and has done nothing; it has never challenged the right of Russian rule in the region, nor has it formulated a policy regarding future self-determination in the Central Asian republics.

This timidity has been due to an American understanding of the extreme Soviet reaction against any official discussion of Central Asia. The Russians would consider this a precipitate provocation. Raising the issue would sharply antagonize the Soviet Union, and what could we gain by it? Further, we face the danger of raising nationalist hopes in Central Asia without being able or willing to support them. If the United States suddenly made an issue of the colonial situation in Central Asia, peoples there would take this as a signal that this country encourages their efforts to achieve independence. If local movements then rose in response, the United States would have a commitment to rally by them. Fearing both a terrible turn in relations with the Soviet Union and responsibility for developments in Central Asia, the United States government has refrained from meddling.

The sensitivity of the Central Asian question is reason for caution, but not for avoiding the issue. Two reasons argue in favor of raising this matter: it is consistent with the U.S. policy since World War I of opposing all colonial rule and favoring self-determination, and it serves our purposes. A cautious discussion of Russian rule in Central Asia can cause the Soviet Union great embarrassment in international circles, and possibly can contribute to the dismantling of its empire.

How might the topic best be brought up by the U.S. government? By addressing the world at large, not the Russians or the Central Asians. We must avoid any suggestion of encouragement to the Third World peoples of the Soviet Union, for we want no responsibility for fomenting unrest.[6] This would only poison relations with the USSR and force us to be accountable for uncontrollable developments there.

Rather than try directly to influence events in the Soviet Union, we should make the world aware of the situation there. Were the United States, for example, to submit Central Asia as a topic for discussion at the United Nations Committee on Decolonization, this alone would make the matter an international issue. Such discussion would put the Soviet Union on the defensive, and it might have particular influence on Muslims, who feel strongly for their coreligionists.

The current American emphasis on human rights has met with a cool international response, because it embarrasses most of the world. It works with countries that depend on us, but has proven totally ineffectual against the Soviet Union. In contrast, a campaign against colonialism would win wide international support. In other words, the United States and its allies need not wage this campaign on their own against the USSR. It should be enough to raise the issue, and then let the Third World countries apply pressure on the Soviet Union. Their displeasure carries far more weight than ours since they, unlike us, are potential allies.

The U.S. task, then, is to make the Third World aware of the situation in the Soviet Union. The European colonies, such as the Ukraine, will concern the Third World very little, but it will take great interest in Central Asia, an area of Third World peoples ruled by Europeans. By making known the situation in Central Asia, we may not only cause the Soviet Union to lose its prestige as an anti-imperialist power, but Third World pressure might speed up the formation of nations within the Soviet Union and lead to the release of its many colonies. Needless to say, this has enormous implications for the whole future of the USSR.

The more the Third World knows about Third World peoples in Soviet Central Asia, the better for both those peoples and for ourselves. As the Central Asians grow in numbers and gain political consciousness, their obscurity and invisibility will end. Their status as the last major Third World peoples under European rule will become a major matter of international concern in the coming years.

IV

The Economic Problem

11

ANTHONY SMITH

The Case of
Dependency Theory

The dependency theory of national development. Interaction between national and international economic enterprise. Horizontal and vertical dimensions of the dependency approach to Third World issues. Academic theories. Fact against theory in Latin America. The strength of nationalism. Marxist and capitalist views of the North-South situation. Internal movements in the Third World. The need to understand the logic of change.

Until recently, literature on the problems of development in the industrializing areas of the globe—the "South" or Third World—has tended to concentrate on the *internal* dynamics of change in these regions, such things as party structures, ethnic and class conflict, urbanization, land tenure systems, and the like. Third World countries are *contrasted* with the industrial societies of the North in the understanding that the different characteristics of the two regions can be seen as representative of different "stages" of development. In the last few years, all this has been called into question—as indeed it should be—by a group of writers who, whatever their differences, share the view that the various stages of development among world societies should not so much be contrasted as *linked*, and that these linkages should be understood to express the evolution of forces that can be studied only at the level of world, not local, history. To study the Third World is thus to study the history and nature of imperialism as it rose in the North and expanded into the South, shaping local society in its image.

This new school of thinking calls its approach *dependency theory*, thereby stressing the way in which the Third World "depends" in its economic, social, and political structures on the formative influence of northern imperialist domination. From the perspective of dependency theory, the conventional way of studying Third World "development" or "modernization" in the United States is an exercise in ideological obfuscation, deliberate or otherwise, designed to conceal the way imperialism works. Dependency theory does this by focusing theoretical attention on the South alone, as though it can be meaningfully understood apart from the greater global history to which it belongs. In this manner, the imperialist system disguises its power, shielding itself from ideological attack.

There is little question that the theoretical underpinnings of United States professional literature and academic course organization have hereby received a serious challenge. The models of political development, which for nearly twenty years were the stuff of American writing and the foundation of many a brave career, are now disputed in no uncertain terms. Nor does this seem to be just a coincidence, coming as it does in the aftermath of Vietnam and the rise in petroleum prices; evidently the real power of the Third World in international affairs is coming to be matched by a more aggressive literature on its behalf. As the force of southern nationalism expresses itself more powerfully in concrete terms, so it seeks conceptual arms as well—and finds them in dependency theory. For dependency theory locates the terrible current problems of Third World economic development in past northern exploitation of the South. And the theory calls for a reordering of the international balance of power so that these problems may be solved. In the anti-imperialist struggle, the theory sees the expression of a southern nationalist determination to achieve genuine independence in the international system and to ameliorate living standards of the poorest in the Third World.

It is important, of course, to recognize the differences among those who can be classified after their Latin American appellation as *dependencistas.* Latin Americans, Asians, and Africans, not to mention North Americans, Europeans, and socialist country experts, figure in their ranks. With so many adherents in so many parts of the world, with a literature in its modern form over twenty years old (although able to trace its lineage back to Lenin and Hobson, if not earlier), and with inevitably different lines of theoretical exposition and sharp disagreements among them, it is nevertheless essential to see dependency theory as a school. For, whatever the internal differences, it has generally shared assumptions and commonly agreed upon enemies. Indeed, the unity and importance of dependency theory proponents is such that they must be seen as a school in a broader than strictly academic sense. For dependency theory represents the intellectual meeting ground of Marxism and certain important forms of nationalism in the Third World, and it thereby serves as the ideological underpinning of a "united front" among these groups, directed against what it sees as the local power of northern imperialism. To be sure, dependency theory contains explicit preferences for the form of domestic social organization it favors for the South—usually some variant of socialism—and thus cannot be expected to attract all southern nationalists to its banner. But the primary ambition of the *dependencistas* at this point in time is to struggle at the level of the nation and the international system for what they see as a better world. In this respect especially, dependency theory appeals to a broad spectrum of nationalists in the South.

This chapter is intended neither as a comprehensive survey of the dependency literature nor as an effort to assess its practical significance as an ideological force mobilizing nationalist sentiment in the South today. Rather, I hope simply to examine what seems to me to be the most important theoretical assumption of this school, and to subject it and its chief corollaries to a thoroughgoing criticism. My concern is not to debunk completely the theory, nor to deny the genuine insights it has into the process of Third World development. Instead, my intention is to show that dependency theory has its limitations in coming to grips with the contemporary problems of the Third World, and that the failure to recognize these limitations converts much of the literature into a partisan ideology every bit as closed to criticism—and ultimately just as unable to see crucial aspects of reality—as the "bourgeois" approach to Third World development the *dependencistas* so sharply attack. Unless otherwise indicated, the writers referred to all may be considered to belong to the dependency school.

The cardinal assumption of the dependency school is Hegel's admonition that the whole has a logic greater than the sum of its parts. Concretely put, this means that whether we are interested in individual psychology or the fate of nations, we must approach our subject by seeing it on the broadest relevant canvas where all the factors influencing its development are present. This is the level of the "whole," the "totality." It is crucial to understand that an analysis conducted at a lower level of interaction, at the level of a "part," will never show us, of itself, this greater pattern. To the contrary, the "part" can only be understood by its place within the "whole," which alone gives it meaning. In the case of Third World development today, it should be fairly apparent what this approach entails: it means that such issues can only be comprehended *globally,* and this along two dimensions, one of which may be called vertical or historical, the other to be seen as horizontal, or involving the entire international system. Any attempt to see issues of Third World development on a more reduced scale, so the dependency school would hold, must fail, succumbing to the illusion that a "part" is explicable in its own terms alone. In a word, to study the South, one must study imperialism—its origin, its present dynamic, its likely future evolution. In this light it will be seen that *the development and wealth of the North and the underdevelopment and poverty of the South are a function of one another.*

Concrete examples may make this point more clearly. Immanuel Wallerstein (1974), perhaps the dean of the dependency school in North America, has insisted that the dynamism of the West has come precisely from the ability of its economic order to escape local political controls and to work its way on a world level, at which point alone it can be meaningfully studied. Similarly, Samir Amin (1974), an Egyptian with a wide reputation in Western Europe, wrote that,

apart from a few "ethnographic reserves," all contemporary societies are integrated into a world system. Not a single concrete socio-economic formation of our time can be understood except as part of this world system.

In the African context, for instance, Walter Rodney (1973) writes that underdevelopment

expresses a particular relationship of exploitation: namely, the exploitation of one country by another. . . . The underdevelopment with which the world is now preoccupied is a product of capitalist, imperialist and colonialist exploitation.

Apparently, even the word "tribe" must be struck from our vocabulary. According to Colin Leys (1974), the word can only be used between quotation marks:

"Tribalism" is a creation of colonialism. It has little or nothing to do with pre-colonial relations between tribes. . . . In neo-colonial

Africa, class formation and the development of tribalism accompany each other.

It is in this same vein that André Gunder Frank (1972), writing of Latin America, can speak of the "development of underdevelopment," while Stanley and Barbara Stein (1970) report that, in considering contemporary problems, they

view Latin America as a continent of inadequate and disappointing fulfillment and seek to pinpoint the coordinates of sustained backwardness in examining the process of economic change in a dependent, peripheral, or colonial area.

Asian development can be fitted into the same mold, as Frances Moulder (1977) explains; the backwardness of China relative to Japan is attributed to the fact that the former was more incorporated into the European-dominated international system than the latter. Finally, many of these studies refer with praise to Paul Baran's (1956) earlier efforts to study Indian economic development in much the same terms:

there can be no doubt that had the amount of economic surplus that Britain has torn from India been invested in India, India's economic development to date would have borne little similarity to the actual somber record. . . . India, if left to herself, might have found in the course of time a shorter and surely less tortuous road toward a better and richer society.

The charge, it should be emphasized, is moral as well as historical: the links between North and South, which may be historically demonstrated to exist, are at the same time morally culpable, in the sense of being directly responsible for the widespread misery in the Third World. "The lot of more than a billion people of the developing world continues to deteriorate as a result of the trends in international economic relations," declares the opening sentence of the Charter of Algiers, founding document of the Group of 77, the name given to the international association of Third World countries (now numbering well over one hundred). A concrete example of this process was offered by Salvadore Allende on the occasion of the Third United Nations Conference on

Trade and Development, held in Chile in 1972. In 1931, Allende declared, foreign copper companies invested about $30 million in Chile. Over the ensuing years, at least $4 billion was repatriated to the United States in profits—but no fresh capital was added to this original sum. And this in a nation of ten million people, where estimates say half a million children are today mentally damaged as a result of malnutrition. By Allende's account, this development came about when a self-interested local elite, concerned to fill its own pockets but unmindful of the national interest, created a large external public debt to encourage such investment from abroad. Thus, in 1971, some one-third of the total export earnings of Chile had to service a debt, in his words, "largely contracted in order to offset the damage done by an unfair trade system, to defray the costs of the establishment of foreign enterprises on our territory, [and] to cope with the speculative exploitation of our resources."

Such statements could be multiplied many times over by citations from a wide range of southern writers and politicians and their supporters in the North. These arguments about the character of the international system are ultimately moral: they lodge responsibility for the South's condition on a system of investment, trade, and finance run by the North for its own profit. Thus, the Charter of Economic Rights and Duties of States, voted by the UN General Assembly in January 1975 upon the recommendation of President Echeverría of Mexico, maintains that the South has the "right" to nationalize foreign investments strictly according to local laws, and to enter into commodity cartels to raise and stabilize the prices of raw materials, whereas it is the "duty" of the North to accept such arrangements.

In a formal sense, the argument has merit. Like the claims in the United States today for "affirmative action" and "reparations" by minority groups, so southern countries affirm that the international system has worked to their detriment even as it has furthered the prosperity of the North. The established procedures by which the international economic system is run are only apparently neutral, therefore, and on closer inspection may be seen to serve the interests of one group at the expense of another.

To be persuasive, however, the argument needs to be empirically valid as well as formally sound. Does the international system linking South to North actually exist in the fashion described? The question is, first of all, scientific, and only thereafter normative.

The most fundamental criticism to be made of the world view of dependency theory in this respect is that its manner of exalting what I have called the "whole," the "totality," gives to the international system dominated by northern capitalism a power far greater and more coordinated than it actually possesses with respect to the "parts," or the countries of the Third World. Not that the system lacks coherence and means of protecting itself. When regimes threaten to nationalize foreign enterprises, for example, they may expect to receive less investments of this sort in the future and suffer international credit restrictions, which may, in turn, raise the risk of civil disorder as internal economic conditions become unstable. But this is no reason for which to exaggerate the coordination and power of the international system, which is actually much more fluid than dependency theory allows. Dependency theorists establish a tyranny of the whole over the parts which closer inspection makes difficult to accept.

Even in the heyday of imperialism, there were definite limits on what the Europeans could hope to accomplish, and a clear local component to the character of their rule in the South. Consider, for example, the breathtaking exaggeration of the man generally considered to be the father of dependency theory in the United States, Paul Baran (1956:149–50), writing on India under British rule:

Thus, the British administration of India systematically destroyed all the fibres and foundations of Indian society. Its land and taxation policy ruined India's village economy and substituted for it the parasitic landowners and moneylenders. Its commercial policy destroyed the Indian artisan and created the infamous slums of the Indian cities filled with millions of starved and diseased paupers. Its economic policy broke down whatever beginnings there were of an indigenous industrial development and promoted the proliferations of speculators, petty businessmen, agents, and sharks of all descriptions.

And it might be recalled from above that Baran felt that "India, if left to herself, might have found in the course of time a shorter and surely less tortuous road toward a better and richer society." The obvious objection to this line of argument, however, is that it grants far too much power to the British (for evil or otherwise), while it gives far too little credit to the power of Indian traditions and institutions. India before the British was not without sin, nor were the British the authors of unmitigated evil. "Parasitic landowners and moneylenders" were present before the British arrival; British "commercial policy" is now believed to have "destroyed" far fewer native artisans than was previously thought; British economic policy certainly did far more to create the foundations for the industrialization of India than to "break down whatever beginnings there were"; British "land and taxation policy," rather than "ruining" the village economy, was surely far less exploitive than that under the Great Mogul in Delhi; and British "administration," far from destroying "all the fibres and foundations of Indian society," in fact adopted the policy of most conquerors of large populations and adapted itself rather well to indigenous ways.

To be sure, India might have fared better; between roughly 1880 and World War I, British policy definitely worked as a handicap on Indian industrialization. But regressive Indian forces were at work as well. The Great Mutiny of 1857 had demonstrated to the British that local forces resisting change had to be handled with care. And the multiple problems of India today, more than thirty years since independence, can only be marginally associated with the British rule of over a century, evidence again that the British presence did not permeate every level of Indian life.

As the case of British India suggests for today, the international system is far more fluid than dependency theorists allow, and its impact on southern societies is therefore both weaker and more varied than they would expect. As a consequence, theoretical room must be made to understand the real power of initiative southern states possess, both in regard to local affairs and to the international system. For there is no blueprint, implicit or explicit, which keeps the South the perpetual "hewer of wood and drawer of water," as is commonly alleged. Where is the strategy to prevent southern industrialization, monopolize raw materials, break up domestically integrated markets, oppose regional integration plans, accentuate a still greater international division of labor favoring the developed nations? Where is the strategy similar to German policy toward southeastern Europe from the late nineteenth century through World War II or, less premeditatedly, British policy toward the industrialization of its dependencies prior to World War I? To the contrary, as we shall see below, there is strong evidence that most southern states today enjoy an autonomy from the influence of the international system that should not be underestimated (just as it should not be exaggerated). Indeed, there is reason to believe this has long been the case; historians of the Near East, South Asia, and the Far East have insisted time and again that local cultures have adapted themselves to the momentary dominance of the Europeans, only to assert themselves more vigorously as alien power declined. It is an unjustifiable act of condescension to suppose these local traditions simply disappeared in the face of the European onslaught. It is especially surprising to see those who call themselves southern nationalists overlook the strength of the identities of these local cultures for the sake of damning the allegedly all-pervasive influence of the North.

The international system might also be called fluid in the sense that, by its very operation, it prepares the ground for changes in the relative power of states within it. For example, World Bank and United States Department of Commerce statistics show that, by the end of 1975, Algeria had run up an external public debt of over $9 billion, and that the United

States had become the country's chief creditor and trading partner. Certainly it would be difficult to maintain that Algeria was hereby reduced to a dependent status in the international system, its autonomy reduced, and its economy open to exploitation. To the contrary, it would appear that Algeria is practicing that trick of the martial arts whereby the strength of an opponent is turned against himself: Algeria cooperates with the international system in order better to escape its control.

Is Algeria an exception? It would seem not. For perhaps twenty years, statistics put out by the United Nations and the Organization for Economic Cooperation and Development (OECD) report, manufacturing output in the Third World has increased faster than these economies in general, and faster than the rate of manufacturing output in the capitalist states of the North. One of the principal arguments against colonialism and neocolonialism was precisely that they retarded such progress, but the available figures argue strongly that this is no longer the case.

The most striking demonstration comes from the statistics for the middle 1970s, when the so-called "middle income" Third World countries—those with per capita incomes of $200 to $700 a year—managed to increase their manufacturing output by around 8 percent annually, while the OECD countries registered a zero annual increase. These figures demonstrate both the vigor and the independence of manufacturing in the Third World. The index numbers of industrial production for all southern countries are especially revealing in this regard (see Table 1).

For so long it was such a sacrosanct article of faith that the Third World could not develop, given the logic of the international system, that still today many dependency theorists simply deny that southern industrialization is occurring. They state—incorrectly—that light, not heavy, industry is the only growth sector, or that industrial output or employment is not so dynamic when compared to population growth or other economic sectors.

Table 1

Industrial Output as a Percentage of 1970 Production in Developed and Developing Market Countries

Year	Heavy Industry (1)[a]	Heavy Industry (2)[b]	Light Industry (1)[a]	Light Industry (2)[b]	Total (1)[a]	Total (2)[b]
1960	53	43	66	64	57	54
1974	122	148	114	127	119	137
1975	112	150	110	132	111	141
1976	123	165	120	141	122	152

Source: United Nations, *Bulletin of Monthly Statistics* (August 1977).
[a]Developed market countries.
[b]Developing market countries.

Failing these arguments, the dependency theorists may maintain that there are developments sponsored by the international system which effectively counter whatever favorable trends exist in the South—for example, through "decapitalization" and "denationalization." The preferred manner of establishing the so-called "decapitalization" of the South is to present capital flows between North and South, showing that more leaves the Third World than enters—an apparent indication of exploitation. Thus, with respect to Latin America, Dale Johnson (Cockroft 1972) writes, "between 1950 and 1961, 2,962 million dollars of U.S. private capital flowed into the seven principal countries of Latin America, while the return flow was 6,875 million dollars." But in and of themselves, what do these figures mean? Unless we know what this balance of investment in Latin America or to the amount of output generated, such sums tell us very little indeed.

Reports by the United States Department of Commerce provide statistics which suggest how dubious Johnson's charges are. In 1975, for example, United States private investment in Latin American manufacturing totaled $178 million. At the same time, American corporations remitted to this country $359 million in profits, and another $211 million in royalties and fees. Some years do not show such a heavy outflow to the United States, but 1975 would seem to correspond to the *dependencista* expectation: American firms "decapitalized" Latin America of $392 million that year in terms of manufacturing alone. However, compared to total United States investments in manufacturing of $8.6 billion, the sum repatriated—4.6 percent—hardly represents an extortionist outflow. This sum of $392 million appears all the more trivial when compared to the total sales of North American manufacturing affiliates in Latin America in 1974: $20.9 billion. Either as return on capital invested or on volume of business generated, the amount of money claimed by United States enterprises for use at home can only with difficulty be seen as perpetuating the international second-class status of the South. The opposite could more properly be argued.

A second charge against North American investments is that they "denationalize" industry in the South—that they buy up profitable, progressive firms in the Third World, leaving the less interesting ventures to the local bourgeoisie. Thus, Richard Barnet and Ronald Mueller (1974) report that a Harvard Business School study for the period 1958–1967 shows North Americans acquiring southern property on every side: "About 46 per cent of all manufacturing operations established in the period were takeovers of existing domestic industry." Messrs. Barnet and Mueller neglect to inform the reader, however, that this same study shows that through liquidations or expropriations, or sales of an entire affiliate or a considerable portion thereof, United States interests had divested themselves of nearly as many manufacturing concerns as they had acquired: 332 lost versus 337 gained. A more crucial statistic might be the value of affiliates bought and sold, not the number. Here, figures are hard to find, but the Department of Commerce does report that, for 1975 and 1976, United States manufacturing firms sold off about as much in value of their southern affiliates as they acquired through takeovers..

A final question has to do with the industrial sector in which foreign investments are located. Here again, the pattern seems clear: increasingly in the Third World foreigners are forbidden to invest, except in those domains where local capital and know-how are deficient. This has meant a progressive movement out of some fields and into others by American investors, with the foreigners generally holding the most advanced and remunerative industries. From the perspective of dependency theory, this spells the technological subservience of the South to the North. But it might just as easily be argued that such a strategy is the best way for the South to get technology transferred to it from the North, and that whatever gains the North thereby realizes are small compared with the benefits achieved by the South. It might be recalled that ever since Lenin the Soviet Union has encouraged something like this kind of investment, with the long-range ambition, of course, to emerge technologically superior to the capitalist countries.

It should not for a moment be forgotten that these economic exchanges are occurring within a political context dominated by the American defeat in Vietnam. For the nearly five hundred years of European expansion across the globe, southern weakness militarily put a clear limit to political strength. Colonialism's demise may have ended the direct political control of North over South, but there was always the threat of military intervention if southern regimes failed to respect northern interests. Thus it had been in Asia since the First Opium War in 1840. Vietnam meant the end of this tradition, at least on the grand scale, as should be apparent when the current reality is compared with the brave words of George Liska (1967):

The Vietnamese War . . . may well come to rank on a par with the two world wars as a conflict that marked an epoch in America's progress toward definition of her role as a world power. . . . This role implies the necessity to define—by force if necessary—the terms on which regional balances of power are evolved and American access to individual regions is secured. . . . Had it been less dramatized, the Vietnamese War would have been an ideal ground for evolving, training, and breaking in . . . a combined political-military establishment as well as for educating the American people to changing facts of life. It may still prove retrospectively to have been such.

It was under the shadow of the victory of Vietnamese nationalism that Arab nationalism scored its stunning success in raising petroleum prices late in 1973. In 1972, Organization of Petroleum Exporting Countries (OPEC) states received $29 billion for their exports, some 7 percent of world trade by value; but by 1975 their exports totaled $114 billion, accounting for about 13 percent of world commerce (down from 16 percent in 1974). While OPEC's ability has in certain respects hurt the rest of the Third World, its success is part of the general rise of southern states internationally, as the figures presented earlier on industrial development pointedly suggest.

How can we best explain the growing relative strength of the South in relation with the North? Any number of factors may be pointed out, including the stimulation of contact with the North through aid, trade, and investment. But the force which appears to me to constitute the single most decisive factor in the emergence of the South internationally is the growing power there of the various state organizations. To an important degree, there has always been genuine political muscle in the South on the part of the local inhabitants. For example, in the case of India, Mahatma Gandhi repeatedly insisted on the absurdity of so few Britishers—in the 1930s, some 4,000 civil servants, 60,000 soldiers, and 90,000 businessmen and clergy—billeting themselves upon a country of 300 million persons. British success depended upon a fragile network of local collaborators, including economic elites, warrior tribes, traditional power holders, and minority groups endangered by other Indians. Throughout the European colonial empires, such a brokerage system between the foreign authorities and the local population could be found. Its structure was generally a decisive influence on the character of postwar decolonization. From the rise of the Young Turks and the Chinese Republicans under Sun Yat-sen in the early years of this century, the history of political organization in the South has generally tended to confirm the power of local politicians at the expense of the international system. Vietnam and the success of OPEC are only the most dramatic signs of this process.

For the most part, dependency theorists dispute these developments. "The essence of neo-colonialism is that the State which is subject to it is, in theory, independent and has all the outward trappings of international sovereignty. In reality its economic system and thus its political policy is directed from outside." So wrote Kwame Nkrumah (1966) when he was still chief-of-state of Ghana and before he was toppled by local political opposition. Most dependency theorists subscribe to this modern expression of Marxism, which sees in ruling groups the expression of class interest, and—in finding the contemporary ruling class to be an international bourgeoisie—sees virtually all state structures, apart from those of resolutely socialist states, as tools of international capitalism.

But it is not only those with a Marxist bias who see the power of the international system throughout the fabric of southern life. The sheer magnitude of European trade with the Third World also seemed to point in the same direction. In 1820, world trade was valued at some 341 million pounds sterling, and British investments abroad—no other country engaged in such activity—totaled perhaps 10 million pounds. But by 1880 world trade topped 3 billion pounds, while British foreign investment came to some 200 million pounds and probably accounted for no better than half the European and North American investments abroad. How could such economic dynamism fail to have its impact on the preindustrial areas of the world, seen by these capitalist powers as sources of raw materials and markets as well as geostrategic stakes in rivalries centered in Europe? As a consequence, virtually any area of the South examined by the end of the nineteenth century will show the imprint of European penetration, and it is not difficult to establish a *prima facie* case for the point of view of dependency theory. However, when these various southern areas are placed side by side, and not looked at as separate cases, it is the differences among them that appear as well.

A simple comparison illustrates the point. By 1880, Argentina and Egypt each had received some 20 to 25 million pounds sterling of British investment and each was permeated with the British presence. But Egypt was on the verge of collapse (which came in 1882), while Argentina was moving into position as Great Britain's most important economic satellite in Latin America. In short, while the outward thrust of European power in the nineteenth century was generally the same (although account must be taken of geostrategic considerations), the European impact varied widely in Africa, Asia, the Middle East, and Latin America. And to understand the variety of receptions the Europeans got, it is necessary to understand local political conditions and their ability to cope with the foreign challenge. Focusing on the dynamics of European expansion, then documenting its impact on the South, is not enough.

A number of Latin Americanists recently have tried to address the question of the state in order to understand, in terms of dependency theory, the rise there of authoritarian-bureaucratic regimes since the mid-1960s. Even writers who had earlier been critical of the theory have apparently now decided it is a useful tool to comprehend this question. The general schema of their approach has run along the following lines: the international system forced a style of industrialization on Latin America (import substitution) which, by the 1950s, was playing out; the result was increased civil turmoil and a polarization of forces, with the right backed by the United States. Ultimately, this right-wing action proved successful—at least in the short run—because of the support brought to it by multinational corporations eager to invest in

Latin America once stability there was assured. The force of the international system, essentially in its economic relations, thus molded the character of the Latin American state.

Once again, however, the problem is not to determine whether the international system has affected the form of the state in Latin America—surely it has—so much as to evaluate the degree of the contribution and to see it alongside domestic factors. And it would appear that, in their concern to relate local experiences to outside influences, *dependencistas* have once again systematically underestimated the importance of internal forces. Thus, three hundred years of rule by Catholic Spain and Portugal left Latin America with a legacy of authoritarian government characterized by a corporatist ideology, patron-client relations, and regional *caudillo* authority still alive.

More recent developments have contributed still more importantly to the authoritarian governments of today. World War I and the Great Depression brought such populist leaders as Vargas in Brazil and Perón in Argentina to power, men dedicated to mass mobilization in order to curb the local power of foreigners and their local collaborators (chiefly the landed oligarchs of the export sector). In a sense, then, Latin America "decolonized" in the 1930s, with populist nationalism ascendant. The economic crises of the 1950s made these populist coalitions untenable, and the local political situations polarized. But the structures within which these events occurred had been created in a period of opposition to the international system.

Argentina and Brazil fit this pattern, but the case of Mexico is particularly illustrative: the *Partido Revolucionario Institucional* ruling Mexico since the end of the revolution of 1910–1917 (although under various names) took the most decisive steps in its institutionalization of an authoritarian corporatist structure around 1938, at the very time the Cárdenas government was dramatically expropriating American utility and oil companies in Mexico. It would thus appear that domestic factors, and not simply the dependent status of

Latin America internationally, must be respected if one is to understand the current spread of authoritarianism throughout the continent.

Of course, it would not serve our understanding of contemporary international relations to go to the other extreme from dependency theory, to assert blindly the preeminence of local factors in Third World development. For over a century now, northern trade and investment, combined with occasional military intervention, have indeed vitally affected the economic and political development of the South. Today, most of these countries depend on the international connection for military know-how and espionage services, and for aid, trade, and investment as an integral part of preserving the peace domestically and assuring regional rank. For few of these states have acquired political institutions appropriate to the social forces they must integrate and control. Geographic, ethnic, and class interests are seldom aggregated effectively through party structures, while bureaucracies, which determine the ability of governments to act competently, are often inefficient or corrupt. Conflicts with neighboring states invariably compound these problems, as regional balances of power establish themselves in the wake of decolonization. In such circumstances of incipient civil and regional upheaval, the international connection can take on great political significance. Dependency theory seems to me to be especially accurate when it speaks of the outcome of these local struggles in terms of their intersection with the forces of the international system.

The point of this chapter has not been, therefore, to deny the interconnectedness of global developments today, nor to doubt the extensive influence the North has on the South by virtue of its far greater relative power and the linkages connecting the two areas. I have tried to establish instead some measure of the South's autonomy from the North despite these factors, some respect for southern traditions, institutions, and determination, which have historical importance irrespective of northern imperialism. I have tried to indicate as well the ambiguities and contradictions of the international system, which mean that, even in those domains where the North is strong, the present logic of change may be that it is sponsoring the relative growth in power of the South.

For some two hundred years now, the industrial revolution has been spreading outward from Great Britain. Just as the first nation to gain international predominance as a result of these technological breakthroughs has passed from the center stage of history, so there is good reason to suspect that the future will see the growing importance of states still industrializing. Such developments will result in good measure from the international system itself.

Dependency theory obscures these points, making imperialism more all-pervasive and self-perpetuating than is the case. It may serve the political needs of certain groups to see the power of the North in this light, but there is no reason those of us without such needs should subscribe to a world view so distant from reality.

12

RICHARD E. BISSELL

Political Origins of
the NIEO

Economic and political assumptions behind the NIEO. Mercantile morality and the economic scapegoat in historical perspective. The dowry of emerging ex-colonies. Nationalist ambitions of Third World leaders. Machine politics and the NIEO. Funds, and the capitalist pressure of multinational corporations. The tension between economics and politics.

To the Western mind trained in capitalist economics, the "new international economic order" (NIEO) has a reasonably clear agenda: (1) stabilizing commodity prices, (2) controlling the impact of multinational corporations, (3) easing the transfer of technology to developing countries, and

(4) increasing the rate of transfer of real resources to developing countries. Despite the existence of real economic problems that fit such categories, solutions have been elusive. Discussions have avoided the underlying political disagreements. Western leaders, following their own training, have considered economic problems as discrete entities, and Third World leaders have deliberately avoided bringing their political problems onto the agenda. In doing so, negotiators find that they are frequently unable to obtain precise definitions of economic problems, and that there is not a finite conception of future economic needs in developing countries.

This chapter will contend that such imprecision derives from readily observable political problems that will never be met by narrowly construed economic discussions. By using the political bases of the NIEO, the new generations of political leadership search for economic tools to assure stability of their fragile political orders.

HISTORICAL BACKGROUND

To a large degree, the NIEO is simply a reinvention of the wheel to carry the burden of social change. NIEOs, in various forms, have been carried through at historical points in many societies, and generally as a response to unbearable social tensions. The history of the entrepreneurial middle class is one of commercial success followed by expropriation by the ruling classes. Nietzsche was not proposing a new ideology when he wrote that "Merchant and pirate were for a long period one and the same person. Even today mercantile morality is really nothing but a refinement of piratical morality."

The devastating effect of this view can be seen in many cultural examples. The Chinese evolved a code of social hierarchies during the Chou dynasty: warrior-administrators at the top, peasants second, artisans third, with merchants at the bottom so as to ensure their susceptibility to expropriation. This notion of rights and privileges was transferred to Japan as well, where the aristocracy exercised its right to confiscate a merchant's wealth when the debt of the upper class became unbearable—witness the 1705 incident when the Japanese head of state accused the Yodoya family, richest of the Osaka merchants, of "unbefitting ostentation," and took away all of their fortune (Reischauer and Fairbank 1958:55, 636). Jewish merchants in medieval Europe frequently suffered the same fate, and Ibo merchants in Nigeria encountered the same attitudes in the late 1960s.

The search for an economic scapegoat in human history is as common as crop failures, and where societies are divided into three layers, the temptation to point the finger at the middle is overwhelming. The poor can confiscate from the middleman merchant by riot, and the rich can confiscate by fiat. In the present global economy, where it is manifestly impossible to provide for the material expectations of all countries, there has been a protracted search for the middleman to blame.

The NIEO is an international attack on the middle-class entrepreneur. The curious aspect of the NIEO, however, is that the attack has been deflected from the rich countries–the greatest pressure has been brought on the Western economic interests in the Third World that play a middle-class role. The entrepreneurial, but physically powerless, roles of expatriate individuals and industries in the national societies of the Third World are being confiscated in an ages-old move to deal with social and political unrest. In the short term, Third World leaders need to find economic scapegoats to explain the unfulfilled expectations to their own people; the long-term effect is to reduce the role of international entrepreneurship, as all commerce is subjected to strict governmental control through each aspect of the NIEO.

Economic nationalism is not a new issue. The growth of autarky in the 1930s is acknowledged to have undermined world peace. Many factors have contributed to this autarky in the 1970s, some economic and some political. The economic

forces are considered in another chapter. Two political forces
will be examined here: the generational changes in the Third
World, and the drive for stability by Third World leaderships
in shaky nationalistic orders.

THE GENERATION OF THE NIEO

The essential problem of political generations was indicated
by Harold Isaacs (1977:39–56), when he noted that the move
from power-seeking to power-wielding required leaders ''to
cross the great divide between nationalist dreams and national
realities.'' In effect, ''romantic nationalism'' gave way to
more mundane forces, with Third World elites not fully understanding the extent of the transformation. Those elites felt
that it would be possible for the former colonial powers to
transfer tangible resources as readily as they had handed over
the symbolic trappings of independence. And, for some time
after independence, the West did transfer aid and support in a
vague gesture of atonement for the colonial period, and in the
naive belief that the decolonized areas might need a simple
dowry to be pushed along the road to rapid economic development.

Such aid, on a meaningful scale, lasted only until the Vietnam war and 1973 oil crisis. After all, the ambivalence of the
West about colonialism—a political order quickly abandoned
when the costs of maintaining it put any stress on political
and economic tranquility in the metropoles—took an entirely
different form with regard to gifts to former colonies. The
developed countries of both East and West are not eager to
give away something for nothing, and certainly not in
exchange for Third World ideological attacks on
''neocolonialism.'' The current arguments of the NIEO involve both demands for tangible assets and attacks on the
legitimacy of Western capitalism, but the developed states
cannot concede ground on either issue without imperiling
their domestic orders.

A "sea change" is occurring in the training and education of the emerging generation of Third World leaders. Those who took power at the time of independence had been educated in the West—not necessarily at the best universities, but that was not essential. It was a virtual prerequisite that nationalist leaders spend some extended time abroad, forming linkages with exiled fellow nationalists from their own countries and others. The leaders to whom the West was willing to transfer power were those who could speak and understand the vocabulary of Western ideals and institutions. The formative experience achieved by spending years in exile in another, powerful culture with universal influence created a sense of vision in early nationalists that enabled them to transcend many of the discouraging aspects of economic backwardness in their own societies. That distance between the leaders and the people injected a dynamism into the societies that resulted in change and growth.

The leadership class now emerging in much of the Third World, however, is increasingly home-grown. Thirty years have passed since much of Asia achieved independence, and nearly twenty years for most of Africa. Today, time spent abroad is kept to a minimum, for politics has been domesticated. During the tenure of General Acheampong as Ghanaian head of state (1973–1978), people in Accra joked about his unwillingness to travel further than Togo. But the general replied that it had nothing to do with politics or threats to his rule; he simply had no desire to go further.

Domesticated politics also means that aspirant leaders need to remain at home for their training. Even among the military, the focus is increasingly domestic—witness the fall-off of interest in Latin America for the Canal Zone school run by the United States for young officers. The growth of service academies and universities in the Third World in the 1960s and 1970s is phenomenal. Inevitably, independence meant founding national universities. The University of Khartoum was established in the Sudan in 1956; in the Ivory Coast, the University of Abidjan in 1964. In Malaysia, universities were founded in 1962, 1969, 1970, and 1973; and in Nigeria, only the university at Ibadan existed at independence, yet by 1975 the number had increased to fourteen. To an increasing degree, potential Third World leaders, both civilian and military, are educated at home, and sent abroad only for brief technical training. There is thus no tendency to internalize a Western code of civil and military behavior as had been done by many of the leaders at independence. Ironically, many such "national universities" were funded in the past and currently by universities and philanthropies in the metropoles—with apparently little regard for the ultimate political impact of such training.

A second feature of this emerging generation of leaders is their lack of interest in capitalist incentives. The reasons for this are several: the failure to spend extended time in the West, leading to little intuitive understanding of the workings of a capitalist economy; the ideology of decolonization, which contained the germ of anticapitalism, for any aspect of the colonial social order is seen as anathema; a general lack of respect for the concept of contract, the foundation stone of a capitalist economic order (see Bozeman 1971); and, perhaps most important, the desire to remove power centers that are potential rivals to the young national governments. Thus, both Third World calls for *authenticité,* reversion to traditional (non-Western) values, and the reaction against European and Western economic institutions are clearly related to a global antagonism toward capitalism. A working capitalist system requires a respect for the long term, a willingness to commit people and resources for the future, an ability to organize a society sufficiently to carry out those commitments, and the strength to compete in an open economic framework. On all four scores, much of the Third World drops by the wayside. Some governments have taken up the challenge—Brazil, Korea, Kenya, the ASEAN (Association of Southeast Asian Nations) states, and others—but in many cases the experiences of the last several decades have eroded the interest of the weaker, domestically oriented leaders in a capitalist order.

The West went through several phases to reach a functioning capitalist system, including a number of aborted efforts. Thus, there is no reason to assume that the Third World in general will *not* eventually become as capitalist as the West. The creation of numerous fragile political entities since the second world war, however, has established obstacles to the capitalist development of many societies. Economic power rivals political power, and insecure politicians will exclude the rival entrepreneurial forces to insure their survival. Of greatest interest to us, however, is the absence of conditions in many new nations even to participate in an international capitalist order. Consider, for example, the abrogation of contracts in the last few years in the area of long-term debt. North Korea has simply suspended all debt repayments. Negotiations for rescheduling debts have become routine; the estimated value of multilateral debt reschedulings has risen from about $100 million in 1960 to $800 million annually in the post-1973 period. Such depreciation of debts is a cause for real concern, though not despair. After all, in the nineteenth century both the United States and Russia defaulted with remarkable frequency on European loans (particularly those to railroad-building operations); in one case, the U.S. continued its growth to become the premier capitalist society, and, in the other, the capitalist order was demolished.

One must differentiate within the Third World. Some societies have the underlying values to create, eventually, a competitive capitalist order, and others do not. In 1923, the president *emeritus* of Yale, Dr. Arthur T. Hadley (1923:36–37), wrote of the character of Americans who developed the Western United States:

They were accustomed to judge men by what they did and not by what they professed. And this saved them from intolerance. They were enthusiastically devoted to their country and to its government; but they asked little of that government except that it should protect land titles and appoint honest judges. They were admirably fitted by temperament and training to carry the theory of free competition to its logical conclusion and reach the kind of result which Adam Smith or John Stuart Mill would have predicted.

In the Third World today there are echoes of that spirit; in both Brazil and South Africa, for instance, there have been calls by significant elites within the last year for a reduction in governmental control after periods of directed economic growth. Their interest in the international welfare state known as NIEO is of marginal importance.

A third feature of the present generation of Third World leaders is their response to the problem of governing polyethnic societies. At the time of independence, many Third World leaders inherited political institutions without any domestic legitimacy. In subsequent years, "coming to terms" with the lack of domestic support has resulted in several different kinds of politics: totalitarianism in some cases (with dubious prospects for longevity), and in others, machine politics, which attempts to create a political consensus among ethnic groups. The hallmarks of such political systems are patronage, favors, bribery, and other responses to particularistic needs that Westerners would term less-desirable politics. But both Aristide Zolberg (1966) and Myron Weiner (1962), scholarly observers of different areas of the Third World, have appropriately identified the utility of the political machine in bringing traditional populations into the same political system (see also Scott 1969:1142–58). The political machines compensate for the fact that formal legislative mechanisms cannot channel the demands of traditional population groups unfamiliar with democratic, individualistic politics. In providing readily available bargaining groups on domestic political and economic issues, the political machine may not replicate the parliamentary politics of the developed West, but, for the Third World, it is better than no politics at all—i.e., disintegration of the state, or the indefinite perpetuation of authoritarian rule.

What interests us here, however, are the implications of machine politics for the new international economic order. They fall into several categories.

(a) Since corrupt politics operates at a deficit, the machine politics of the Third World must be subsidized. The price of bringing people into the political process is usually monetary, and the ability of new governments to raise money (presumably through taxation) is limited. Keeping people involved in a political machine requires the government to have more money to hand out to the people than it takes from them. If the government operates without a deficit, in fact, the people will see no vested interest in working within the political system (since their needs are short term), and they are close enough to the subsistence level to ignore the government. In that way, postcolonial attempts in the Third World to continue the European practice of squeezing excess capital out of the farmers has frequently failed, as the farmer simply moved his produce across the border for better prices. At present, Ghanaian farmers are carrying 50,000 to 100,000 tons of cocoa across the border illegally each year.

Governments faced by such challenges have three choices: do nothing, extort produce from farmers by force (rarely successful), or obtain financial support from overseas to pay farmers *and* grease the wheels of corrupt urban politics. There are exceptions, of course: the OPEC (Organization of Petroleum Exporting Countries) nations were in the enviable position of extorting money from oil importers after 1973, and some nations have economic sense. A recent report by *West Africa* noted that "the Liberian economy has been badly hit by falling prices for iron ore—its principal export. Government revenue is, surprisingly, standing up well in spite of this because of improved methods of tax gathering and because of high agricultural yields and prices." Liberian politics, of course, has been accumulating legitimacy far longer than most Third World governments, simply by longevity of existence.

(b) In the urban areas, Europeans have been replaced by Third World personnel, with important side effects. During the colonial period, various implicit subsidies of colonial op-

erations existed—for example, in the form of retirement benefits for expatriate civil servants. Thus, salaries did not have
to be appreciably higher than European standards to attract
personnel, for there was a long-term assurance of financial
security from the metropole. Two conditions have changed.
First, external assurance no longer exists for indigenous personnel, and with the credit-worthiness of many governments
uncertain, governmental elites in the Third World are tempted
to establish private pension plans (Swiss bank accounts, family industries) as compensation. Second, politics is routinely
turbulent, which suggests to elites that their tenure in office
will be short. The societies are not seen to hold the solutions
to their economic problems in their own hands, and given the
vagaries of international politics and aid flows, any disruption
can cause the fall of public leaders. Thus, the accumulation
of "retirement funds" must be done in a short time, leading
to greater demands on the political machine. It is now unusual for a leader to be removed without public discussion of
financial irregularities.

(c) The instability of external sources of funds for political
machines in the Third World has led to startling snatching of
new sources of revenue. The evolution of the widespread
nationalization of assets owes much to the demands of local
political machines. The need for jobs can be satisfied in part
by placing people in staff positions in nationalized firms.
Short-term cash requirements can be aided by retaining formerly repatriated profits inside the country—at the disposal of
the government. The need to pay off foreign owners can be
avoided by issuing bonds, and then renegotiating the debt.
And the rival power centers represented by foreign investors
that dominate the cash economies of small Third World countries are thus eliminated. In the process, the infrastructure of
power built by foreign entrepreneurs is placed at the disposal
of the government and the political machine.

The only problem, of course, is that long-term growth suffers, as foreign capitalists lose interest in further investment.
Nevertheless, the purposes of the political machine are

fulfilled: short-term political gains at the cost of long-term economic growth. Unfortunately, the logical end result of such historical momentum has already happened: Uganda has been reduced to the position of an international bartering agent, with planes carrying twice-weekly loads of coffee beans to Britain, and returning with equal amounts of palace goods and essential spare parts.

THE SEARCH FOR STABILITY

For their own survival, Third World leaders attempt to channel all foreign influences through governmental mechanisms. The enhancement of political legitimacy is their overriding objective. Some nations rode the tiger of economic growth and social change, and have been successful. Others went for the ride and, to paraphrase the limerick, came back inside. The message from the latter no longer reflects an abiding devotion to economic growth; their dominant concern is regime-survival. They feel it would be better for their nations' links with the international system to atrophy than for the government to lose control of them. The international marketplace is a cacophony of events that cannot be understood, and the flow of those events must be slowed down by governmental controls. These leaders want to restrict the number of foreign influences in their countries, for even the leadership cadre is confused by the number and complexity of foreign economic influences. The influences of such an outlook on the NIEO are quite evident.

Regarding commodities, the Third World attempts to stabilize export earnings. Since political machines cannot put aside surplus earnings for difficult years, and long-term planning is discouraged, periodic declines in commodity prices precipitate political crises in exporting countries. People with marginal loyalty to the national government are rarely willing to absorb the costs of such export shortfalls themselves, and most governments are not sufficiently developed to enforce the sharing of hard times by the entire population. In such circumstances, the fragile political coalitions that govern most Third World countries must obtain major subsidies in times of export shortfalls, or the political coalitions themselves will fall.

The existence of low internal savings rates exacerbates the situation, by restricting the possibilities for financing long-term investment. The people have come to expect governments even to undertake savings plans for the nations. Until "thrift" is given a higher priority in the Third World, as opposed to the present emphasis on "consumption," the developing countries are unlikely to see the transformations of their economies that they so ardently desire. Stabilizing commodity prices ensures consistent levels of consumption-oriented incomes in the Third World—in those well-managed economies, it ensures long-term investment programs—without people having to undertake individual and national measures to cushion the impact of international recessions.

The NIEO also attempts to limit the role of multinational corporations (MNCs) in the global economy. As already mentioned, MNCs threaten the stability of regimes unequipped to deal with the capitalist system. MNCs, in addition, are seen as agents of the former colonial powers, and the goal is to eliminate MNC influence as thoroughly as the world was decolonized. But if the Third World must rely in the long run only on governments and intergovernmental institutions for the necessary investment, they had better be a patient lot. Regime stability and removal of external influences can be achieved, but at a major economic cost.

A major part of the NIEO program deals with the transfer of technology from the developed countries to the Third World. The attempts to regulate such transfers, whether through a generalized "code of conduct," or the establishment of national screening boards for the import of technology, are additional manifestations of distrust for the capitalist process. There is an abiding suspicion that the Third World is somehow paying "too high a price" for imported technology—and that suspicion is heightened by a general insensitivity to the costs of research and development for new technology (similar to the ignorance of the need for internal savings). The desire to coordinate technology imports at the national level is one more effort to increase the "channeling" role of the political leadership. In many cases, as shown in recent American congressional testimony, such government screenings are actually smokescreens for discreet bribe demands. Those societies with policies of open technology imports, as in Asia, have also been showcases of economic growth.

The last NIEO issue of political importance to the Third World is the transfer of real resources on an increasing scale. The financing of new political elites and growing political machines is becoming more burdensome all the time. If population projections are accurate, the provision of basic services in Third World cities will be a staggering job. The degree of potential social disorder represented by urban populations is a frightening statistic for any Third World leader, for a person in an urban area is, by definition, a political influence. The money to preserve social order, through the mechanism of local political machines, is rarely being generated internally.

A variety of sleights of hand have been devised to finance Third World stability. The Third World has proposed, at the law-of-the-sea conferences, that revenues from mining of minerals on the seabed be turned over to them, either directly or through the United Nations. The proposal has not been accepted. In the proceedings of the International Monetary Fund, it was suggested that the creation of special drawing rights (SDRs) be an occasion for giving newly created SDRs to Third World states as one-time donations. A variety of measures were undertaken after 1973 to renegotiate long-term and short-term debts of some countries, as they began to fail to meet interest payments on an increased scale. A special list of the "most needy"—and informally designated the "fourth world"—was published by the United Nations as a focus of special attention, with the latest proposal being the outright cancellation of all debts held by those countries. Only the Scandinavians and British have done so.

Yet there was no proposal, possibly of even greater logic, to suggest that the ''most needy'' might not have the attributes of sovereignty, and should therefore be placed under a state of trusteeship by the United Nations. Such a condition is admitted informally, as French advisors now run the ministries in Chad, Soviet advisors operate the Afghan government, and the operational ministries in Angola are Cuban-staffed. But in formal international negotiations, the only system on the agenda is the manifestly successful economic system of the West—no offer has been made for concessions in the political system of the Third World.

The shape of the NIEO demonstrates the rudimentary awareness among even the poorest of Third World leaders that economic assets can be converted into political power (see Tyler 1977; Bhagwati 1977; Feulner 1976; Sauvant and Hasenpflug 1977). The golden goose must be carefully tended, however, even while stealing the eggs of gold. The NIEO comes close, even without being implemented, to damaging permanently the global economic machine that produced the wealth the Third World so much wants to share.

It is unfortunate that the political pressures underlying the demands of the NIEO are likely to increase in the short term. The conflicts between Third World states, and between them and the developed states, can lead to horribly destructive violence. Where economic systems have been destroyed in the past by political and social irresponsibility, it has taken centuries to put them back together again.

13

NATHANIEL H. LEFF

Beyond the New
International Order*

**Price stability of Third World exports. Resource transfers and
the international income gap. The use of advanced technology
by less-developed countries. The value of improved access to
export markets. The role of multinational corporations. Diplomatic negotiating skill by Third World leaders—hostility or
cooperation? The failure of the Alliance for Progress. The importance of autonomous development. The strain of increased
oil prices on Third World economy. Eurocurrency loans.
Ideological shifts in the U.S.**

*I am grateful to the editors of *Foreign Policy* for permission to utilize here materials which I previously published in that journal.

The call of the developing countries for the creation of a New International Economic Order (NIEO) has aroused widespread interest. Some observers have indeed advocated that the new order be made the centerpiece of future economic and political relations between the United States and the Third World. Before making such a commitment, however, it is worth considering what would be the likely effects if the measures of the NIEO are, in fact, implemented. Such an analysis is the first purpose of this chapter. We then consider the major economic and political shifts which have affected the less-developed countries (LDCs) and the United States since 1972, when the NIEO first received widespread attention. These changes have had important effects on the place of the NIEO in the international policy agenda.

For reasons discussed below, U.S. acceptance of the NIEO would soon lead to a worsening, rather than an improvement, of political relations with the Third World. The prognosis for the economic effects is equally pessimistic. Implementation of the various policy changes which are contemplated—increases and indexation for prices of primary products, vastly expanded resource transfers to the Third World, assured access to technology and markets in the rich countries, and the unquestioned right of LDCs to restructure their relations with multinational corporations—will not lead to substantial economic gains for the Third World. These conclusions may not be intuitively self-evident, so let us examine the reasoning which underlies them.

COMMODITY AGREEMENTS

International agreements to raise and stabilize the prices of raw material products exported by the developing countries have been a prominent theme in the new order. The success of producer cartels in oil and in bauxite has stimulated interest in similar programs for copper, tin, nickel, and primary products in general. In some cases, such cartels may be implemented by Third World exporting countries acting on their own. Financial backing from the Organization of Petroleum Exporting Countries (OPEC) members with excess cash would, of course, increase the feasibility of price support arrangements in more commodities. And active support from the industrialized countries might in principle raise the prices of virtually all primary products in relation to prices of manufactured products.

The potential difficulties involved in maintaining such price support arrangements are clear. Higher and more stable returns will evoke a large increase in world production of primary products. In commodities in which one or two countries are dominant suppliers to the world economy, these countries may be willing to limit supply in the interest of maintaining higher prices. Such curtailment of production is especially feasible if, as in the case of petroleum, the commodities in question are produced in sparsely populated countries without pressing financial needs. Otherwise, however, an International Price Stabilization Agency will be hard pressed to prevent prices from falling, as supply of primary products increases more rapidly than does demand in world markets. Let us assume, however, that with a spirit of international cooperation, and with ample financial support from the more-developed countries, such problems can be resolved. What would be the effects on the Third World of an increase and indexation of commodity prices relative to prices of industrial products?

It is a misconception, of course, to identify primary product production with the less-developed countries, and industrial production with the more-developed countries. In some commodities—for example, cotton, iron ore, and (beet) sugar—countries like the United States, Australia, and France are major international producers. With higher world prices for primary products, more-developed countries may well increase their production of these products (or of substitutes), raising the rich countries' share in world trade or, at the least, replacing their own imports from Third World suppliers.

Sufficiently comprehensive international agreements might, of course, bar such perverse effects stemming from a new international order. More important, however, most Third World countries import as well as export primary products. Consequently, the effects of higher commodity prices on individual developing countries will depend on the price increases which are sustained in specific commodities, and on the composition of each LDC's exports and imports. Taking account of the effects of increased *import* prices on developing countries, the net impact of a higher overall level of commodity prices on many Third World countries is likely to be far less favorable than they may expect. The quantitative effects of commodity agreements on income and growth in the developing countries seem to have been seriously oversold.

INCREASED RESOURCE TRANSFERS

The NIEO would also involve a large increase in resource transfers from the rich to the poor countries. A likely figure for Official Development Assistance under the NIEO would be 0.7 percent of the gross national product of the more-developed countries, a target which Sweden has already attained. The magnitude of the effective increase in aid will, of course, be larger if the more-developed countries accede to another request of the developing countries: cancellation of outstanding Third World debts. For the United States, acceptance of these proposals would involve a rise in public capital flows to a figure greater than $14 billion per annum, more than a tripling of aid from its present levels.

Some observers may question congressional willingness to accept so large an increase in aid. Moreover, the conceptual differences from the present aid program involve a shift which is even greater than the change in dollar magnitudes. To facilitate long-term planning in recipient countries, aid would be granted on the basis of a continuing commitment, not subject to congressional vagaries. And, to avoid the manipulation and dependency relations which marred earlier aid relationships, public capital would now be provided without political strings or administrative control. Finally, far from expecting "gratitude" from Third World countries, Congress would be expected to commit aid within a framework of redressing past and present inequities in the international distribution of income.

All of this seems highly unlikely. But let us assume that these problems can be overcome. What would be the likely effects of a massive increase in resource transfers on the international income gap?

A measure of increased aid would undoubtedly accelerate the pace of economic development in many Third World countries. Increases in aid on the scale contemplated by the NIEO, however, are unlikely to yield commensurate increases in economic growth. Because of human resource and managerial constraints, the capacity to absorb a large volume of investment productively is usually limited (Eckaus 1973). Reflecting limited absorptive capacity, as more and more aid is made available, Third World countries will exhaust their portfolio of high-return investments, and invest in marginal projects which contribute little to growth.

The possibilities for using resource transfers to narrow the international income gap are also limited by other conditions. As proponents of aid have long recognized, on standard Keynesian grounds, a government commitment to a steady flow of aid may well accelerate the pace of economic growth in the more-developed countries. This may exacerbate inequality in the international distribution of income. For, as is well known, the absolute size of the income gap widens if the rich and the poor countries grow at the *same* rate. Further, the prospects for using aid to induce international convergence also depend on such conditions as the pace of population growth in the Third World, and the size of the present difference in income levels between the rich and the poor countries. Given the magnitude of these key parameters, it would be naïve to expect that increased resource transfers will narrow the international income gap perceptibly within a time horizon which is politically meaningful.

IMPROVED ACCESS TO TECHNOLOGY AND MARKETS

Third World leaders have also emphasized the need for improved access to the advanced technology developed in the rich countries. Compliance with these demands will do little to close the international technology gap, however, unless the LDCs implement certain changes in their own policies. Thus, the knowledge and technology necessary to raise agricultural productivity in some crops has, in fact, been available to Third World leaders for years. They have often failed, however, to create extension services, or to follow the input and output pricing policies which are necessary to diffuse the new technology widely among their agricultural producers. A similar failure to diffuse advanced technology which is already available exists in the industrial sector of many developing countries. Government policies in the allocation of credit and foreign exchange have often created a "dualistic" pattern, in which some firms utilize advanced technology and others use backward techniques. This internal technological gap within many Third World countries would not be ameliorated by the measures of the new order.

The demand that the rich countries make their technology more accessible to developing countries has widespread appeal. It is not always clear, however, how implementation of these demands would work in practice. Third World countries already *have* access to advanced technology from numerous sources, such as the consulting and engineering companies which exist in many advanced countries. And, as the relationship between A. D. Little and the government of Algeria testifies, such consulting firms have been willing to serve the aspirations even of radical countries in the Third World. Moreover, the number of international consulting firms and potential supplying countries is sufficiently large to preclude effective collusion with respect to price or inattention to client needs. Because of these conditions, a Third World country which wants to acquire the advanced technology necessary to build and operate, say, a steel mill or a fertilizer plant can, in fact, do so. Even in more sensitive and esoteric areas, supply conditions are such that China has purchased advanced technology for undersea petroleum prospecting (see Harrison 1975).

In addition to consulting firms, LDCs at present have available licensing agreements, management contracts, and turnkey projects as alternative sources of advanced technology. Developing countries have complained that the fees charged by such suppliers are excessive. A new order might, in principle, reduce charges. Note, however, that within the present international system, the governments of developing countries can intervene in negotiations for the transfer of technology, and press for lower payments and more favorable terms. Even such moderate Third World countries as Mexico and Colombia have already implemented such an interventionist policy, and report large savings in their payments for imported technology.

Further, the measures usually proposed to improve access to advanced technology will do little to help the LDCs achieve another major goal—increasing their competitive capacity in relation to multinational corporations. The multinationals' competitive edge depends not only on sophisticated production technology, but also on management techniques in marketing and accounting. Thus, the most advanced production facilities installed in Third World countries will not yield their economic potential if Third World managers do not utilize modern accounting techniques to control productivity, cash balances, and inventories. Third World leaders have shown little interest in acquiring and diffusing such accounting techniques—which are, of course, easily accessible. The relative unimportance of production technology per se can perhaps best be illustrated with some examples. The Third World already possesses the know-how necessary to produce ball-point pens, rubber-soled canvas shoes, and carbonated beverages. Nevertheless, Parker pens, Ked shoes, and Coca Cola are often preferred products in developing countries. The explanation lies not in the multinational corporations' superior production technology, but rather in their marketing techniques. Implementation of the NIEO will do little to change this situation.

Acceptance of another Third World demand—improved access to export markets in the rich countries—would, however, make an important difference for the pace of economic development, at least in some Third World countries. Greater export sales, facilitated by tariff preferences for developing countries and an end to shameful non-tariff barriers in the more-developed countries, would have a number of beneficial effects. With greater foreign exchange earnings, developing countries could import the larger volume of capital goods and raw materials necessary to sustain more rapid growth of output, income, and employment. There is also evidence that domestic saving in developing countries increases with greater exports, so that more domestic capital formation would also be feasible. Finally, export growth in manufactured products would enable producers in developing countries to attain economies of scale, lowering costs and permitting many consumer products to be brought within the reach of broader masses of the local population.

Notwithstanding these important benefits from improved market access, we should also note some potential problems. Some developing countries are more industrialized than others. Brazil or Taiwan, for example, would be better able than, say, Ghana or Sri Lanka to take advantage of the opportunities which tariff preferences would open for expanding sales in the rich countries. Consequently, a generalized tariff preference scheme might not help all—or, indeed, many—developing countries. The more industrialized Third World countries will appropriate the lion's share of the benefits, with little accruing to most Third World countries. Another possibility would be to equalize opportunities for the diverse set of LDCs by creating categories for differential rates of tariff preference. Such a system would not be easy to administer. It would also involve rivalry between Third World countries, and an opportunity for the rich countries to exercise "leverage" against individual developing countries by controlling access to their domestic markets. These political effects of equalizing opportunities would go counter to the whole spirit of the new order.

Further, the place of multinational corporations in improved market access would also have to be clarified. As is well known, despite the many barriers which they encounter, exports of manufactured products from the LDCs to OECD (Organization of Economic Cooperation and Development) countries have, in fact, grown rapidly over the past twenty-five years. Multinational corporations with "sourcing" subsidiaries located in the Third World have had a large role in this expansion of manufactured exports from developing countries. Presumably, multinational corporations with subsidiaries in the Third World would also want to participate in the advantages of generalized tariff preferences. Note also that in negotiations over such participation, multinational corporations have an important bargaining card which is not under the control of the Third World—the possibility of direct sales to their companies' worldwide production and marketing network. Inclusion of multinational corporations in the benefits of improved market access, however, is not what Third World leaders mean when they speak of a new order.

MULTINATIONAL CORPORATIONS

A major redressing of the balance of forces between Third World governments and multinational corporations is, of course, a prominent theme of the NIEO. The proposed restructuring is reflected clearly in the *United Nations Charter of Economic Rights and Duties of Nations*. Article 2 of the charter declares unequivocally that every state has the right:

To nationalize, expropriate, or transfer ownership of foreign property in which case appropriate compensation should be paid by the State adopting such measures, taking into account its relevant laws and regulations and all circumstances that the State considers pertinent.

These provisions may be juridically unimpeachable. In the present context, however, the question is: what would implementation of these conditions imply for the Third World's economic development?

The present lack of international legal sanction for nationalization on terms they themselves decide has not been a major factor deterring Third World countries from expropriating multinational corporations. Rather, in cases where Third World governments have been deterred, it has been mainly because they have felt that they would lose more than they would gain. And, in the post-Suez world, the potential losses to be considered are largely economic—the inflow of new investment and international credits. The numerous examples of expropriations successfully carried out in recent years suggest that, with favorable economic conditions, developing countries will nationalize as they see fit. Universal acceptance of Article 2 in the new order will not change very much in the actual practice of Third World governments.

Increasing juridical recognition of the right of Third World countries to expropriate and compensate as they like will, however, enhance the legitimacy of such actions. Consequently, the NIEO would increase the risk which multinational corporations perceive in the developing countries. This will affect their decisions with respect to new investments and to existing activities in the Third World. Confronted with increased legitimacy for discretionary expropriation, foreign companies will hardly be motivated to take a long-term perspective in efforts at investment, human-resource development, and technology transfer. Further, greater risk can also be expected to reduce the flow of new investment to the Third World. As some Third World governments have seen, imposing conditions which worsen the investment climate for multinational corporations in their countries is often feasible. Unless their country is blessed with special resources like petroleum, however, the LDC government cannot also be assured that foreign firms will actually invest in the country.

From some perspectives, a sharp decline in multinational corporate investment in developing countries might be a good thing. It is unlikely, however, to accelerate the pace of economic development in the Third World. That foreign multinational corporations can be a powerful force for economic development can best be inferred from the behavior of some governments which have been without foreign investment, and which now solicit it actively—for example, Egypt, and East Bloc countries. The experience of India is also instructive here. India has been very successful in safeguarding its rights *vis-à-vis* multinational corporations. For example, because the government considered inequitable the division of the gains which it was offered, it has rejected more than one proposal by foreign firms to build modern fertilizer factories in India. The Indian experience also indicates, however, that independence from multinational corporations is not always associated with economic and technological dynamism. Implementation of the new order's principles with respect to multinational corporations may be expected to lead to a generalization of the "Indian model" to other Third World countries.

THE OVERALL ECONOMIC IMPACT

We can now summarize our discussion concerning the likely effects which the New International Economic Order would have on economic development in the Third World. An increase in public resource transfers to the developing countries would certainly be helpful. Because of limited absorptive capacity, however, increases in aid on the scale contemplated should not be expected to yield commensurate acceleration in the pace of economic development. Other measures such as assured access to technology developed in the rich countries will change little in substance unless developing countries revise some of their internal policies. Similarly, acceptance of the right of Third World governments to nationalize multinational corporations as they see fit will also modify little, for juridical considerations have not been the operative constraint on Third World decisions in this area.

Other new order policies, such as improved access to export markets in the rich countries, can be expected to yield major benefits to some Third World countries and negligible gains to others. Measures to raise prices of primary products will also have differential effects on various developing countries. Individual commodities vary greatly in the extent to which they satisfy the ideal conditions for a Third World producers' cartel; for example, in the availability of substitute products, in the participation of rich countries as competitive suppliers, and in the possibilities for controlling production. Consequently, the price rise which is sustainable will vary between different primary commodities. Moreover, developing countries import as well as export primary commodities. Hence, the net gains to individual Third World countries will be appreciably less than the rise in overall commodity prices.

The foregoing leads to a basic conclusion concerning the likely economic effects of the New International Economic Order. Implementation of the various measures which comprise the NIEO will not lead to a marked narrowing of the international income gap, or to the major economic gains which Third World leaders have been led to expect.

POLITICAL RELATIONS

One may well object that the preceding discussion has missed the essence of the story: the New International Economic Order has to do less with economics than with politics. Thus, it has been suggested, elites in the Third World may have little interest in such Western values as economic growth. Rather, Third World pressures for a new order are essentially an effort at emotional gratification and enhanced status. Consequently, gestures of accommodation on the part of the United States and the more-developed countries would answer their needs. And even if the NIEO did little for the developing countries economically, United States support for such policies would have the enormous benefit of improving political relations with the Third World. In this perspective, even if it yields no economic benefits to the Third World, a new order may be amply justified by giving several years of respite to American officials who must deal with the developing countries.

These views may have a great deal of validity. They also have important limitations. For, although some Third World elites may disdain economic growth per se, they may nevertheless be keenly interested in some things which economic growth permits. Furthermore, in view of the rapid increase of population in the developing countries, pressures will inevitably make themselves felt for more jobs. Economic growth can be helpful in creating additional employment opportunities. Willy-nilly, Third World leaders must be concerned with economic growth or its absence. Consequently, it does not seem productive to base United States relations toward the developing countries on a set of policies—the new order—which will do little to accelerate economic developments.

Furthermore, it is hardly realistic to assume that Third World leaders can be appeased by gestures of accommodation. American policymakers may believe that, by accepting negotiations on the new order, they can use talk to deflect Third World pressures. Such an approach would involve a serious underestimate of the competence of Third World diplomacy. Leaders of the developing countries are fully capable of understanding such stalling tactics. They can also be expected to use such negotiations to their own advantage. Recent experience in negotiations with Third World countries, beginning with Teheran in 1971, suggests that Third World negotiators have, in fact, been far more skillful than some observers in the more-developed countries ever expected. Those observers have apparently underestimated the negotiating prowess of the developing countries, and missed the masterly diplomatic skill which is the reality behind the rhetoric of Third World spokespersons.

Exhibiting this skill, Third World diplomats have already executed the classic maneuver of isolating the "extremists" (U.S. conservatives) and aligning many "moderates" (U.S. progressives) and opinion leaders on their side of the new order debate. The LDCs can be expected to be no less adroit in actual negotiations on a new order. Consequently, such negotiations are likely to take on their own momentum, and to lead to concessions much more far-reaching than American policymakers may expect. Alternatively, negotiations will degenerate into a forum and focus for Third World hostility against the United States.

Finally, and perhaps most seriously over the longer term, United States acceptance of the principles and measures which constitute the new order would itself raise economic expectations in the Third World. For the reasons discussed earlier, however, the actual experience under the new order is not likely to satisfy these hopes. Such a conjunction of heightened expectations and poor experience can be expected to generate disillusion and frustration in the Third World, leading to markedly worsened relations with the United States. If the new order leads to such an outcome, it would hardly serve American political goals.

LEARNING FROM EXPERIENCE

The scenario outlined above may seem unnecessarily pessimistic. It is supported, however, by the denouement of an
earlier experience of United States policy toward Third World
countries, the Alliance for Progress. In that case, too, the
United States reacted to a perceived challenge (Fidel Castro)
by switching from rejection to espousal of ideas and measures
which Latin American leaders had earlier propounded. The
alliance was duly launched, in an atmosphere of good intentions and dedication to a new era in U.S.–Latin American
relations. Further, the United States committed itself to provide $20 billion—a large sum in terms of preinflationary pur-
chasing power—in order to accelerate economic and social
development in Latin America. The alliance also embodied
significant multilateral elements (the *Comité Interamericano
Alianza para el Progreso* [CIAP], the Inter-American Development Bank, and support for the Latin American Free
Trade Association). It also contained important institutional
innovations, such as the Social Development Trust Fund and
the Peace Corps.

The Alliance for Progress may well have helped promote
important economic achievements in Latin America.
Nevertheless, and notwithstanding its good intentions, we
must recognize that the alliance failed to achieve its political
objectives. The effects in terms of relations between the
United States and Latin America were distinctly negative.
Promulgation of the alliance led to heightened expectations.
These could not be sustained, and in Latin America the alliance was soon judged a failure. The ensuing aftermath of
disillusion led to a souring of United States/Latin American
relations.

The experience with the Alliance for Progress suggests
three important conclusions which are relevant in the present

context. First, the United States cannot assure, by its own policies, satisfactory economic and social development in Third World countries—policies implemented by the developing countries themselves are also necessary. Second, to the extent that the United States (or a multilateral agency such as a regional development bank) attempts to influence the developing countries to implement such policies, it creates an intrusive, dependency relation which is intolerable to local elites. Finally, to prevent disillusion and ensuing hostility, the United States should not promise what it cannot deliver. In this perspective, United States acceptance of the New International Economic Order appears even less desirable for political than for economic reasons.

U.S. POLICY AND THE THIRD WORLD

Humanitarian reasons suggest that it would be desirable for the United States to offer international aid that would reduce pauperism in the poorest developing countries. As the efforts at famine relief in Ethiopia show, however, such measures may not always be feasible. Effective administration of large-scale humanitarian programs may well conflict with the preference of Third World elites for autonomy, and for an end to foreign meddling in their affairs. U.S. acceptance of such measures as the International Development Association (IDA) and improved access to markets in the rich countries would also be useful, particularly if they are *not* cast in a new order framework which would raise Third World expectations.

It would also be helpful for the United States to convey to Third World elites the postcolonial perception that their countries' economic and social progress depends most fundamentally on their own decisions with respect to mobilization and utilization of their domestic resources. Such an approach does not imply bleak prospects for development in Third World countries. As in the past, Third World countries which maintain development-oriented investment and exchange-rate policies will experience economic growth. And if autonomy and self-esteem rather than renewed dependency are the object, economic development which is achieved through domestic efforts will be all the more meaningful.

It may well be disagreeable for American spokespersons to address Third World leaders on the virtues of self-help in such areas as domestic saving, internal technology policy, and exchange rates. Americans who find uncongenial a stress on self-reliance rather than external support for development can, however, draw intellectual and ideological support from the works of radical political economists, who have also emphasized the advantages for Third World countries of autonomous development rather than international entrapments (see, for example, Amin 1974). The Chinese, too, have advocated an ideology urging self-help on Third World countries which seek meaningful development. Ideological legitimacy and support from the Chinese for the United States in a reorientation of American economic policies toward the Third World could prove to be an unexpected benefit of the Washington-Peking rapprochement.

Finally, for the reasons we have discussed, U.S. acceptance of the NIEO would soon lead to worsened political relations with the Third World. At the same time, the NIEO would do little for economic development. Indeed, by diverting developing countries from necessary policy measures which are within their own control, the NIEO might well be counterproductive. As such, taking the NIEO as the lodestar for a new era in U.S. relations with the Third World would be a movement in the wrong direction. This may be a disagreeable conclusion. However, as the experience of the Alliance for Progress showed, policies which are conceived with the noblest of intentions, but are grounded in illusion, do not lead to a happy outcome for anyone.

ECONOMIC SHIFTS SINCE PROMULGATION OF THE NIEO

Since the Twenty-Sixth Session of the United Nations, and the ensuing Third World pressures in 1972–1976 on behalf of the NIEO, major international economic and political shifts have occurred. These have changed the policymaking environment both for the United States and for the LDCs. Some discussions of the new order, however, have not realized that these changes have rapidly altered the international policy agenda, including perspectives on the NIEO.

As is now well known, the countries most severely affected by OPEC's quintupling of petroleum prices have been the oil-importing LDCs. The sharp rise in oil prices meant a drastic increase in the foreign exchange receipts necessary for sustaining high rates of economic development. With petroleum costing so much more, LDCs have much less foreign exchange available to pay for the imports of the raw materials and intermediate products which they require for economic expansion. As the experience of the 1950s and 1960s demonstrated, even a process of development based on import substitution necessitates a growing volume of imported inputs.

LDC governments reacted quickly and effectively to the newly imposed import constraint on their development. LDCs borrowed heavily in the Eurocurrency markets in order to finance higher import levels, and thus obtain higher rates of output growth than would otherwise have been possible. The sharp increase in the LDCs' external debt during 1974–1977 thus enabled them to stave off temporarily the impact of higher oil prices on the pace of development.

This policy option for maintaining rapid economic expansion is becoming increasingly unavailable. As Third World debts reach high levels, a flow of new loans to sustain development at the earlier pace appears increasingly unlikely. This is because continuing high rates of output growth in the LDCs require ever-higher levels of imported inputs, and hence ever-increasing absolute magnitudes of foreign borrowing. New loans to the LDCs will be negotiated, if only to "roll over" old debts and avert defaults. But the net volume of imports financed through Eurocurrency borrowing is unlikely to increase sufficiently to enable most LDCs to maintain high rates of economic development.

Developing countries with highly diversified manufactured and agricultural exports may be able to avoid extreme economic slowdown. Diversification is important here, for it permits an LDC to expand its export receipts and import volume without impinging excessively on individual markets in the more-developed countries, and thus evoking higher tariffs or quota restrictions. Brazil is perhaps the prime example of an oil-importing LDC which has followed such a strategy to mitigate the import constraint on its development. But notwithstanding record-breaking export growth and foreign borrowing, Brazil's rate of GNP growth dropped sharply from 10 percent in earlier years to 5 percent in 1977.

As the impact of higher oil prices comes home to roost in LDCs, it does so in a special institutional form. The import constraint on development generally manifests itself through an International Monetary Fund (IMF) policy package to stabilize the LDC's balance of payments and internal inflation. The typical package usually involves an austerity budget, tight credit, and constricted wages. Such measures are designed to reduce the growth of domestic demand and monetary expansion in accordance with the LDC's foreign-exchange availability. The adjustment to lower economic growth is thus implemented via policy measures dictated by an agency of international neocolonialism, the IMF.

Blaming the IMF for the austerity program, however, would be equivalent to condemning the messenger for the message. To see this, imagine the situation of the LDCs facing high petroleum prices, but without the IMF. The LDCs would still have to make the macroeconomic adjustment to a tightened import constraint. Indeed, without the IMF, Third World countries would be worse off, for they would not have access to the fund's low-cost loans. The full economic (and political) burden of adjustment would thus fall completely on themselves. The problem which the oil-importing LDCs now face is not the IMF, but rather the low growth caused by high petroleum prices (see Inter-American Development Bank 1978).

Finally, foreign-exchange receipts of the developing countries have also been hurt by the oil-induced slowdown of the OECD (Organization for Economic Cooperation and Development) economies. As balance-of-payments constraints have reduced growth rates in Western Europe, the imports of these countries from the Third World have also fallen. The prospect is now for intensifying protectionism against many of the products which the oil-importing LDCs export.

POSSIBILITIES FOR AN EXIT

As the somber economic growth prospects of the LDCs loom more sharply, international policy discussions have proceeded in search of solution. For reasons considered below, the measures stressed in the NIEO—commodity agreements, indexation, increased aid—have not received much attention in these deliberations. Rather, the focus has shifted to "technology," and particularly to narrowing the international technology gap. This theme will be highlighted in the 1979 UN Conference on Science and Technology for Development, a conference which is expected to provide the keynote for the Development Decade of the 1980s.

Notwithstanding its magical, "black box" properties, technology is unlikely to solve the short- and medium-term growth problems of the LDCs. The probability of finding "appropriate technologies" which would markedly accelerate the pace of economic expansion in the LDCs is low (Eckaus 1977). In addition, proposed changes in the present system for transfer of technology to developing countries also have their problems. Measures which would reduce the price paid for know-how may in some cases also reduce the quantity and quality of the technology transferred. Policies to increase Third World control over technology transfers may also diminish the flow of new know-how for economic development.

Moreover, the most serious technology gap which LDCs face is usually not international, but internal. In most sectors, there are firms in the developing countries which use technology that is up to international productivity levels. The problem is the technology gap within the LDC—the multitude of other firms which, in a dualistic pattern of development, utilize techniques which are far less productive. This internal gap is the major technology condition which keeps productivity and living standards low in the developing countries, and there is little that international policy measures can do to narrow it. Indeed, for their own reasons, many LDCs have rejected a policy innovation development by the United States for the very purpose of accelerating diffusion of modern technology within the LDCs —the Peace Corps.

Further, as the pace of economic development has slackened, the trade-offs between economic growth and reducing external dependency have become increasingly painful. Dependency with the high rates of economic growth of the pre-1974 era was one thing. Dependency is perceived to have lower costs, however, if it involves possibilities for maintaining expansion in an otherwise bleak economic situation. This shift in LDC perspectives is clear in the treatment now being accorded to multinational corporations (MNCs). As foreign-exchange constraints intensify, some Third World controls are increasingly welcoming MNCs, with their capacity for investment and export promotion. In some cases, the new treatment includes bending, waiving, or reversing measures implemented in the earlier epoch to control MNC activities.

The changing climate for MNCs in the Third World is best understood as a new cycle around a trend. The long-run trend in Third World–MNC relations has been toward increasing LDC self-assertion. The milestones of that trend are clear:

Mexico's petroleum expropriations of 1938; Egypt's seizure of the Suez Canal in 1956; and OPEC's pricing moves in 1973. But within the long-run movement, cycles are also evident in which LDCs alternatively welcome or squeeze foreign investors. Many oil-importing LDCs are now entering a welcoming phase, for, in their present predicament, they find the reduced-dependency theme of the NIEO unhelpful.

If LDCs were to orient their development strategies toward increased economic cooperation among themselves, they might be able to relax the present import constraint on their development. There is little indication, however, that LDC economic policymakers are taking seriously the 1975 Lima Declaration in this regard. Similarly, another possibility might be for Third World countries to adopt a "basic needs" development strategy. This might reduce the dependence of their economies on imported inputs, and enable them to attain higher growth rates despite the limited foreign exchange they can expect to have available. The elites who control most LDCs, however, have shown little interest in pursuing vigorously a development strategy focusing on basic needs. Moreover, it is not even clear that such a strategy would, in fact, lead to high rates of economic expansion. Sri Lanka, a country noted for its basic-needs approach, has not had rapid economic growth. And despite its commitment to providing basic necessities rather than useless gadgets for its population, Cuba has not been able to avoid heavy dependence on a continuing flow of foreign capital (Morawetz 1977).

Thus, not only have perspectives in the developing countries altered considerably since the heyday of the NIEO, but policy measures for escaping from slackening economic growth are not at hand. And even if one is not concerned with growth *per se*, markedly slower rates of economic expansion in the LDCs have obvious implications for increasing unemployment, and hence widening internal income disparities.

THE CHANGING INTERNATIONAL CONTEXT

The international political context within which the New International Economic Order was proposed has also changed drastically. First, within the United States, positions on policies *vis-à-vis* the LDCs have shifted. With stagflation continuing, and longer-term economic prospects worsening in the industrialized world, U.S. policymakers have lost whatever interest they may have had in the cost-raising measures of the NIEO. The main hope of pro-LDC officials in the U.S. government is now to prevent new barriers from being erected to restrict LDC exports, not the dismantling of old ones.

Further, important ideological shifts have also occurred in the U.S. These have undercut the philosophical basis for the massive U.S. resource transfers which were an integral part of the NIEO. U.S. supporters of the developing countries have belatedly come to recognize the importance of reducing LDC dependence for Third World aspirations and for U.S.–LDC relations. They have also come to recognize the inherent inconsistency between a large U.S. developmental role and a reduction in LDC dependence. As the reality of "aid as imperialism" has become clear, the position of Senate liberals like Frank Church toward the LDCs has moved close to a Moynihan policy of benign neglect. This change is ironic, inasmuch as it is out of phase with the present position of LDC policymakers. Irony apart, the current American stance hardly provides the political basis for a vigorous U.S. commitment in support of the NIEO.

The focus of the U.S. development community has, in fact, shifted to a new set of themes: basic needs, human rights, employment growth, and income redistribution in developing countries. Unfortunately, governments in the LDCs do not share U.S. enthusiasm on these issues. The result has been an erosion of dialogue and consensual basis for fruitful collaboration on behalf of the NIEO or in support of the LDCs in general.

Authoritarian governments in the Third World have been incensed by U.S. efforts at promoting human rights in their countries. In the case of Brazil and Chile, this anger has led to rupture of some political and military links. At the same time, LDCs which do guarantee human rights have been put off by the moralizing, interventionism, and inconsistencies of the American policy.

Despite lip service to the goal of reducing unemployment, LDC governments have not been willing to make job-creation a central part of their development strategies. Their lack of enthusiasm in this regard is best seen in the meager policy response to the recommendations of the International Labor Organization's employment missions to Colombia, Kenya, and the Dominican Republic. Similarly, LDC governments have shown a decided disinterest in the American initiative on basic needs. For one thing, such a development pattern does not accord with the consumption preferences of the elites in most LDCs. For another, LDC governments have construed a basic-needs strategy as condemning them to the status of permanent welfare clients, with no prospect for developing to high-consumption levels.

The U.S. focus on the highly skewed income distributions of most LDCs has also intensified U.S.–Third World dissensus. The LDCs negative reaction here clearly reflects their elite's economic interests and their hostility to American interventionism. In addition, emphasis on the social and economic inequalities which prevail within individual LDCs has an important implication in the context of international negotiations on a New International Economic Order. LDC negotiators feel that, with attention drawn to the inequalities rampant in their own societies, they lose the moral advantage which aids them in pressing for a reduction in international inequalities in the distribution of income.*

---

*I owe this observation to Graciella Chichilnisky.

Finally, positions have also changed within the Group of 77. Divergent views have developed as the higher-income LDCs, like Brazil and Korea, have done better in surmounting economic difficulties than have the poorer LDCs. Such a split is evident in the differing positions within the Third World camp on the issue of international debt moratorium. Lack of unanimity as compared with the 1972–1976 years has also appeared, as individual LDCs have scrambled for international investment and export markets.

Most important, it is increasingly clear to oil-importing LDCs that the function of the NIEO issue in international diplomacy is now very different from what they first expected. In the present international context, the prospects for achieving the NIEO are dim. Continued focus on the NIEO issue has thus come to fill a different international role: providing LDC political support to OPEC for its oil-pricing policies. With superb diplomatic skill, OPEC has succeeded in maintaining the allegiance of the oil-importing LDCs— despite the impact of higher petroleum prices on Third World economic growth, foreign debt, and external dependency. OPEC has achieved this feat, not by selling the LDCs oil at substantially concessionary prices, but by offering its support to them on behalf of the NIEO.

As expectations concerning the NIEO have become less sanguine, the illusory nature of OPEC's *quid pro quo* is becoming apparent to the LDCs. Keeping the pot of the NIEO issue boiling is now essentially a tactic for sustaining Third World support of OPEC. The LDCs are increasingly aware just who is being boiled in that pot.

CONCLUSIONS

The main economic objective of the LDCs is now maintenance of a rising flow of imported raw materials, intermediate products, and capital goods in order to sustain their economic development. Because of the severe impact of OPEC's oil prices on the LDCs, that goal is increasingly harder to attain. From 1974 through 1977, many LDCs avoided a drastic drop in economic growth by borrowing in the Eurocurrency market to finance a higher level of imports than would otherwise have been feasible. As external debt has mounted, however, that option is no longer open to most developing countries. Continuing high rates of economic expansion requires ever-growing absolute levels of imported inputs. Foreign loans to sustain a net flow of imports in the necessary magnitudes are not likely to be forthcoming in the future.

For most LDCs, therefore, the prospects for attaining high rates of economic growth in the face of the oil-price import constraint are bleak. International policy measures to permit an exit from this situation are not at hand. Escape via the NIEO is also unlikely. In effect, the economic and political changes which have occurred since 1972–1976 have removed the NIEO from the international policy agenda insofar as one is concerned with helping the developing countries.

What are the realistic possibilities for U.S. policy in this context? We bar, at the outset, forceful U.S. action to lower the relative price of oil to its pre-1974 level. That would enable the oil-importing LDCs to resume economic development at high rates without increasing debt. But it would also disturb our Saudi friends. Consequently, the only course that seems open is expansionary monetary and fiscal policy to maintain American economic growth, and a buoyant world economy for LDC exports. This is hardly a bold new demarche in U.S.–Third World relations. But it does have the advantage of being feasible.

U.S. economic policies toward developing countries will often face a trade-off between promoting economic growth or a dependency relationship which engenders resentment. The United States can do little on its own to accelerate the social and economic development of Third World countries. Our resources and leverage are limited, while the LDCs often have their own preferences and priorities. Consequently, a nonintrusive approach might be, in general, the best overall course for American policy. Such a hands-off stance may not be congenial to traditional American values of activism and involvement. But a nation which has learned to say "No more Vietnams" should profit from a parallel experience to say "No more Alliances for Progress." Otherwise, U.S. policymaking would resemble the post-Napoleonic Bourbons, who "forgot nothing and learned nothing" from their experience in a world which did not conform to their assumptions and preferences.

U.S. policies toward developing countries have, in fact, taken a definite new turn. Broad economic and political commitments have been replaced by specific actions based on perceptions of mutual strategic interests in individual countries. This is what the U.S. has been doing; it might even be the wisest course to follow. Policy pronouncements, however, have not yet caught up with this new reality. As a result, confusion has sometimes been engendered among observers, and perhaps even among participants. Clearer statements on the reality of U.S. policy are, therefore, desirable. U.S.–LDC relations are an issue-area where much would be gained from a de-escalation in rhetoric and a fostering of realistic expectations.

14

WILSON E. SCHMIDT

The Role of Private Capital in Developing the Third World

The search for capital and know-how—beg, borrow, steal, or bargain collectively? The lack of mutual gain in political situations. Intergovernmental transfers and private co-optation. Energizing the rich to help the poor. Exchange rates and the productive use of borrowed funds. Multinational corporations—charges, complaints, and restrictions. Subsidies, and government insurance for private investment.

It is obvious to all that the incomes of the poor people of this world could be increased if they had more capital and know-how with which to work.

It requires only a casual review of the facts to see that the volume of government aid—aid in the sense of gifts and loans at very low interest rates and long maturities—has been stuck at $13 to $14 billion per annum in real terms since the early 1960s. Despite the enormous growth in the real income of the rich countries' governments, they have not been willing to give more. This is a reality.

The outlook for stealing is also limited. After their success in forming the OPEC (Organization of Petroleum Exporting Countries) cartel and the less substantial achievements of the International Bauxite Association, the poor countries have few commodities left that are so readily cartelizable. This, too, is a reality.

Faced with these facts, the poor countries have gone to collective bargaining for a New International Economic Order (NIEO), demanding of rich governments in a variety of international fora almost every conceivable dispensation, subsidy, and privilege one could imagine. Their efforts to gain more aid receipts, starting with the United Nations Conference on Trade and Development in 1964, failed; I doubt that the new efforts will be more productive, for the myth that it is better to give than receive has been broken.

THE NEED FOR MUTUAL GAINS

The problem lies in the fact that there is no mutual gain in aid except in patently political situations. The donor gives up real resources; the poor country gains real resources. It is sometimes thought that by accelerating economic growth abroad through aid, we increase the market for our exports. Higher incomes abroad no doubt do increase our exports. But the absurdity of an argument that aid somehow, therefore, pays for itself is revealed by the fact that private merchants or manufacturers only give samples to their customers; aid to develop their customers is not part of their marketing strategy. The outlook for intergovernmental transfers of resources is grim indeed.

What, then, should the poor do? The answer is for them to give something in return for what they need—something that is tangible, real, and worthwhile, so that the *private* sector of the rich world is co-opted into their progress. The idea of mutual gain is fundamental to energizing the rich to help the poor.

Both the opportunity provided by this prescription, and the poverty of the aid approach, can be demonstrated by a simple numerical example. Suppose the return on capital in a poor country is 20 percent, while the return on capital in a rich country is 10 percent. If the rich country's government gives the poor nation $5 per annum for each of the next twenty years, the rich country is poorer by that amount, while the poor country is equally richer. If the rich country's government loans $25 for twenty years at zero interest, the poor country gains $5 per annum by investing the $25 at 20 percent; the rich country loses $2.50 per annum, because it could have invested the $25 at home at 10 percent. *But* if the rich country were to loan $100 at 15 percent interest for twenty years, the poor country would still gain $5 per annum (investing the $100 at 20 percent, but paying 15 percent interest), *and* the rich country would gain $5 per annum, earning $15 on the loan as compared to $10 at home. Only in the last example is there mutual gain. It hardly takes much understanding of human behavior to see that the transfer of resources is much more likely to materialize when there is mutual gain.

What is required for mutual gain is that the return on capital in the poor countries exceed that of the rich countries. There is a fair amount of evidence that this is the case. At least, this is what I deduce from casual reading of project feasibility reports of the World Bank over the years, and this observation seems to be supported by at least some of the literature surveyed by Nathaniel Leff (1975).

THE BURGEONING INTERNATIONAL CAPITAL MARKET

There is a great deal of money to be had out there. What does not seem to be fully recognized by the poor countries is that there is an international capital market open to them as well as to the rich, from which they can borrow on terms more cheaply than they can invest at home. In 1977 alone, $74 billion in capital was transferred among countries through international bond issues and Eurocurrency credits. This international capital market has exploded from a mere $8 billion in 1970. The poor countries began to catch on to it in 1968, when the Ivory Coast borrowed $10 million. The poor countries' use of the market has grown from $375 million in 1970 to $16.2 billion in 1977, far faster than the sums obtained by the rich countries. What is striking, however, is that two countries—Brazil and Mexico—account for almost half of the borrowing by the poor countries in 1977 and have, in fact, dominated the figures through much of the decade. Some countries do not even want to borrow on this market. The Indian government in 1973 limited such borrowing for fear of alienating lenders on soft terms—low interest rates and long maturities—which is surely a comment on the donors' policies, if not on the Indians themselves. Clearly, there is money out there for qualified borrowers who desire it.

To qualify, a nation needs to convince the creditor that it can repay the debt and cover the interest in the currency of the lender. If it can do this continuously, it need never really repay, because the creditor will be eager to repeat and expand the loan or credit when it comes due.

What makes a country credit-worthy in the eyes of private international lenders is complicated. It includes a variety of features of the borrower that are measurable, such as the portion of a nation's foreign currency earnings that need to be set aside to cover the amortization and interest on existing external debt. It also includes a variety of features that are truly immeasurable, such as how good the financial managers of the government are, and how ready is their access to the chief of state.

Cutting through the details, the real issue in credit-worthiness is whether the borrowing nation can be expected to come up with the foreign currency to repay the principal and cover the interest. This, in turn, depends on the condition of its balance of payments—the flows in and out of the country of foreign currency.

The two keys to the balance of payments of a country are (1) its exchange rate system, and (2) the productive use of the externally borrowed funds.

The bulk of the poor countries maintain fixed exchange rates between their currencies and another currency or a group of currencies. They far too often employ exchange controls to limit their citizens' demands for foreign currency and, in doing so, maintain overvalued currencies which, in turn, restrict their exports, because their prices are too high in foreign markets. They seem forever short of foreign exchange. Needless to say, this makes them less credit-worthy.

A costly side effect of the fixed exchange rate system employed by so many poor countries is that they waste their own resources. The central banks of the poor countries hold reserves of foreign currency of around $50 billion (this figure excludes members of the Organization of Petroleum Exporting Countries [OPEC]). One reason they do this is to protect their exchange rates; these reserves can be drawn upon when export receipts fall or import requirements rise instead of allowing the exchange rate to depreciate. These reverse investments to the rich countries probably yield from 6 to 10 percent—there are no figures—which means, in this world of inflation, a zero real return. Were these resources invested at home by the poor, they would, at 20 percent, yield $10 billion per annum, a figure not far from recent aid levels of $13 to $14 billion. (This, of course, is a rough figure, open to a number of objections, including the possibility that, if these funds were not held by central banks, private citizens would, instead, have to hold them. But this objection is doubtful when one considers that the simultaneous removal of both the fixed rates and exchange controls would bring home capital illicitly kept abroad by residents because of the exchange controls.) No one forces the poor nations to fix their exchange rates. Since April 1978, each country has been free under the rules of the International Monetary Fund to choose its own exchange rate system. Most of the rich countries have wisely chosen to allow their currencies to float, albeit in a managed way.

The second requirement for credit-worthiness is that the borrowed funds be employed productively—either directly or indirectly. This, in fact, is intimately related to repaying the funds in foreign currency and to the exchange rate system. To repay the borrowed funds and the interest, the debtor nation must raise its exports or cut its imports to gain the foreign exchange to repay the debt. This, in turn, means that it must produce more goods and services than it previously used at home, providing a surplus to be exported. By employing the borrowed funds productively, the national output is increased automatically, providing the spare goods and services required. If the exchange rate does not unduly restrict the sale of exports or unduly subsidize the purchase of imports, the extra output will be smoothly converted into foreign currency.

The seeming contradiction with an earlier point by Nathaniel Leff (Chapter 13) is thus also reconciled. He has argued that "the continuing high rates of output growth . . . require ever-higher levels of imported inputs, and hence ever-increasing absolute magnitudes of foreign borrowing." The availability of capital to finance such imports is indeed limited, as he has argued, but with floating exchange rates an adjustment in import levels would be automatic.

A number of the poor countries have unwisely restricted the use of the international capital markets to fund projects which would directly yield foreign exchange, either by substituting for imports or expanding exports. In doing so, they have greatly constrained their borrowing opportunities. Such policies rest on a lack of understanding of how the balance of payments adjusts to exchange rate changes. If the externally borrowed funds have been used wisely in projects unrelated to trade, they will yield a return in local currency; when that currency is used to buy foreign exchange to repay debt, the debtor's exchange rate will depreciate, automatically stimulating exports and constricting imports. The export surplus provides the required foreign exchange. There is no requirement that external funds generate foreign currency directly, as long as the authorities are willing to let the exchange rate change.

THE MULTINATIONAL CORPORATION

The other major source of resources which has been less than fully exploited is that of the multinational corporations. Because they are large and transcend national borders, these corporations have access to enormous amounts of capital. In the early 1970s, such companies in market economies had $165 billion invested abroad. Perhaps a fourth of this was in poor countries. American companies alone had invested $30 billion in the poor nations, out of a total of $137 billion invested abroad by the end of 1976.

The benefits which accrue to the poor countries go well beyond the provision of capital. They provide jobs. A recent estimate put the jobs generated by American multinationals in poor countries at 1.5 million. They provide training to local citizens. They provide scarce entrepreneurial and managerial talent. They provide production know-how, market information, and sales organizations. They provide markets for local suppliers. Because they are multinational, they connect the poor with the world, widening their horizons and increasing their opportunities. And they even provide a conduit for tax funds from the rich nations; e.g., under U.S. law, a multinational corporation's tax liability to the Internal Revenue Service (IRS) is reduced, within limits, to the extent that it pays income taxes abroad.

Despite these benefits, the normal rhetoric of the day has the multinational corporation as the villain of the piece. The catalog of charges: stifling local entrepreneurs, employing too little labor per unit of capital by virtue of transferring excessively advanced technology, evasion of taxes, production of products that the poor buy but ought not to be allowed to have, excessive charges for know-how, absorbing poor countries' savings through local borrowing, bribery, charging excessive prices behind tariff protection, dependence on head-office decisions that can adversely affect the jobs, foreign exchange receipts, and real income of the host nation, etc.

It is difficult for me to feel sorry for a corporation—after all, it is not a natural person. But sometimes it is subject to absolutely ludicrous complaints. How well do I remember a citizen of one poor country berating a petroleum company for importing drilling mud and not buying it locally during the rainy season. Obviously the company used local mud; what had to be imported were the essential additives, some of them in great bulk, to prevent blowouts, etc.

Some of the charges appear to be flat wrong. Some are right, but only if one grants certain assumptions about the good society, which assumptions are arguable. Some are right, but miss the culprit. Some are, in fact, backhanded compliments, for they amount only to the argument that the host country is not getting as much as it should from the multinational, rather than arguing that the multinational is doing harm.

The charge that the multinationals use more capital-intensive techniques of production, implying fewer jobs in the host countries, appears to be wrong. A number of studies confirm this conclusion. One particularly interesting one (Lecraw 1977) reports that multinationals from both the West and the East exhibited lower capital/labor ratios than their domestic counterparts in over two hundred manufacturing firms in Thailand.

The charge that the multinationals produce goods that people ought not to have—e.g., Coca Cola—somehow misses the misery of the poor, the relief that such simple pleasures provide from grinding poverty. I doubt that those who make such charges would wish to dictate or even comment on the religious choices of the poor; why should they dictate or comment on their other consumption patterns?

Tax evasion is said to arise through transfer-pricing. For example, if a foreign affiliate of an American parent corporation produces a product which becomes a component of another product produced by the parent in the United States, the price charged for the component determines where the profit is. Opportunities for profit-shifting, and thus tax evasion, occur as long as these are not arm's length transactions. Research in this area fails to point net in any particular direction. In any event, it is clear from the data that the host countries receive substantial revenue from the subsidiaries of multinationals and, therefore, this is the backhanded kind of compliment that the host country did not get enough.

The complaint that multinationals charge excessive prices behind protection from imports misses the culprit. Added to this complaint is the addendum that the excessive profits are then taken out of the country, a complaint that at first appears to be correct, because we have shown that the external funds must be used productively if they are to provide the extra goods and services required to increase exports to pay the earnings transferred abroad. The proper answer to the charge is that if, in fact, the protection reduces the real income of the country, the protection should not have been afforded to the product in the first place by the host government. Furthermore, the fact that the income may be taken out of the country is irrelevant; if local investors instead of foreign investors provided the resources, the country's real income is still reduced, because the local investors' investible funds are wasted in projects with artificially inflated returns.

With respect to bribery, it obviously does exist. The odd element in the picture is that it is the multinational, and not its critics, who should complain. Unfortunately, in many poor countries corruption in government is the standard. To get action, a bribe must be paid. This raises the costs to the multinational. The necessity to bribe is a deterrent to investment. It is, indeed, unfortunate that the laws, regulations, and procedures of many poor countries put officials in a position to demand bribes. The thief is the one who accepts the bribe, or the government which gives such people positions of power.

There are a variety of methods by which the poor countries deter the inflow of capital and know-how through multinational corporations. One is plain, perhaps unintended, harassment. For example, a number of years ago I had a casual conversation with an American middle manager in a very poor country. He told me that he had just solved a very serious problem—namely, getting a work permit for a highly skilled welder to come into the country for a brief period of time. He had solved his problem by bribing the clerk at an airline company to inform him when a certain high official of the government would next be flying out of the country. When he later got that information, he further bribed another clerk to reserve a seat next to the official. In the course of the flight, he raised the problem of the work permit, the official invited him to visit his office when he returned from the trip, and after that meeting the work permit was issued. That struck me as a hard way to do business.

Another deterrent is the threat of expropriation. During 1946–1973, no less than $2 to $3 billion of U.S. investment in poor countries was expropriated (not including the nationalization of Middle East petroleum producers). Presumably, the risk of appropriation deters some investments altogether. In other cases, it causes the multinational to commit less capital to the host country while still achieving the scale of operations it desires. It can do this, for example, by borrowing capital in the host country for some of the investment in plant and equipment, thus reducing the amount of the parent's assets at risk. Alternatively, it can sell equipment to a host country leasing corporation, which leases the equipment to the parent's subsidiary. Both techniques reduce the net transfer of capital to the poor country. By borrowing locally, it does not put its money into the country in the first place. By leasing, it gets its money for the equipment immediately by selling the equipment to the local leasing company.

Obviously, multinationals do not like to have their assets expropriated. But if they are, they would then like fair compensation for them, as is thought to be the rule of international law. This, however, has been a serious problem. One estimate puts uncompensated losses at $6 billion in the postwar period. As one United Nations study recently put it (Center on Transnational Corporations 1978:10),

Although compensation in the event of nationalization is usually guaranteed under investment laws, legislation tends to be vague concerning the criteria for the assessment of compensation and the modalities of compensation payments. Consequently, disagreements over the amount of compensation due to a nationalized enterprise have become a frequent source of investment disputes.

Another deterrent to multinational investment is the frequent requirement in the poor countries of some minimum amount of local control and ownership (sometimes majority)—by either the host government or local nationals—of foreign-owned subsidiaries. Clearly, all other things being equal, a parent corporation would prefer to own 100 percent of its foreign subsidiary, if for no other reason than it makes the operation simpler. (As I write this, IBM is pulling out of Nigeria because the Nigerian government insists that 40 percent of its subsidiary be owned by Nigerians.) The adverse effect of Colombia's requirement, along with other restrictions under the Andean Common Market, that foreign corporations divest their majority ownership, is shown by the fact that in the four years after the decision (December 1970), registration of new foreign investments in Colombia averaged $31.4 million per year, compared with $114.7 million per year in the preceding four years. The sad part of this is that the host country puts up cash that it needs badly for other purposes, and puts it in the place of funds that otherwise would be available from abroad. I recall my utter amazement when one government in a poor country insisted on owning half of a small refinery which the foreign investor was willing to carry 100 percent. The government's presence surely would not have made it more efficient, and thus added nothing to the national welfare. What the government wanted was the income, when projects elsewhere in the economy cried out for financing. In its own national interest, one would have thought, the government would have at least insisted that the foreign investor put the relinquished funds somewhere else in the economy.

Still another deterrent is the limitation imposed by some governments of poor countries on the transfer of profits of foreign subsidiaries to their parent corporations, and thus to their stockholders. Some impose limits on payments of royalties for patents and know-how. Some restrict the payments of externally owned debt. And some place limits on the repatriation of capital originally invested.

Obviously, all of these controls limit the freedom of action of the multinational and, therefore, make foreign investment less attractive to them. More specifically, the delays in the repatriation of profits have dramatic effects on the rate of return from foreign investment, because compound interest takes its toll. Thus, an American parent corporation which can invest at home at 15 percent will find that its yield on foreign investment whose income is blocked for five years will fall by 25 percent, as compared to the situation where it can repatriate the foreign income annually. Future managers of multinational corporations are now being tutored in the concept of the terminal rate of return—the return they obtain after the profits are unblocked. As foreign investment decisions are most often based on rates of return, such restrictions markedly reduce the incentive to invest.

What is so senseless about restrictions on the repatriation of profits is that, as explained above, profitable foreign investment produces a rise in the national output which, if the exchange rate is allowed to move, automatically transfers the profits at no net cost to the nation. The multinationals are often charged with taking more money out of the country than they bring in. Even if this were the case, this argument shows that it is costless as long as the original capital invested is employed productively.

Finally, many of the poor countries prohibit foreign investment in selected areas. Some of these may make sense, such as national defense industries. But others, like those of banking and insurance, do not. The capital and money markets of many of the poor countries are sorely underdeveloped; the presence of more bank and non-bank financial institutions would help to relieve the glaring defects in the mechanisms for allocating scarce capital within the poor countries. Particularly objectionable are the restrictions—such as those imposed in India and in the Andean Common Market countries—on foreign investment in industries already "adequately serviced" by existing enterprises. By dulling the threat of competition, the performance of the existing countries clearly is worsened.

Having mentioned the wide variety of restrictions on foreign investment imposed by poor countries, note should be taken of the incentives which many of those same countries provide to foreign investors. These often take the form of exemptions from various import duties on raw materials and components, as well as income-tax holidays. As anyone familiar with the notion of gains from trade knows, the exemptions from import duties are, with or without foreign investment, a step in the right direction from the standpoint of the poor country. The income-tax holidays are, however, a useless incentive, as we shall see below.

THE PROBLEM OF SUBSIDIES
AND MUTUAL GAINS

We began by emphasizing the importance of mutual gain if the private sector of the rich countries were to be co-opted into the progress of the poor. When looked at from the standpoint of the rich countries, the extent of mutual gain is suspect by reason of the policies of their governments.

The United States government has for years provided insurance to American foreign investors against losses due to wars, civil disorders, expropriation, and currency inconvertibility. In 1974, the Congress mandated that the Overseas Private Investment Corporation (OPIC) increase private participation in these activities, and ultimately withdraw completely from direct underwriting of these risks by 1979–1980. Subsequent to the mandate, OPIC made major efforts to gain the participation of private insurance companies in its portfolio, but this has largely failed, presumably because the risks are too great, given the premia. The Carter administration has recommended that OPIC be continued without the mandate for privatization.

Failure to attract private insurers suggests that there is no true mutuality of interest. In effect, OPIC is a subsidy. The rate of return to the United States, given the risks, does not exceed the rate of return on investments at home. If it did, OPIC would not be necessary. In such circumstances, *if some public purpose* is served by providing help to the poor countries where investors will not go without such guarantees, the optimal policy is no investment at all. Instead of subsidizing private investment by continuing OPIC, the Carter administration should replace it with a straight grant to the poor, because it is cheaper, as a simple numerical example will show.

Reversing the constellation of yields on investment assumed earlier, imagine that the return on capital in the poor country is 10 percent, while in the rich country the return is 20 percent. Clearly, there is no loan or investment which will benefit both the rich and the poor country simultaneously, inasmuch as the lender (investor) would require 20 percent or more, whereas the poor country gains only if the charge for the capital is less than 10 percent. If the rich country's government were to subsidize the loan (investment) to the extent of 11 percent, both the *private* lender (investor) and the poor country would gain. For example, the lender (investor) could charge 9.5 percent on a loan of $100; the poor country would gain $0.50 per annum by investing the funds at 10 percent, and the private lender (investor) would gain $0.50 with a 9.5 percent return, plus the 11 percent subsidy included, compared with a 20 percent return at home. But the true cost to the rich *nation* is $10.50 per annum, because the rich country obtains a return of 9.5 percent from abroad, but foregoes a return of 20 percent at home on the $100 loan or investment. It would, in fact, be far cheaper simply to give the poor country $0.50 per annum. There is no loan on any terms which would benefit the poor country and also cost the rich country less than $0.50. Subsidized loans or investments are not the economical option when the yield on capital in the poor country falls short of that in the rich country. Hence, even if some public purpose is served, OPIC is not the answer.

The other reason why the notion of mutual gain is suspect stems from the U.S. tax code. As suggested earlier, the multinational corporation provides the poor with a conduit to the U.S. Treasury. Within certain limits, the Internal Revenue Service permits American investors to take a credit against their U.S. income tax liability for income taxes levied by foreign governments on the income they earn abroad. The consequences of this for mutual gains can be seen from a numerical example.

The United States actually loses real income on some of our investments, because multinationals choose between foreign and domestic projects on the basis of their comparative returns after taxes. For example, suppose a multinational has a choice between a domestic and a foreign project, both of which yield $100 before taxes, and both of which require the same investment. If the foreign corporate tax rate is 40 percent, while the U.S. corporate tax rate is 50 percent, the domestic project yields $50 to the company (with the other $50 going to the IRS), while the foreign project yields $50 (with $40 going to the foreign government and, because of credit, only $10 going to the IRS). Here we see that the U.S. credit declines if the host country provides an income-tax holiday, so that the $40 foreign tax falls and the after-tax profit on the foreign project remains unchanged, making the tax holiday ineffective.

Since the after-tax return is the same, the multinational would be indifferent between the two projects. But if the company flipped a coin and the foreign project won, America would lose. The reason is that the United States gets only $60 of foreign currency with which to buy foreign goods and services from the earnings of the foreign project, whereas the United States gets $100 of additional goods and services from the domestic project. The total amount of goods and services available to Americans as a whole is $40 lower than it could be. In effect, foreigners take $40 of the output in one case, and none in the other. If the investment were made at home, our taxes could be $40 lower.

This situation would be rectified if the U.S. tax code were amended to reduce the U.S. corporate tax rate on income from domestic investments to offset the effect of the credit. The same result could be achieved if the code allowed the American corporation to deduct as costs (rather than credit) foreign taxes in computing its tax liability to the IRS. In that event, the investment committee would be choosing between a foreign project that yielded only $30 after all taxes ($100 gross income minus $40 foreign taxes equals $60 net income before U.S. taxes; $60 less the U.S. corporate income tax rate of 50 percent equals $30) and a domestic project which yielded $50 after all taxes. It thus would prefer the domestic project, and the United States real income, measured in terms of goods and services available to it, would be higher than it otherwise would be.

One estimate, clearly rough, suggests that annual American investment in the poor countries would decline by half if the deduction were substituted for the credit. That still leaves a substantial flow of capital to help the poor, a flow which would be enhanced if the poor would reduce their restrictions on private foreign investment. After adjusting the U.S. tax laws and rescinding OPIC, there would be a mutuality of gain.

CONCLUSION

Benjamin Franklin may have been a great diplomat, a fine editor of the Declaration of Independence, and perhaps a superb flier of kites, but he was a lousy economist: "He that goes aborrowing goes asorrowing." "A man may, if he knows not how to save as he gets, keep his nose to the grindstone." Franklin obviously did not perceive the value of capital markets. He did not see that, by borrowing the savings of others, the grindstone and the nose are soon parted.

As long as the rate of return on capital in the poor countries is higher than in the rich countries, a fact for which there is fairly persuasive evidence, there is a possibility of mutual gains by the transfer of capital from the rich to the poor countries. By offering a tangible return to the rich, the poor can co-opt the private sector of the rich countries into their progress, gaining the benefits of their capital and know-how. With aid levels roughly constant in real terms since the early 1960s, and with the outlook for further stealing limited, capital transfers that provide mutual gains are the most viable option to enhance the economic well-being of the poor.

Unfortunately, the poor countries have not taken full advantage of the international capital market, which has grown rapidly in the 1970s. Because they employ fixed exchange rate systems in so many cases, their ability to repay debts is weakened and their credit-worthiness impaired, making them less attractive to lenders than they otherwise would be.

Furthermore, the poor countries have imposed a variety of obstacles to investment by multinational corporations, institutions which have great access to capital and knowledge which could be put to work in the poor nations to the benefit of both. Complaints about the performance of the multinationals are flat wrong, miss the culprit, or are really backhanded compliments amounting to the charge that they do not do enough for the poor.

To insure the mutual gains to the rich countries, some adjustment in the tax system of the rich countries is required, along with the cessation of such subsidies as insurance against various losses.

V

Conclusion

15

W. SCOTT THOMPSON

A World of Parts

Military regimes and supplies in the Third World. The problem with human rights and U.S. policy. Economic development and the Western response. Foreign aid. The Soviet policy in Third World countries. Moscow's military strategy. The balance of influence.

Among the lessons that a policymaker might derive from this volume, one clear point emerges from virtually every chapter, and that is that we live in a world of parts. Certainly, for policy purposes, there is no "Third World," but a world of regions and countries with which it is in our interest—and theirs—to deal separately. Other more specific lessons cluster themselves in three natural areas relating to internal political order in states of the Third World, to economic realities in those countries in the international system, and to the relationship of these political and economic realities to international order.

POLITICAL ORDER

What is most striking throughout the Third World—and so little understood—is the seeming uniformity of a large role for the military, and the low level of human rights. These are variables, as Finer and Lipset have taught us, but questions of policy relevance proceed from the basic observations. How pertinent, for example, is an arbitrary ceiling on arms transfers to Third World countries? Aside from the obvious willingness of competitive suppliers to fill the vacuum, there is the more important point that *insecurity* is growing nearly everywhere in the Third World. This is, first of all, a result of the deteriorating internal conditions of political order, whose causes Dennis Austin has investigated, and second, because of the not unrelated growth of conflicts between neighbors over boundaries, resources—indeed, all the traditional sources of conflict. Yet another cause is ethnic diversity within Third World states, leading to civil strife in every region of the Third World, and to war in some states.

Whether the attempt to prevent states from buying arms deals with symptoms or causes is not wholly clear. But in many instances it is obvious that a refusal to sell arms to an American friend may, in fact, increase international insecurity, where our adversaries have shown no similar reluctance in arming their client. The continued difficulty the Shah of Iran has in persuading the U.S. government to supply his armed forces with sophisticated weaponry is ironic indeed, particularly in view of the ease with which Iran's smaller neighbor, Iraq, buys everything on its shopping list from Moscow. True, there has been a vastly increased rate of arms purchases by all the states of the Persian Gulf. But there has also been a vast increase in the size of the stakes there, given both the increased value today of oil as a commodity, and its probably greater value tomorrow as Soviet and American domestic oil supplies continue to diminish. Iran's role as a peacekeeper in the region—particularly now that the British security presence is negligible—is critical, and depends on American arsenals.

By the same token, it may not be the highest wisdom to meddle in the affairs of military regimes that make an effort to civilianize themselves. American attempts to produce a civilian government from honest elections in Bolivia in mid-1978 were noble in intent, but in method, little different from time-honored interventions of earlier days throughout the hemisphere. There is no brief in this argument for military rule as such; but a clear view of political reality should encourage an understanding of why it is so difficult to lower the profile of the military in the Third World, given the weakness of all other institutions. It should also reveal why it is so difficult for the United States to achieve its ends through the very interventions so decried in recent years, when these were undertaken on behalf of more conservative governments. In short, Third World countries must find a basis for political order on their own. This limits the American role to preventing any other superpower from attempting to impose its favored solutions—and that will be a more than sufficient task for American statecraft in the years ahead.

"Human rights" is also a complicated question. Everyone is "for" human rights in the United States. The principal problem with human rights as a foreign policy preoccupation is one of leverage. It does little good to ask an authoritarian government—let alone a totalitarian one—to cease being authoritarian and to release its political prisoners (whose imprisonment is the critical manifestation of the very character of the government), unless one has power with which to back up one's demand. Small wonder, then, that the American human rights drive of recent times, for all the idealism behind it, has been effective only in the relatively powerless Third World and among our allies and close friends, from whom

Washington can withhold credits, arms, and state visits. But what of all those who care not at all for Washington's good opinion? The point is best seen with respect to the Soviet Union, which has tightened its repression in the very middle of important negotiations with Washington.

But one need not go so far. Has the good example of, for instance, Philippine president Ferdinand Marcos, in releasing numerous detainees—supposedly as a result of American pressure—impressed as supposedly humane a leader as Julius Nyerere of Tanzania, where several thousand political prisoners are still held, and whose relations with Washington remain frosty? And what about the largest less-developed country in the world, the People's Republic of China? While State Department human rights "enforcers" look for excesses by the Republic of China, they excuse their own absence even of criticism of the mainland on the grounds that they have no information—indeed. And it was mid-1978 before presidential concern was registered for the genocide in Cambodia, but concern for the 153 political prisoners of the Republic of Korea came early. The lesson seems to be: keep quiet, and do it on a big scale, if you wish to avoid American wrath.

Other problems in a human rights policy include the danger of ethnocentrism—of setting American standards for a part of the world where the problem is, in the first instance, establishing order. A standard should be set—but without arrogance or presumption. It might be better, for example, to use multinational institutions as leverage against the worst offenders in human rights, who happen not to be America's allies and friends in the Third World. The United States might well temper its enthusiasm for paying UN bills so long as the Human Rights Commission continues to refuse to investigate the human rights situation in Uganda. The UN Decolonization Committee of Twenty-Four might be pressed to put the position of the Central Asian colonies of the Soviet Union on its agenda, for reasons both of human rights and decolonization. There is no intrinsic reason why a UN committee cannot put a superpower in the dock; the Committee of Twenty-Four has been investigating the "colonial" status of Puerto Rico for years.

Another point is one of style—to talk less and do more. A Somali, reacting to what he charged as Ethiopian genocide in the Ogaden, said, "We had some trust in the international advocates of human rights. But we found their concern was hollow. *They are the empty vessels which make the most noise.*"

ECONOMIC REALITIES

By now there should be little doubt about what *works* in the economic development of Third World countries. One need not confine his view to the miracle economies of free-market Asia. One can look at a jaunty little country like Tunisia which, despite the absence of many natural resources or more oil than suffices for internal needs, will join the four major African oil exporters in the "thousand dollars a year per capita" league in the early 1980s. Tunisia will be in the same class as Algeria, not because of vast deposits of gas, but because of a freer economy and better use of skilled manpower.

One can compare the Ivory Coast with two countries that started out at roughly the same level. Guinea broke with France in 1958 when the Ivory Coast chose continued close association, and Guinea's Marxist government is one of the few governments of any sort that can boast of a continued slide downhill for its people ever since. The regime survives because a capitalist bauxite enclave supplies enough foreign exchange for the president's ambassadors and for the distribution worldwide of his Marxist encyclicals. Guinea's condition is pitiful, while the Ivory Coast has moved into the upper-middle range of African states. Ghana started out as the richest country of black Africa, but chose various forms of managed economies over the years, and its relative position to the Ivory Coast next door has slipped continuously. Basic commodities are no longer available. It might have been arguable a decade ago that the Ivory Coast's conspicuous wealth in the capital did not trickle down to the villages, but no recent visitor could easily make that argument, now that the modern infrastructure and amenities have reached into every corner of the country.

Yet a predisposition *against* the market economy persists throughout the Third World, in part for the political reasons described by Richard Bissell. But there is also the apologetic character of the American—and Western—response. Radical countries make the running in the essentially political forums of the New International Economic Organization (NIEO). The West accepts the terminology and parameters of discussion determined by these states. Admittedly, substantive concessions do not follow accordingly, but the gap between the framework and what is achieved increases Third World frustration. Perhaps it is time to narrow the gap by patronizing less, and by saying quite frankly that the United States, for one, does not agree that a massive transfer of Western wealth would solve Third World problems.

Certainly the ghosts of many aid programs should now be laid to rest, with the arguments advanced herein by Schmidt, Bauer, and Yamey. There may very well be—and I would argue that there often is—a political case to be made for foreign aid; for example, to save a government which would otherwise fall and leave the country open to external manipulation. That is surely the only good case that can be made for the Western bail-out of Zaïre's government in the aftermath of the Cuban-aided invasion of Shaba province in 1978. But such situations are the exception. The absence of aid programs has hardly prevented other great powers from garnering influence in the Third World. The Soviet Union has, for all intents and purposes, ceased to grant economic aid to the Third World, save for direct subventions to Cuba and technical assistance to client governments like Ethiopia and Afghanistan. Even so, the amount is a tiny fraction of American aid. Moscow makes a virtue of necessity. It proclaims that it has no responsibility to help the poor countries, having had no responsibility in "hamstringing the social and economic effort of the developing countries" originally, as one Soviet writer put it. So the Soviets export the one thing they are good at—guns—and those they supply at double the rate now as compared with the first half of the 1970s.

Since aid on a larger scale will not be forthcoming from the United States in the foreseeable future, we too might as well make a virtue of necessity. It may well be time to say that, except at times of humanitarian necessity, Third World countries should not expect aid; rather should they concentrate, as Nathaniel Leff has suggested, on closing the *internal* gap that is so glaring between ruling elite and everybody else—so much greater a gap than that between Third and First Worlds.

There is a paradigm available of a major power looking primarily to its own interests and maximizing its influence worldwide. It is of Gaullist France. A Tunisian diplomat in 1966, at the height of Gaullist influence, said,

France is the only country that openly breaks the UN embargo on the sale of arms to South Africa. It defies Africa and tests its nuclear weaponry on the Sahara. It maintains a string of neo-colonized states to whom it gives its only aid, in the form of budgetary subventions. And yet which major power of the world is the most prestigious in the Third World? France. Which leader is the most influential? Charles de Gaulle.

De Gaulle's style was to be attentive to Third World aspirations without pretending an ability to solve their problems—and all the while forthrightly looking to French interests. The United States does not have to tackle every world problem to sustain a position of respect; least of all does it have to humor the least responsible elements within the Third World, the ones calling themselves the "progressive" states.

Probably the most important point about economic issues for policymakers concerns the relative unimportance of economics. After the Vietnamese war, it became the fashion in the United States to extol the role of economics in determining world political issues; indeed, as the North Vietnamese tanks and divisions stormed across the demilitarized zone, ending the war in an American defeat, the notion that military force solved nothing grew in sanctity. As Russian ships bombarded rebel-held ports in Eritrea, the American ambassador to the United Nations developed his view—one echoed throughout the U.S. government—that even Marxist governments would have to trade with us and become involved in our system. But, of course, the governments, before the use of gunboats, had not been Marxist. Edward Luttwak has argued herein that *ex post facto* legitimizations for whatever happens are rapidly forthcoming these days. The fashionable argument, in fact, says that American economics will be used as the excuse to cover the adversary's determinative military action. It is time that the role and level of economic and political issues be seen for what they are in the Third World.

We are led quite naturally to *international politics* and the Third World. The first point to remember is how involved the West is with the Third World in its security. Our alliances, however tattered, all include or involve Third World countries. Even NATO during recent years has made the question of its supporting flanks—from Africa across to the Persian Gulf—a prime question. Two Third World countries, Iran and Saudi Arabia, both of which outrank many industrial states in gross national product and per capita income—are among the most important states in the world from the Western point of view, and a principal prize from the Soviet point of view.

The Soviet Union, for its part, is building an alliance system in the Third World. It is no mirror image of the West's; Moscow smartly determined to avoid those exposed dimensions of the Western security system that hobble it: thus the use of surrogate troops, the prohibition on shore visits by Soviet sailors, the absence of formal, explicit alliances where treaties of friendship and political understandings will do. Its location, mostly along the critical Western sea lines of communication between the Persian Gulf and the Western industrial customers, is hardly fortuitous. Outposts like Afghanistan, which helps Moscow to outflank Iran and to extend the outer boundaries of the continental Soviet system, and new positions, like those in Ethiopia, help Moscow outflank the Persian Gulf—indeed, the whole Middle East. So about the strategic significance of the Third World there should be no doubt.

Ironically, despite the fact that most of the conflict acted out on the battlefield since World War II has taken place in the Third World, it has become fashionable in Washington to say that these areas are *not* strategically significant; it was a misperception to have seen them as such, and to have fought over their loyalties or over the endurance of one regime or another, or so the argument goes. Misperception or no misperception, it is, alas, not something that can be decided unilaterally. Those who said Angola was "not important," and prevented an effective American response to Soviet-Cuban aggression, were simply ignoring the communist perception, which was the opposite. Today, the most critical region on earth, as many strategists see it, is the Persian Gulf. It is there, rather than on the Central European front, that sparks might most easily light a third world war. And this is a region in which no peaceful changes of power have occurred in memory. So the Third World is becoming more, not less, strategically significant.

It thus becomes ironic for American legislators now to insist that foreign aid "be for people," rather than for countries in strategically significant locations. Aid is, in any case, always for "people" (though Nathaniel Leff points out that it is difficult to get it into the right hands, however high the motives). While it is a worthy aim to help the poorest, the fact remains that political needs will necessitate the use of the remaining American tools of statecraft to shore up weak regimes or reward helpful ones. That is not *Realpolitik,* it is simple realism.

The irony in the Soviet challenge to the West in the Third World is that it has any credibility at all. Western experience and involvement—both political and economic, throughout Asia, Africa, and Latin America—is greater by orders of magnitude in most countries there. Where the methods of communism have been applied to the economies, disaster has uniformly resulted. If resentment of the role of the colonial powers exists in places, that is a diminishing asset for enemies of Western–Third World partnership, as the disparity between colonizer and former colony continues to narrow. Perhaps Western political models have only limited relevance to these plural, unstructured states, but the Western tradition of freedom at least sets a standard whereby Third World states can minimize the excesses as they struggle to find an indigenous and satisfactory solution to the problem of order. The communist model is crude and unsophisticated, one of little insight, simply calling for the unlimited use of brute force to ''solve'' delicate problems—in fact, to obliterate them.

Even in the area of disposable military power for use in the Third World, the West remains preeminent, theoretically at least. Indeed, the one area of the military balance between East and West in which the West—and the United States in particular—has a substantial edge, is in the projection of power. Yet that edge, in marines, landing craft, the whole panoply of power, is vitiated by two factors, which in turn vitiate all the other advantages to which the West should, by rights, be entitled. The first is that the Soviets are narrowing the American lead, not least by employing surrogates like Cubans and East Germans to do their hard chores, but also by building up their capabilities in long-term transport, amphibious ships, and so forth. More important, this buildup is complemented by the combination of greater will which Moscow possesses compared to Washington, and which flows from the unparalleled strategic stockpiling of nuclear missiles, submarines, and bombers. An American advantage in the ratio of marines over Soviet naval infantry—even if still eight to one, as it is today—will mean little if a credible Soviet counterforce capability effectively inhibits us even from threatening to intervene where our interests are engaged.

Thus, although all the Western political and economic advantages can count for something, they can all be negated by a sufficiently ruthless Soviet purpose, one taking advantage of a new Soviet superiority in strategic weaponry. It might be well to recall Max Beloff's well-expressed thought—that the Third World is less interested in which side is going to be nicer, than "in which side is going to come out on top."

NOTES

4. Dennis Austin: "Prospero's Island"

1. The first conference was in 1966, when seventy-seven nations joined together. They were as diverse as Afghanistan, Brazil, El Salvador, India, Saudi Arabia, Togo, and Yugoslavia. Others joined subsequently, to bring the number to over one hundred. By 1974, there was a good deal of talk about a "New International Economic Order," and distinctions began to be drawn between subcategories of the more or less developed countries; but still the basis of diplomacy and organization remained that of the notion of there being two or three "worlds."

2. A few simple statistics. Monthly wage rates in the textile industry in 1977 were: Japan £269, UK £180, Hong Kong £76, South Korea £59. Steel output per man year: Japan 690 tons, UK 116 tons, South Korea 280 tons. Costs of steel production per ton: South Korea (hot-rolled steel) $180, UK $300; South Korea (cold-rolled steel) $230, UK $385. Present plans include the production of 2 million cars by 1991, including 40 percent for export. See *The Times* [London] (1978).

3. As in the West Indies. "In global terms, Jamaica and Trinidad are microterritories, but in the Commonwealth Caribbean they are giants without which the less-developed countries of the eastern Caribbean cannot survive" (Payne 1978).

4. "Since 1974 there has been no available information on the composition of the cabinet except for the reported deaths of several cabinet ministers." Description of the government of Equatorial Guinea under Francisco Nguema (Amnesty International 1978:303).

5. S. E. Finer: "The Military and Politics in the Third World"

1. On the mechanics of the *coup*, see Finer (1976), and especially Luttwak (1969).

2. "It is a partnership in all science; a partnership in all art; a partnership in every virtue and in all perfection. As the ends of such a partnership cannot be obtained in many generations, it becomes a partnership not only between those who are living, but between those who are living, those who are dead, and those who are to be born" (Lubbock 1893:223).

3. See the admirable essay of Professor Kossok (German Democratic Republic) in Janowitz and van Doorn (1971:403–24).

4. Nordlinger himself points this out (1970:1147, n. 51).

6. Peter T. Bauer, Basil S. Yamey: "The Third World and the West: An Economic Perspective"

1. Here are three representative statements:

"Two-thirds of mankind—more than two billion individuals—remain entrapped in a cruel web of circumstances that severely limits their right to the necessities of life. . . . The misery of the underdeveloped world is today a dynamic misery, continuously broadened and deepened by a population growth that is totally unprecedented in history'' (McNamara 1973:30).

A statement in the preamble to the *Declaration of the Establishment of a New International Economic Order* includes ''neo-colonialism in all its forms'' and the ''remaining vestiges of alien and colonial domination'' among ''the greatest obstacles to the . . . progress of the developing countries'' (United Nations 1975:5).

''Complete decolonisation . . . and the liquidation of the remnants of colonialism in all its forms . . . is a necessary condition for economic development'' (General Principle Fourteen of the First United Nations Conference on Trade and Development [UNCTAD] 1964).

2. The following observations by Rudyard Kipling (Carrington 1970:165) are of interest: ''Neither at Penang, Singapur, nor this place have I seen a single Chinaman asleep while daylight lasted. Nor have I seen twenty men who were obviously loafing. . . .

''This much, however, seems certain. If we had control over as many Chinamen as we have natives of India, and had given them one tithe of the cosseting, the painful pushing forward, and studious, even nervous, regard of their interests and aspirations that we have given India, we should long ago have been expelled from, or have reaped the reward of, the richest land on the face of the earth.''

3. ''For mankind as a whole there has actually been no progress at all [in the 20th century]. . . . As Mr. H. W. Singer has rightly pointed out, world real income per head and with it the standard of living of the average human being, is probably lower than 25 years ago, and perhaps lower than in 1900, because the nations that have rapidly raised their economic standards have been a shrinking proportion of the total world population'' (Myrdal 1956:2).

The concept and measurement of ''progress'' for ''mankind as a whole'' raise philosophical problems on which there can be legitimate differences of opinion. But it is undoubtedly ill conceived to equate progress or even changes in economic standards with changes in per capita income as conventionally measured, or to ignore in such statements the large increase in world population as well as in the average expectation of life in both rich and poor countries.

Moreover, national income estimates and comparisons involving Third World countries are subject to vast errors and biases which vitiate their use as a basis for analysis or policy. Professor D. Usher (1968, quoted in Bauer and Yamey 1977:26) has shown that such errors and biases amount to several hundred percent.

4. Professor John C. Caldwell (1976:321–66) discusses the high level of fertility of people in Southern Nigeria who use modern contraceptives. He also examines the benefits parents continue to derive from large families in Lagos and Ibadan, its two principal cities.

5. See also an article in the *Washington Post* (4 July 1977). Hanlon and Agarwal (1977) base their article in large part on a report of a team headed by Professor D. Banerji. They observe: ''The Western aid agencies . . . either kept quiet or applauded the sterilisation programme. World Bank President Robert McNamara took time off his busy schedule during his Indian visit to call upon the Indian Health and Family Planning Minister to congratulate him for the Indian Government's 'political will and determination' in popularising family planning. This was during November, 1976, at the height of the compulsory sterilisation campaign.''

6. Aspects of Burma's economic history are relevant for several of our themes. Burma developed into the world's leading exporter of rice before the second world war. Peasants responded to the expansion of the market for Asian products after the opening of the Suez Canal. They migrated in large numbers to Lower Burma from the subsistence agriculture of Upper Burma, and reclaimed land from marsh and jungle. Their activities, largely financed by Indian (Chettyar) lenders, were assisted by the flow of workers from India to meet seasonal demands.

Since the second world war, the government of independent Burma has engaged in large-scale state intervention, and has been opposed to foreign trade and enterprise. Burma is now "an object lesson in the disaster that can follow the resolute application of western-conceived socialist polities" (*The Times* [London], 13 September 1976). It has stagnated, possibly even retrogressed.

7. It is worth noting how readily state educational activities can turn into the exercise of pressure, especially in the Third World. In parts of Indonesia, each local authority now keeps an "up-to-date map showing the contraceptive practice of every fertile couple, so that fieldworkers can concentrate their efforts." And there is an experimental program to provide "awards to villages with good records in family planning." The various activities have been supported by the World Bank and by the United Nations Fund for Population Activities (*The Times* [London], 7 June 1978).

8. In accordance with accepted usage, aid here means official aid, as distinct both from private investment and from charity. We also include in aid the grant element in subsidized loans, debt cancellation, and certain kinds of international commodity schemes. Since the early 1960s there has been a tendency for the term *resource* or *wealth transfers* to replace the term *aid.*

9. Compare also an article by Peter T. Bauer and Cranley Onslow in *The Times* [London], 15 November 1977.

10. The reader may ask whether the usual proposition that aid promotes growth has not been examined statistically. In fact, statistical studies which have been made show at best a weak and inconclusive association (see Pearson et al. 1969:49; Görgens 1976). In any case, such studies are based on changes in estimated per capita national income, which, for conceptual, analytical, and technical statistical reasons, cannot be relied on to reflect changes in living standards or economic conditions. Further, such studies cannot determine what would have happened without aid. This difficulty arises because of the familiar problem of discerning the causal relationship between specified variables when a situation or process is affected by numerous past and present influences operating with various time lags, and often interacting with each other.

11. We may note parenthetically that the performance of these functions does not normally mean close control over people's lives and activities. This may be one reason why many exponents of the current ideology on development are unperturbed when governments engage in comprehensive planning or other forms of large-scale collectivization while simultaneously they neglect their elementary functions. The ideologues seem more interested in controlling people's lives than in their spiritual or material well-being.

12. The following example may perhaps illustrate the extremes which are averaged and aggregated in the concept of the Third World. In Papua New Guinea there are people only recently emerged from the Stone Age. The Third World also includes Mexico. In that country, a method of producing lead oxide has been de-

veloped and is to be used in a plant being set up in Holland by Mexican engineers. A Mexican system for cleaning the air surrounding paper mills is being marketed in Canada and Sweden. In Mexico City, a key process in the production of the contraceptive pill was developed.

13. The specific trade and technology transfer proposals of the NIEO are part and parcel of the overriding demand for wealth transfers.

10. Daniel Pipes: "The Third World Peoples of Soviet Central Asia"

1. In order to concentrate on Third World peoples, this chapter ignores the equally important Russian expansion westwards into Europe. Central Asians do not constitute all the Third World peoples in the Soviet Union by any means, but they are the largest in number and the most important of them.

2. The term "Russian" in reference to settlers in Central Asia also includes other Slavic speakers, primarily Ukrainians.

3. This is true without even considering the European republics (Estonia, Latvia, Lithuania, White Russia, the Ukraine, and Moldavia) or the satellites in Eastern Europe (Poland, East Germany, Czechoslovakia, Hungary, Romania, Bulgaria) and Mongolia.

4. Only the People's Republic of China rivals in size the Soviet empire. It includes some 40 million non-Han Chinese, including Manchus, Mongols, Koreans, Turks, and Tibetans. As in the Soviet Union, Turks constitute the largest minority. The Chinese case also fits classic colonial patterns, perhaps more closely than the Soviet Union, although the Chinese, of course, are not Europeans.

5. For a brief account, see Rywkin (1975:277–78).

6. This does not preclude us from expanding radio broadcasts to Central Asia. The Voice of America currently programs only one hour daily, and Radio Liberty programs five hours. Increased programing would hasten the processes described here.

REFERENCES

Ahmed, Imitiaz. 1971. "Secularization." *Seminar* 144 (August).

Allworth, E., ed. 1967. *Central Asia: A Century of Russian Rule.* New York: Columbia University Press.

————. 1973. *The Nationality Question in Soviet Central Asia.* New York: Praeger.

Amin, Samir. 1974. *Accumulation on a World Scale.* Trans. Brian Pearce. New York: Monthly Review Press.

Amnesty International. 1978. *Africa South of the Sahara 1977–1978.* London: Europa Publications.

Ardener, E. W. 1954. "Some Ibo Attitudes to Skin Pigmentation." *Man* 100–101 (May).

Baran, Paul. 1956. *The Political Economy of Growth.* 2d ed. New York: Monthly Review Press.

Barnet, Richard, and Mueller, Ronald. 1974. *Global Reach.* New York: Simon and Schuster.

Bastide, Roger. 1968. "Color, Racism and Christianity." In *Color and Race,* ed. John Hope Franklin. Boston: Houghton Mifflin Company.

Bauer, Peter T. 1976. *Dissent on Development.* Cambridge, MA: Harvard University Press.

————, and Yamey, Basil S. 1977. "Against the New Economic Order." *Commentary* (April).

Bebler, A. 1962. *Military Rule in Africa.* New York: Praeger.

Berreman, Gerald D. 1972. "Race, Caste, and Other Invidious Distinctions in Social Stratification." *Race* 13 (April).

Béteille, André. 1968. "Race and Descent as Social Categories in India." In *Color and Race,* ed. John Hope Franklin. Boston: Houghton Mifflin Company.

Bhagwati, Jagdish N., ed. 1977. *The New International Economic Order: The North-South Debate.* Boston: MIT Press.

————, and Eckaus, R. S., eds. 1973. *Development and Planning.* Cambridge, MA: MIT Press.

Bodrogligeti, A. J. E. 1975. "The Classical Islam Heritage of Eastern Middle Turkic as Reflected in the Lexikon of Modern Literary Uzbek." *Canadian Slavonic Papers* 17.

Bourricaud, François. 1965. "Indian Mestizo and Cholo as Symbols in the Peruvian System of Stratification." In *Ethnicity Theory and Experience,* ed. Nathan Glazer and Daniel P. Moynihan. Cambridge, MA: Harvard University Press.

Bozeman, Adda. 1971. *The Future of Law in a Multicultural World*. Princeton, NJ: Princeton University Press.

Brewer, Marilyn B., and Campbell, Donald T. 1976. *Ethnocentrism and Intergroup Attitudes, East African Evidence*. New York: John Wiley.

Bronfenbrenner, M. 1976. "Predatory Poverty on the Offensive: The UNCTAD Record." *Economic Development and Cultural Change* (July).

Burrows, Edwin G. 1947. *Hawaiian Americans*. New Haven: Yale University Press.

Caldwell, John C. 1976. "Toward a Restatement of Demographic Transition Theory." *Population and Development Review* (September/December).

Carrington, Charles. 1970. *Rudyard Kipling*. Harmondsworth: Penguin.

Center on Transnational Corporations. 1978. *National Legislation and Regulations Relating to Transnational Corporations*. New York: United Nations.

Cockroft, James D., et al. 1972. *Dependence and Underdevelopment: Latin America's Political Economy*. New York: Anchor Books.

Cohen, Ronald. 1970. "Social Stratification in Bornu." In *Social Stratification in Africa*, ed. Arthur Tuden and Leonard Plotnicov. New York: The Free Press.

Connor, Walker. 1972. "Nation-Building or Nation-Destroying?" *World Politics* 24 (April).

Das Gupta, Jystirandra. 1974. "Ethnicity, Language Demands, and National Development." *Ethnicity* 1.

Dreyer, June Teufel. 1977. "The Kazakhs in China." In *Ethnic Conflict in International Relations*, ed. Astri Suhrke and Lela G. Noble. New York: Praeger.

Duran, James. 1974. "The Ecology of Ethnic Groups from a Kenyan Perspective." *Ethnicity* 1.

Eckaus, Richard S. 1973. "Absorptive Capacity as a Constraint Due to Maturation Process." In *Development and Planning*, ed. J. N. Bhagwati and R. S. Eckhaus. Cambridge, MA: MIT Press.

———. 1977. *Appropriate Technologies for Developing Countries*. Washington, DC: National Academy of Science.

d'Encausse, Hélène, and Schram, Stuart. 1969. *Marxism and Asia*. London: Allen Lang Penguin Press.

Engels, Friedrich. 1848. "French Rule in Algeria." *The Northern Star* (22 January). Quoted in Karl Marx, *On Colonialism and Modernization*, ed. S. Avineri. Garden City, NY: Doubleday and Co.

Enloe, Cynthia H. 1973. *Ethnic Conflict and Political Development*. Boston: Little, Brown and Co.

Esman, Milton J. 1965. "Communal Conflict in Southeast Asia." In *Ethnicity Theory and Experience*, ed. Nathan Glazer and Daniel P. Moynihan. Cambridge, MA: Harvard University Press.

Ferguson, J. H. 1961. *Latin America: The Balance of Race Redressed*. London: Oxford University Press.

Feulner, Edwin J. 1976. *Congress and the New International Economic Order*. Washington, DC: The Heritage Foundation.

Finer, S. E. 1976. *The Man on Horseback: The Role of the Military in Politics*. 2d ed. London: Penguin Press.

Fishman, J., Ferguson, C. A., and Das Gupta, J., eds. 1968. *Language Problems of Developing Nations*. New York: John Wiley.

Frank, André Gunder. 1972. "The Development of Underdevelopment." In *Dependence and Underdevelopment: Latin America's Political Economy*, James D. Cockroft et al. New York: Anchor Books.

Franklin, John Hope. 1968. *Color and Race*. Boston: Houghton Mifflin Company.

Glazer, Nathan, and Moynihan, Daniel P., eds. 1975. *Ethnicity Theory and Experience*. Cambridge, MA: Harvard University Press.

Görgens, E. 1976. "Development Aid—An Obstacle to Economic Growth in Developing Countries?" *The German Economic Review* 14.

Gosovic, Branislav, and Ruggie, John Gerrard. 1976. "On the Creation of a New International Economic Order: Issue Linkage and the Seventh Special Session of the UN General Assembly." *International Organization* 30 (Spring).

Hadley, Arthur Twining. 1923. *Economic Problems of Democracy*. New York: Macmillan.

Halpern, M. 1962. "Middle East Armies and the New Middle Class." In *The Rule of the Military in Underdeveloped Countries*, ed. J. J. Johnson. Princeton, NJ: Princeton University Press.

———. 1963. *The Politics of Social Change in the Middle East*. Princeton, NJ: Princeton University Press.

Hamilton, Gary. 1977. "Ethnicity and Regionalism: Some Factors Influencing Chinese Identities in Southeast Asia." *Ethnicity* 4.

Hanlon, J., and Agarwal, A. 1977. "Mass Sterilisation at Gunpoint." *New Scientist* [London] (5 May).

Hanna, William J., and Hanna, Judith L. 1969. *Urban Dynamics in Black Africa*. Washington, DC: Center for Research in Social Systems, American University.

Harrison, S. 1975. "Time Bomb in East Asia." *Foreign Policy* (Fall).

Huntington, Samuel. 1969. *Political Order in Changing Societies*. New Haven: Yale University Press.

Inter-American Development Bank. 1978. *Latin American Energy and Oil: Present Situation and Prospects*. Washington, DC: Inter-American Development Bank.

Isaacs, Harold R. 1977. "Fathers and Sons and Daughters and National Development." In *Political Generations and Political Development*, ed. Richard J. Samuels. Lexington, MA: D. C. Heath.

Jackman, R. W. 1976. "Politicians in Uniform: Military Governments and Social Change in the Third World." *American Political Science Review* 70, 4.

Janowitz, M., and van Doorn, J., eds. 1971. *On Military Intervention*. Rotterdam: Rotterdam University Press.

Johnson, J. J., ed. 1962. *The Rule of the Military in Underdeveloped Countries.* Princeton, NJ: Princeton University Press.

Julliard, Jacques. 1978. "For a New 'Internationale.'" *The New York Review of Books* 25 (20 July).

Kearney, Robert N. 1978. "Language and the Rise of Tamil Separatism in Sri Lanka." *Asian Survey* 18 (May).

Keynes, John Maynard. 1961. *General Theory of Employment, Interest and Money.* London: Macmillan.

Kuper, Leo, and Smith, M. G., eds. 1971. *Pluralism in Africa.* Berkeley, CA: University of California Press.

Lecraw, D. 1977. "Direct Investment by Firms from Less-Developed Countries." *Oxford Economic Papers* (November).

Leff, Nathaniel. 1975. "Rates of Return to Capital, Savings, and Investment in Developing Countries." *Kyklos* (December).

Lewis, Bernard. 1958. *The Arabs in History.* London: Arrow Books.

———. 1970. "Race and Colour in Islam." *Encounter* 35 (August).

Lewis, R. A., et al. 1975. "Modernization, Population Change, and Nationality in Soviet Central Asia and Kazakhstan." *Canadian Slavonic Papers* 17.

Leys, Colin. 1974. *Underdevelopment in Kenya: The Political Economy of Neocolonialism, 1964–1971.* Berkeley, CA: University of California Press.

Liska, George. 1967. *Imperial America.* Baltimore, MD: Johns Hopkins Press.

Lubbock, Sir J., ed. 1893. *Selections from the Speeches and Writings of Edmund Burke.* London.

Luttwak, Edward. 1969. *Coup d'Etat: A Practical Handbook.* London: Penguin Press.

McKinlay, R. D., and Cohan, A. S. 1974. "Military Coups, Military Regimes and Social Change." Mimeo. Prepared for delivery at the APSA Annual Meeting (September).

———. 1976. "Performance and Instability in Military and Nonmilitary Regime Systems." *American Political Science Review* 70, 3.

McNamara, Robert. 1973. *One Hundred Countries, Two Billion People: The Dimensions of Development.* London: Pall Mall Press.

Mandelbaum, David. 1972. *Society in India.* Vol. 2. Berkeley, CA: University of California Press.

Manoni, O. 1956. *Prospero and Caliban.* New York: Praeger.

Markovitz, Irving L. 1977. *Power and Class in Africa.* Englewood Cliffs, NJ: Prentice-Hall.

Marx, Karl. 1960. "The Future Results of the British Role in India." In *On Colonialism,* Karl Marx and Friedrich Engels. Moscow: Foreign Languages Publishing House.

———. 1968. *On Colonialism and Modernization,* ed. S. Avineri. Garden City, NY: Doubleday and Co.

———, and Engels, Friedrich. 1959. *Gesamtausgabe.* Vol. 6. Institute for Marxism-Leninism of the Central Committee of the Socialist Unity Party. Berlin: Dietz Verlag.

———. 1953. *Letters to Americans*. New York: International Publishers.

———, and Engels, Friedrich. 1960. *On Colonialism*. Moscow: Foreign Languages Publishing House.

Mason, Philip, ed. 1967. *India and Ceylon: Unity and Diversity*. London: Oxford University Press.

Menges, Karl H. 1967. "People, Languages, and Migrations." In *Central Asia: A Century of Russian Rule,* ed. E. Allworth. New York: Columbia University Press.

Ministry of Education [Kenya]. 1967. *Triannual Survey, 1964–1966, and Annual Report for 1966*. Nairobi: Government Printer.

Moore, Carlos. 1974–1975. "Were Marx and Engels Racists?: The Prolet-ARYAN Outlook of Marxism." *Berkeley Journal of Sociology* 19.

Morawetz, David. 1977. "Economic Lessons from Some Small Socialist Countries." Paper presented to the American Economic Association (December).

Morris-Jones, W. H. 1967. "Language and Religion within the Indian Union." In *India and Ceylon: Unity and Diversity,* ed. Philip Mason. London: Oxford University Press.

Moulder, Frances. 1977. *Japan, China and the Modern World Economy*. New York: Cambridge University Press.

Moutafakis, George. 1977. "The Role of Minorities in the Modern Middle East Societies." *Middle East Review* 9 (Winter).

Myint, H. 1971. *Economic Theory and the Underdeveloped Countries*. London: Oxford University Press.

Myrdal, Gunnar. 1968. *Asian Drama: An Inquiry into the Poverty of Nations*. New York: Pantheon Press.

———. 1956. *An International Economy*. London: Routledge.

Nkrumah, Kwame. 1966. *Neocolonialism*. New York: International Publishers.

Nordlinger, Eric. 1970. "Soldiers in Mufti: The Impact of Military Rule upon Economic and Social Change in the Non-Western States." *American Political Science Review* 64, 4 (December).

Nove, A., and Newth, J. A. 1967. *The Soviet Middle East*. London: George Allyn and Unwin.

Nun, J. 1970. "The Middle Class *Coup*." In *The Politics of Conformity in Latin America,* ed. C. Véliz. Oxford: Oxford University Press.

Parkes, H. B. 1960. *A History of Mexico*. Boston: Houghton Mifflin Company.

Patterson, Orlando. 1965. "Context and Choice in Ethnic Allegiance: A Theoretical Framework and Caribbean Case Study." In *Ethnicity Theory and Experience,* ed. Nathan Glazer and Daniel P. Moynihan. Cambridge, MA: Harvard University Press.

Payne, A. J. 1978. *Caribbean Integration*. Manchester: University of Manchester Press.

Pearson, Lester B., et al. 1969. *Partners in Development: Report of the Commission on International Development*. New York: Praeger.

Pipes, Richard. 1965. "Reflections on the Nationality Problems in the Soviet Union." In *Ethnicity Theory and Experience,* ed. Nathan Glazer and Daniel P. Moynihan. Cambridge, MA: Harvard University Press.

Purcell, Victor. 1965. *The Chinese in Southeast Asia.* London: Oxford University Press.

Pye, Lucien. 1965. "China: Ethnic Minorities and National Security." In *Ethnicity Theory and Experience,* ed. Nathan Glazer and Daniel P. Moynihan. Cambridge, MA: Harvard University Press.

Reischauer, Edwin O., and Fairbank, John K. 1958. *East Asia: The Great Tradition.* Boston: Houghton Mifflin.

Rodney, Walter. 1973. *How Europe Underdeveloped Africa.* London: Bogle-L'Ouverture.

Rywkin, M. 1975. "Religion, Modern Nationalism and Political Power in Soviet Central Asia." *Canadian Slavonic Papers* 17.

Samuels, Richard J., ed. 1977. *Political Generations and Political Development.* Lexington, MA: D. C. Heath.

Santa Cruz, Hernan. 1971 (rev. 1976). *Racial Discrimination.* New York: United Nations.

Sauvant, Karl P., and Hasenpflug, Hajo, eds. 1977. *The New International Economic Order: Confrontation or Cooperation between North and South?* Boulder, CO: Westview Press.

Schmitter, Philippe. 1971. "Military Intervention, Political Competitiveness and Public Policy in Latin America, 1950–1967." In *On Military Intervention,* ed. M. Janowitz and J. van Doorn. Rotterdam: Rotterdam University Press.

Scott, James C. 1969. "Corruption, Machine Politics, and Political Change." *American Political Science Review* 63.

Sebring, James. 1972. "The Formation of New Castes: A Probable Case from North India." *American Anthropologist* 74 (June).

Segrera, Martïn. 1974. *Los Racismos in America Latina: Sus Colonialismos Externos e Internos.* Buenos Aires: Ediciones Bastilla.

Sherwin-White, A. N. 1967. *Racial Prejudice in Imperial Rome.* Cambridge: Cambridge University Press.

Shorish, M. M. 1975. "Soviet Developmental Strategies in Central Asia." *Canadian Slavonic Papers* 17.

Smith, M. G. 1971. "Pluralism in Precolonial African Societies." In *Pluralism in Africa,* ed. Leo Kuper and M. G. Smith. Berkeley, CA: University of California Press.

Southall, Aidan. 1961a. "Kinship, Friendship and the Network of Relations in Kiseny, Kampala." In *Social Change in Modern Africa,* ed. Aidan Southall. London: Oxford University Press.

———. 1961b. *Social Change in Modern Africa.* London: Oxford University Press.

Srinivas, M. N. 1962. *Caste in Modern India.* New York: Asia Publishing House.

Stein, Stanley, and Stein, Barbara. 1970. *The Colonial Heritage of Latin America.* New York: Oxford University Press.

Suhrke, Astri, and Noble, Lela G. 1977. *Ethnic Conflict in International Relations*. New York: Praeger.

Suyin, Han. 1971. "Race Relations and the Third World." *Race* 13 (April).

Thompson, W. R. 1973. *The Grievances of Military Coup-Makers*. Beverly Hills, CA: Sage Publications.

The Times [London]. 1978. "The Awakening Industrial Giant." 15, 16 March.

Tinker, Hugh. 1969. "The International Race Studies Programme: The Institute of Race Relations." *Race* 11 (October).

Tuden, Arthur, and Plotnicov, Leonard, eds. 1970. *Social Stratification in Africa*. New York: The Free Press.

Tyler, William G. 1977. *Issues and Prospects for the New International Economic Order*. Lexington, MA: D. C. Heath.

Ul Haq, Mahabub. 1976. *The Poverty Curtain: Choices for the Third World*. New York: Columbia University Press.

United Nations. 1975. *Report on the Sixth Special Session of the United Nations General Assembly*. London: Her Majesty's Stationery Office.

Usher, D. 1968. *The Price Mechanism and the Meaning of National Income Statistics*. Oxford: Clarendon Press.

van den Berghe, Pierre L. 1967. *Race and Racism*. New York: John Wiley.

Véliz, C., ed. 1970. *The Politics of Conformity in Latin America*. Oxford: Oxford University Press.

von Grunebaum, Gustave. 1946. *Medieval Islam*. Chicago: University of Chicago Press.

Wagatsuma, Hiroshi. 1968. "The Social Perception of Skin Color in Japan." In *Color and Race,* ed. John Hope Franklin. Boston: Houghton Mifflin Company.

Wallerstein, Immanuel. 1974. *The Modern World-System*. New York: Academic Press.

Weiner, Myron. 1962. *The Politics of Scarcity*. Chicago: University of Chicago Press.

Wixman, R. 1973. "Recent Assimilation Trends in Soviet Central Asia." In *The Nationality Question in Soviet Central Asia,* ed. E. Allworth. New York: Praeger.

Zolberg, Aristide. 1966. *Creating Political Order: The Party-States of West Africa*. Chicago: Rand McNally.

ABOUT THE AUTHORS

DENNIS AUSTIN, Professor of Government at the University of Manchester in England, is well known for his studies of African and Indian nations formerly associated with Great Britain. His most recent books include *The Commonwealth in Eclipse* (1972), *Politics in Africa* (1978), and the forthcoming *Sri Lanka and Ghana* (1979).

PETER T. BAUER is Professor of Economics at the London School of Economics and Political Science, University of London, and a Fellow of the British Academy. His primary interest is in economic development in underdeveloped countries, a subject of many of his books and articles published within the past twenty years. He is the author of *Aspects of Nigerian Development* (1974), and his latest book is *Dissent on Development* (1976).

MAX BELOFF, a specialist in history, government, and public administration, is Emeritus Gladstone Professor of Government and Public Administration and Fellow, St. Antony's College, University of Oxford, and Principal of the University College at Buckingham, England. His many writings include articles published in English, French, and Italian journals, and a number of books, three of which are *The Balance of Power* (1967), *The United States and the Unity of Europe* (1963), and *The Intellectual in Politics* (1970).

RICHARD E. BISSELL, Managing Editor of *ORBIS,* is a research associate at the Foreign Policy Research Institute, Visiting Professor of Political Science at Temple University, and a lecturer on political science at the University of Pennsylvania. He is the author of "Southern Africa: Testing Détente," in *The Soviet Threat: Myths and Realities,* edited by Grayson Kirk and Nils H. Wessell (1978), "The Role of the International Oil Companies," *Current History* (May/June 1978), and *Southern Africa in the World: Autonomy or Interdependence?* (1978).

DANIEL J. ELAZAR is Director, Center for the Study of Federalism, at Temple University, and President of the Jerusalem Institute for Federal Studies in Israel. He is consultant to private and governmental groups, including the U.S. Advisory Commission on Intergovernmental Relations, and since 1966 has been a lecturer in the U.S. Civil Service Commission Executive Training Program. A prolific writer, his books include *American Federalism: A View from the States* (rev. ed. 1972), sections of which have been widely reprinted, and the forthcoming *Federal Democracy.*

S. E. FINER is Gladstone Professor of Government and Public Administration at the University of Oxford, and former Chairman of the Political Studies Association of the United Kingdom. His many publications include *A Primer of Public Administration* (1950), *Comparative Government* (1970), and *The Man on Horseback: The Role of the Military in Politics* (2d edition 1976).

ALLAN E. GOODMAN, currently serving as an Assistant National Intelligence Officer in the CIA's National Foreign Assessment Center, is a specialist on the politics of developing countries. He is also Adjunct Professor of Diplomacy at Georgetown University, School of Foreign Service, and teaches courses on the theory and practice of international negotiations. His articles on international affairs are widely published, and his books include *The Lost Peace: America's Search for a Negotiated Settlement of the Vietnam War* (1977), *Negotiating While Fighting: The Diary of Admiral C. Turner Joy at the Korean Armistice Conference* (1977), and *Politics in War: The Bases of Political Community in South Vietnam* (1973).

NATHANIEL H. LEFF, Professor of Business Economics and International Business at the Graduate School of Business, Columbia University, is particularly interested in the economics of developing countries in Latin America. He is the author of *Economic Policy-Making and Development in Brazil, 1947–1964* (1968; published in Brazil in 1977), and of a number of articles in English and Portuguese, including "The Rate of Return to Capital, Saving, and Investment in Developing Countries," *Kyklos* (December 1975), and the forthcoming "Entrepreneurship and Economic Development: The Problem Revisited," to be printed in *Journal of Economic Literature.*

SEYMOUR MARTIN LIPSET is known internationally for his studies of political sociology and social stratification. He is Professor of Political Science and Sociology at Stanford University and Senior Fellow in the Hoover Institution. His many books and articles include *Political Man: The Social Bases of Politics* (1960), which won the MacIver Award, *Revolution and Counterrevolution* (1968), and, written with Earl Raab, *The Politics of Unreason: Right-Wing Extremism in the U.S. 1790–1970* (rev. ed. 1978), which received the Gunnar Myrdal Prize. He is the author of "Equity and Equality in Public Wage Policy" in *Public Employee Unions*, published by the Institute for Contemporary Studies in 1977, and both editor and contributor to the Institute's book on *Emerging Coalitions in American Politics* (1978).

EDWARD N. LUTTWAK is Research Professor, Georgetown University, and Senior Fellow at the Center for Strategic and International Studies at that university. He is a former consultant at the U.S. Department of Defense. His many published works include *Coup d'état* (1968, 1969), translated into thirteen languages, and chapters in the Institute for Contemporary Studies publication *Defending America*, "European Insecurity and American Policy," and, in the forthcoming *Perceptions of the Superpower Military Balances* edited by Donald C. Daniel, "The Missing Dimension of U.S. Defense Policy."

DANIEL PIPES, William Rainey Harper Teaching Fellow in the College of the University of Chicago, specializes in Middle Eastern affairs and has studied in West Germany, Egypt, and Tunisia. His published articles include "Turks in Early Muslim Service," *Journal of Turkish Studies* (1978), "The Strategic Rationale for Military Slavery," *Journal of Strategic Studies* (1978), and "Black Troops in Early Muslim Armies," *International Journal of African Historical Studies* (in press).

WILSON E. SCHMIDT is Professor of Economics and Director for International Programs in the Center for the Study of Public Choice at Virginia Polytechnic Institute and State University. A consultant to government agencies on policy questions of international finance and economic development, his many writings include "Trade Relations: Areas of Conflict and Congruence," in *Latin American–United States Economic Interactions: Conflict, Accommodation, and Policy for the Future,* edited by Robert Williams, W. S. Glade, and Carl Schmitt (1974), and "U.S. Capital Export Policy: Backdoor Mercantilism," in *U.S. Taxation of American Business Abroad* (1975).

ANTHONY SMITH is Associate Professor of Political Science at Tufts University. His publications include *The French Stake in Algeria, 1945–1962* and *The Third World and American Foreign Policy since 1945*, both forthcoming, and an article on dependency theory to be published in the January 1979 edition of *World Politics*.

W. SCOTT THOMPSON, Associate Professor of International Politics at the Fletcher School of Law and Diplomacy, is a former assistant to the Secretary of Defense (1975–1976). He has been a visiting research professor at the University of the Philippines and at Chualongkorn University in Thailand, and is a member of the Council on Foreign Relations, International Institute of Strategic Studies. He has written widely, including the chapter ''The Projection of Soviet Power'' in *Defending America*, published by the Institute for Contemporary Studies in 1977, and his books include *Ghana's Foreign Policy (1957–66: Diplomacy, Ideology, and the New State* (1969), *Unequal Partners: Philippine and Thai Relations with the United States* (1975), and *Lessons of Vietnam* (1976).

BASIL S. YAMEY is Professor of Economics at the London School of Economics and Political Science, University of London, and a Fellow of the British Academy. He was a member of the official British Monopolies and Mergers Commission from 1966 to 1978, and has published a number of books and articles on economics and related subjects. He is the author of *The Economics of Futures Trading*, published in 1976.

INDEX

317

SELECTED PUBLICATIONS FROM
THE INSTITUTE FOR CONTEMPORARY STUDIES
260 California Street, San Francisco, California 94111

Catalog available upon request

THE CALIFORNIA COASTAL PLAN: A CRITIQUE
$5.95. 199 pages. Publication date: March 1976.
ISBN 0-917616-04-9
Library of Congress No. 76-7715
Contributors: Eugene Bardach, Daniel K. Benjamin, Thomas E. Borcherd-
ing, Ross D. Eckert, H. Edward Frech, M. Bruce Johnson, Ronald N.
Lafferty, Walter J. Mead, Daniel Orr, Donald M. Pach, Michael R.
Peevey.

THE CRISIS IN SOCIAL SECURITY: PROBLEMS AND PROSPECTS
$5.95. 214 pages. Publication date: April 1977; 2d ed., rev., 1978.
ISBN 0-917616-16-2, 0-917616-25-1
Library of Congress No. 77-72542
Contributors: Michael J. Boskin, George F. Break, Rita Ricardo Campbell,
Edward Cowan, Martin Feldstein, Milton Friedman, Douglas R.
Munro, Donald O. Parsons, Carl V. Patton, Joseph A.Pechman, Sher-
win Rosen, W. Kip Viscusi, Richard J. Zeckhauser.

DEFENDING AMERICA: TOWARD A NEW ROLE IN THE POST-
DETENTE WORLD
$13.95 (hardbound only). 255 pages. Publication date: April 1977 by
Basic Books (New York).
ISBN 0-465-01585-9
Library of Congress No. 76-43479
Contributors: Robert Conquest, Theodore Draper, Gregory Grossman, Walter
Z. Laqueur, Edward N. Luttwak, Charles Burton Marshall, Paul H.
Nitze, Norman Polmar, Eugene V. Rostow, Leonard Schapiro, James
R. Schlesinger, Paul Seabury, W. Scott Thompson, Albert Wohlstet-
ter.

EMERGING COALITIONS IN AMERICAN POLITICS
$6.95. 530 pages. Publication date: June 1978.
ISBN 0-917616-22-7
Library of Congress No. 78-53414

329

Contributors: Jack Bass, David S. Broder, Jerome M. Clubb, Edward H. Crane III, Walter De Vries, Andrew M. Greeley, Tom Hayden, S. I. Hayakawa, Milton Himmelfarb, Richard Jensen, Paul Kleppner, Everett Carll Ladd, Jr., Seymour Martin Lipset, Robert A. Nisbet, Michael Novak, Gary R. Orren, Nelson W. Polsby, Joseph L. Rauh, Jr., Stanley Rothman, William A. Rusher, William Schneider, Jesse M. Unruh, Ben J. Wattenberg.

FEDERAL TAX REFORM: MYTHS AND REALITIES
$5.95. 270 pages. Publication date: September 1978.
ISBN 0-917616-32-4
Library of Congress No. 78-61661
Contributors: Robert J. Barro, Michael J. Boskin, George F. Break, Jerry R. Green, Laurence J. Kotlikoff, Mordecai Kurz, Peter Mieszkowski, John B. Shoven, Paul J. Taubman, John Whalley.

GOVERNMENT CREDIT ALLOCATION: WHERE DO WE GO FROM HERE?
$4.95. 208 pages. Publication date: November 1975.
ISBN O-917616-02-2
Library of Congress No. 75-32951
Contributors: George Benston, Karl Brunner, Dwight Jaffe, Omotunde Johnson, Edward J. Kane, Thomas Mayer, Allen H. Meltzer.

NEW DIRECTIONS IN PUBLIC HEALTH CARE: AN EVALUATION OF PROPOSALS FOR NATIONAL HEALTH INSURANCE
$5.95. 277 pages. Publication date: May 1976.
ISBN 0-917616-06-5
Library of Congress No. 76-9522
Contributors: Martin S. Feldstein, Thomas D. Hall, Leon R. Kass, Keith B. Leffler, Cotton M. Lindsay, Mark V. Pauly, Charles E. Phelps, Thomas C. Schelling, Arthur Seldon.

NO LAND IS AN ISLAND: INDIVIDUAL RIGHTS AND GOVERN-MENT CONTROL OF LAND USE
$5.95. 221 pages. Publication date: November 1975.
ISBN 0-917616-03-0
Library of Congress No. 75-38415
Contributors: Benjamin F. Bobo, B. Bruce-Briggs, Connie Cheney, A. Lawrence Chickering, Robert B. Ekelund, Jr., W. Philip Gramm, Donald G. Hagman, Robert B. Hawkins, Jr., M. Bruce Johnson, Jan Krasnowiecki, John McClaughry, Donald M. Pach, Bernard H. Siegan, Ann Louise Strong, Morris K. Udall.

NO TIME TO CONFUSE: A CRITIQUE OF THE FORD FOUNDA-
TION'S ENERGY POLICY PROJECT *A TIME TO CHOOSE AMERICA'S
ENERGY FUTURE*

$4.95. 156 pages. Publication date: February 1975.
ISBN 0–917616–01–4
Library of Congress No. 75–10230

Contributors: Morris A. Adelman, Armen A. Alchian, James C. DeHaven,
George W. Hilton, M. Bruce Johnson, Herman Kahn, Walter J. Mead,
Arnold B. Moore, Thomas Gale Moore, William H. Riker.

ONCE IS ENOUGH: THE TAXATION OF CORPORATE EQUITY
INCOME

$2.00. 32 pages. Publication date: May 1977.
ISBN 0–917616–23–5
Library of Congress No. 77–670132

Author: Charles E. McLure, Jr.

OPTIONS FOR U.S. ENERGY POLICY

$5.95. 317 pages. Publication date: September 1977.
ISBN 0–917616–20–0
Library of Congress No. 77–89094

Contributors: Albert Carnesale, Stanley M. Greenfield, Fred S. Hoffman,
Edward J. Mitchell, William R. Moffat, Richard Nehring, Robert
S. Pindyck, Norman C. Rasmussen, Davis J. Rose, Henry S. Rowen,
James L. Sweeney, Arthur W. Wright.

PARENTS, TEACHERS, AND CHILDREN: PROSPECTS FOR CHOICE
IN AMERICAN EDUCATION

$5.95. 336 pages. Publication date: June 1977.
ISBN 0–917616–18–9
Library of Congress No. 77–79164

Contributors: James S. Coleman, John E. Coons, William H. Cornog,
Denis P. Doyle, E. Babette Edwards, Nathan Glazer, Andrew
M. Greeley, R. Kent Greenawalt, Marvin Lazerson, William
C. McCready, Michael Novak, John P. O'Dwyer, Robert Singleton,
Thomas Sowell, Stephen D. Sugarman, Richard E. Wagner.

THE POLITICS OF PLANNING: A REVIEW AND CRITIQUE OF
CENTRALIZED ECONOMIC PLANNING

$5.95. 352 pages. Publication date: March 1976.
ISBN 0–917616–05–7
Library of Congress No. 76–7714

HC59.1
T456
332

\$790206254

Contributors: B. Bruce-Briggs, James Buchanan, A. Lawrence Chickering, Ralph Harris, Robert B. Hawkins, Jr., George Hilton, Richard Mancke, Richard Muth, Vincent Ostrom, Svetozar Pejovich, Myron Sharpe, John Sheahan, Herbert Stein, Gordon Tullock, Ernest van den Haag, Paul H. Weaver, Murray L. Weidenbaum, Hans Willgerodt, Peter P. Witonski.

PUBLIC EMPLOYEE UNIONS: A STUDY OF THE CRISIS IN PUBLIC SECTOR LABOR RELATIONS

$5.95. 251 pages. Publication date: June 1976; 2d ed., rev., 1977.
ISBN 0–917616–08–1, 0–917616–24–3
Library of Congress No. 76–17444

Contributors: A. Lawrence Chickering, Jack D. Douglas, Raymond D. Horton, Theodore W. Kheel, David Lewin, Seymour Martin Lipset, Harvey C. Mansfield, Jr., George Meany, Robert A. Nisbet, Daniel Orr, A. H. Raskin, Wes Uhlman, Harry H. Wellington, Charles B. Wheeler, Jr., Ralph K. Winter, Jr., Jerry Wurf.

REGULATING BUSINESS: THE SEARCH FOR AN OPTIMUM

$5.95. 300 pages. Publication date: April 1978
ISBN 0–917616–27–8
Library of Congress No. 78–50678

Contributors: Chris Argyris, A. Lawrence Chickering, Penny Hollander Feldman, Richard H. Holton, Donald P. Jacobs, Alfred E. Kahn, Paul W. MacAvoy, Almarin Phillips, V. Kerry Smith, Paul H. Weaver, Richard J. Zeckhauser.

WATER BANKING: HOW TO STOP WASTING AGRICULTURAL WATER

$2.00. 56 pages. Publication date: January 1978.
ISBN 0–917616–26–X
Library of Congress No. 78–50766

Authors: Sotirios Angelides, Eugene Bardach.

HC 59.7
T456

$790206254